The User Unconscious

The User Unconscious

ON AFFECT, MEDIA, AND MEASURE

Patricia Ticineto Clough

UNIVERSITY OF MINNESOTA PRESS
Minneapolis
London

Published by the University of Minnesota Press
111 Third Avenue South, Suite 290
Minneapolis, MN 55401-2520
http://www.upress.umn.edu

Printed in the United States of America on acid-free paper

The University of Minnesota is an equal-opportunity educator and employer.

25 24 23 22 21 20 19 18   10 9 8 7 6 5 4 3 2 1

Names: Clough, Patricia Ticineto, author.
Title: The user unconscious : on affect, media, and measure / Patricia Ticineto Clough.
Description: Minneapolis : University of Minnesota Press, [2018] | Includes
    bibliographical references and index.
Identifiers: LCCN 2017042833 | ISBN 978-1-5179-0421-0 (hc) |
    ISBN 978-1-5179-0422-7 (pb)
Subjects: LCSH: Affect (Psychology). | Experience. | Unconsciousness. |
    Interpersonal relations. | Social sciences—Philosophy.
Classification: LCC BF175.5.A35 U84 2018 | DDC 303.48/3–dc23
LC record available at https://lccn.loc.gov/2017042833

For Lucy and Clara, with love,
always, just your Mimi

Contents

Introduction

At a time when it seems urgent to reenvision the potential for productive interventions in the present and near future, the essays collected here look to the past two decades of the twenty-first century. Originally published between 2007 and 2016, the essays were written in the aftermath of the bombing of the World Trade Center, the 2008 financial crisis, and the worldwide intensification of militarism and policing, leading me to grapple with the tightening relationship of neoliberalism, biopolitics, and the expansion of digital media and computational technologies. During this time I also turned my attention to affect, objects, and other-than-human agencies, drawing on the perspectives of speculative realisms, object-oriented ontologies, and new materialisms. Over these same years, the analyses of media, especially digital media, were extended to computational technologies that provide the infrastructure for the expansion and multiplication of the operations and functions of social media, the internet, and technologies of surveillance and control.

Taken together, the essays point to what early-twenty-first-century critical theory, philosophy, and media studies of the past still have to offer us in facing the near future as digital media and computational technologies, neoliberalism, and biopolitics continue to reach into the ontological grounds of human subjectivity and sociality, both in their operating on nonconscious, bodily responses or affect and in their flooding the domain of connectivity with other-than-human agencies or datafication. Moving from *the affective turn* to *the datalogical turn,* the essays propose that what in important about early-twenty-first-century critical theory, philosophy, and media studies is their recognition of an *originary technicity* in ongoing processes of denaturalization and their insistence on the indeterminacy immanent to human and other-than-human agencies.[1] The recognition of originary technicity and the insistence on indeterminacy are not in themselves liberatory or, for that matter, inclined to any particular politics, as recent world events have been a stunning reminder. Yet, the relationship of originary technicity and indeterminacy to digital media and computational technologies must be more clearly understood so as to make possible interventions against neoliberalism's further giving way to its own illiberality and biopolitics becoming more violently racist, sexist, and xenophobic, making many live in near unlivable conditions.

I have treated indeterminacy and originary technicity in prior works. In *Autoaffection*, I took indeterminacy to be a matter of the intimate link between subjective unconscious processes and what I referred to as their "technical substrates," and even earlier, in *The End(s) of Ethnography*, I referred to unconscious processes in terms of "writing technologies of the subject."[2] In what follows, especially in a number of experimental compositions collected here, I have once again taken up unconscious processes and originary technicity. The experimental compositions were produced to evoke the unconscious processes that have informed my engagement with early-twenty-first-century critical theory, media studies, and philosophy. In turn, they urge a more general reconsideration of unconscious processes and experimental composition in relationship to the transformation that measure is undergoing with the expansion of digital media and computational technologies. Although not yet fully developed in the essays that follow, the experimental compositions gesture toward what I will describe in this introduction as the "user unconscious" in order to rethink subjectivity and sociality in the shift from the private and the public to the personal and the networked.

THE AFFECTIVE TURN, ONTOLOGY, AND MEASURE

While the turn to affect in critical theory and philosophy first focused primarily on the precognitive, preconscious capacities of human subjectivity inhering in bodily matter, it nonetheless also critically engaged technologies of surveillance and control central to war, terrorism, and counterterrorism. These technologies deepened the relationship of neoliberalism to the shift in governance from disciplining the individual subject to regularizing populations, or what I have called "population racism."[3] I first used this term to extend Michel Foucault's discussion of biopolitics and state racism to the everyday unequal distribution of life chances or affective capacities managed through the statistics and demographics of the technical solutions of policy and programming.[4] In the 2011 publication of "Gendered Security / National Security: Political Branding and Population Racism" (included in this collection), appearing in our coedited *Beyond Biopolitics,* Craig Willse and I further developed the concept.[5] We proposed that, with war, terrorism, and counterterrorism, population racism was operating at a global scale beyond the nation-state and had been doing so in some version or another at least since colonialism and slavery, a matter of gender and sexuality as well. While recognizing the longer history of population racism, we argued that the relation between technicality and measure at the heart of its biopolitical intent was becoming more central to governance and economy, thus making the ontological effects of the relationship of affective capacities, measure, digital media, and computational technologies a critical concern for theory, philosophy, and media studies.

Of course, the focus on population did not mean that the individual was not a biopolitical target of an affective politics or that affect was not a matter of a politics of human emotions, feelings, and moods. But a number of affect theorists, myself among them, also were drawn to think that the capacity to affect and be affected is not only a matter of the human individual or human population, but a capacity at every scale of matter, as "intensity," "incipient action," indeterminate, and dynamic, as Brian Massumi would put it.[6] As such, affect, he famously argued, is autonomous from that which it inhabits as its indeterminacy. Affect always is in excess of its capture or its measure, making its measure a vexing issue. Already there was considerable debate about the (im)measurability of affect when, in a 2007 publication, "Notes toward a Theory of Affect-Itself" (included in this collection), I and my graduate students and coauthors argued that measuring affect required rethinking measure and materiality, both the materiality of affect and the affectivity of matter.[7]

"Notes toward a Theory of Affect-Itself" was our response to Marxist theorists who were rethinking labor as affective and questioning how to measure the exploitation of labor in the production of affective capacities as valuable. We proposed that affect is measurable, but not in the terms by which Marx measured exploitation—that is, the laborers' expenditure of energy over hours, producing a surplus value over the wage. We argued instead that capital was setting out a domain for the investment in and an accumulation of affect by abstracting human affect to affect-itself: it is affect-itself that labors, not only the body of the laborer taken as an auto-poietic organism. In making this argument, we were moving affect outside the realm of human subjectivity and the autopoietic body-as-organism.

"Notes toward a Theory of Affect-Itself" also was our response to feminist theorists who were rethinking bodily matter in ways other than the discursive construction of the human body then dominant in feminist thought. At that time, we were particularly drawn to the work of Tiziana Terranova and Luciana Parisi, who reinforced our own critique of the thermodynamically closed autopoietic body-as-organism, arguing instead for the body as machinic assemblage that is "neither mechanistic nor organismic, but a matter of affectivity, fluids and energy flows, alluring the disparate to each other as well as sustaining the continuous."[8] For Terranova and Parisi, this "post-cybernetic" understanding of the body was not only a matter of a shift in economy and governance to neoliberal-ism and what Deleuze called a "control society."[9] It also was a matter of the investments of science and technology that introduced into life what Keith Ansell Pearson had referred to as a "techno-ontological threshold" that undermined the opposition of the living and the inert, the organic and the nonorganic.[10] In placing technicity on the same ontological plane as being or recognizing an originary technicity, there also was a gesturing to other-than-human agencies, depriviledging or decentering the conscious subject and human experience and, again, necessitating a rethinking of measure. [11]

In "Notes toward a Theory of Affect-Itself," we also drew on David Bohm's treatment of measure in relationship to quantum theory and in-formation, in which he argued that matter is informational or self-forming and, so, when measuring matter, "to say that we are simply measuring an intrinsic property" is inappropriate.[12] What actually happens is a par-ticipation of the measuring and the measured in which the participation in one another is affective; that is, it produces a multiplier-effect, with quantum effects feeding forward and back over all scales of matter. We concluded that to propose that matter is affective involves conceiving affect as measurable where measuring affect would be itself affective. In being affective, affect is self-measuring, always indeterminate or productive of an excess of affect with every measure.

In the 2012 publication of "War by Other Means: What Difference Do(es) the Graphic(s) Make?" (included in this collection), I would return to the matter of measuring affect and population racism in an analysis of the 2008 publication *I Live Here,* a boxed collection of four books, each a collage-like composition of journal entries, stories, and photographs embedded in graphic novellas about the war in Chechnya, the ethnic cleansing at the Burmese border, the disappearance and death of women around the maquiladoras near the Mexican border, and the AIDS epidemic in Malawi, Africa.[13] Linking the graphic style to the production of a global victimization, I treated population racism as the aesthetic of an affective economy in which racialized populations are made a figure both in the ongoing appeal for war and in the ongoing appeal for a humanitarian response to war, as well as disease, abuse, and violence. The graphic graphics offer their viewers an identification with the figure of victimization in ways that endlessly move viewers in an affective circuit, giving them the sense of being both victimizing and victimized, accusing and accused, shaming and shamed, claiming innocence and feeling guilty. The graphics work to engage their viewers in war, including war by other means dependent on the productive measure of affect or the production of an affective excess in aestheticizing population racism as political "brand."

In "War by Other Means," I would not only return to the matter of measuring affect, but I would go further to take up affective measuring in general, proposing that affective measuring is the measure of what is indeterminate, already dynamic, or lively. As such, affective measuring, as I put it, was "beyond probability," the probability that Michel Foucault had argued was the measure *par excellence* of biopolitics (29). Affective measuring functions differently; affective measuring, as I put it then, is "a probe for the improbable," the indeterminate, or the not-yet of futurity (ibid.). I concluded that affective measure generated "an enthrallment with measure" that turns measure into the "alluring evidence of an already present future" (ibid.). The already present future was a reference to what had been described as a preemptive logic in which the future was brought into the present affectively, blocking an actual opening to the future. The fear of terrorism incited by counterterrorist strategies against terrorism's mere possibility was the example Massumi offered in his influential essay on neoconservative neoliberalism and what he called "ontopower," the essay also appearing in Willse's and my collection *Beyond Biopolitics*.[14]

In developing the relationship of neoconservativism and neoliberalism, Massumi would refer to war, terrorism, and counterterrorism, as well as to "natural" disasters, like Hurricane Katrina. Arguing that the neoliberal economy was not only a matter of human capital but also, more broadly, a matter of the affective capacity of all matter, all life, Massumi defined ontopower as an "environmental power" that "returns to life's unliveable conditions of emergence in order to bring it back, redirecting its incipience to alter emergent effects" (30). More than or other than discipline and a biopolitics of population, ontopower works on the "conditions of emergence" in the economic environment of neoliberalism, which, post-9/11, became more securely enjoined to a neoconservative governmental use of ontopower in the form of what Massumi described as "command power."[15] Striking only when there is a crisis so as to otherwise leave the neoliberal economy to its "natural" undulations, command power nonetheless seeks to preempt crisis by continuously monitoring the social and the biophysical environments for their affect or mood, affectively creating a crisis-oriented sociality and, thereby, allowing government to act indirectly on the economy, seemingly by other than economic means. In Massumi's development of the ontopower as command power, affective capacity again was linked to an incipience at all scales of matter and to capitalist interest in affect-itself that, in "War by Other Means," I argued was making it necessary to rethink measure, probability, and the improbable.

"War by Other Means" would appear in Athina Karatzogianni's and Adi Kuntsman's 2012 *Digital Cultures and the Politics of Emotion* alongside Parisi's article "Nanoarchitectures: The Synthetic Design of Extensions and Thoughts,"[16] in which she would reiterate that matter's capacity to affect and be affected was "disincarnating affect from a bio-physical body and a thinking mind in what is a culture of data programming and data explosion" (36). For Parisi, nanodesign is only an affective trigger for the production of novelty in matter, exposing "what atoms and molecules already do in the physical world," while the algorithms applied are "not mere simulations of what already exists" (ibid.). In proposing that indeterminacy is immanent not only to the physical world but also to the nonrepresentational operation of algorithms themselves, Parisi oriented thinking about ontology and measure in a way that differed from other feminists scholars, Karen Barad for one, a difference that I would explore further in "Feminist Theory: Bodies, Science, and Technology" (included in this collection).[17] "Nanoarchitectures" not only led me to rethink feminist theory, but it turned my attention to algorithms in the context of an explosion of data and data programming in a control society or a postbiopolitical society.

In her later work on the algorithms that operate on massive amounts of data, what has been called "big data," Parisi further argued that algorithms no longer aim exclusively to predict or calculate probabilities, but rather, operate so that "any set of instructions is conditioned by what cannot be calculated," by the incomputable quantities of data that disclose "the holes, gaps, irregularities, and anomalies within the formal order of sequence."[18] This is "the residual power of algorithms," she argued: "They have the capacity to unleash novelty in biological, physical and mathematical forms" (13). For Parisi, computation had become speculative, "beyond probability and cybernetic control," as postprobabilistic uncertainties or incomputable data operate to allow for the arrival of novelty (137). Drawing on a number of mathematicians who addressed the information between 0s and 1s and on Alfred North Whitehead's philosophy, Parisi's treatment of algorithms turned from a preemptive power to a prehensive one, since the environment of affective responses was no longer the primary target and interest of power, as Massumi's ontopower implied. Instead, the "incomputable" in the operation of the algorithm itself became central, what Parisi, in "Nanoarchitectures," had called "the primacy of quantic complexity in logos," which she proposed challenges the privilege of human cognition and consciousness (47). Parisi's treatments of algorithms would give support to what, in "War by Other Means," I had proposed about affective measure: that it had become aesthetic.

A footnote was attached to this description of affective measure indicating that, in my taking measure as aesthetic, I was referencing recent discussions about ontology in which Graham Harman, for one, had argued that "aesthetics is first philosophy" and, as such, "causality is alluring."[19] Challenging what had been taken to be causality as well as measure, the turn to aesthetics as causality became a way of rethinking Western thought and its privileging of human reason, consciousness, and cognition at a time when other-than-human agencies were becoming ubiquitous in everyday life. Object-oriented philosophers, speculative realists, and new materialists, as well as those critical theorists influenced by Deleuze and Whitehead, engaged these other-than-human agencies, recognizing the philosophical lineages to which they belonged, ones that risked a panpsychism or the vitalism of all things.

Aesthetic causality was accompanied by a rethinking of ontology in terms of the capacity of all things, including humans, to affect and be affected, to attract and repel. As Steven Shaviro would put it: "It is only aesthetically, beyond understanding and will, that I can appreciate the actus of the thing being what it is, in what Harman calls 'the sheer sincerity of existence.'"[20] Aesthetic causality involves "feeling an object for its own sake" (7). Yet, this is not a matter of the sublime or of human consciousness or cognition simply failing or being limited; rather it is about the ontology of the object, its capacity to feel and be felt by other objects and, in doing so, to be "slightly or massively changed, caused to become different things" (10). Arguing, as Harman had, that "the aesthetic dimension is the causal dimension," Timothy Morton proposed that the object differs from itself and, as such, causality happens "because this dance of nonidentity is taking place on the ontological inside of an object," from which the forces of repulsion or attraction radiate and are a "lure to feeling."[21] The object thus has the capacity to mediate change; mediation is immanent to it.

My critical engagement with aesthetic measure resonated not only with the turn to ontology but also with approaches to economy in terms of an "aesthetic capitalism," to use Shaviro's term, which, in "War by Other Means," I took to be the economy informing the aestheticizing of population racism. Whether labeling capitalism as aesthetic or as a knowledge economy, an information economy, or an affect economy, there was a growing awareness of the ongoing transformation of production and the materiality of commodities. Nigel Thrift had argued that commodities were no longer discrete goods to be consumed and, in their consumption, realize surplus value.[22] Instead, the commodity now pointed to a process that is "intended" to produce nothing but more process as its surplus value. More specifically, the intention is to orient the surplus of process toward inventiveness, or as Thrift put it, "to commodify the push of will with the aim of producing enhanced 'invention power'" (142). The commodity had become a mediatic object, alluring and affective. For Thrift, this involved not only what is already sellable but also, increasingly, what can be appropriated for selling, or more likely renting, since now consumers often pay to use a commodity, or rather, participate in a process for a given amount of time. No longer "alienating," commodification instead "requires buy-in, literally and metaphorically" (143). In these terms, consumption, production, and distribution collapse into circulation through what Thrift called "an expressive infrastructure" that was displacing the social system as sociality became a matter of an ongoing transmission of affect (ibid.).

I was drawn to treat affective measure in terms of an aesthetic causality and a speculative realism with the hope that it might lead the social sciences, especially sociology, my institutionally based discipline, to take up critical theory, media studies, and philosophy. Not only was causality being reconceived at the same time that there was a return to realism, albeit a speculative realism, in the wake of the poststructural emphasis on language and textuality. There also was a rethinking of other-than-human agencies, probability, and algorithms at a time that datafication of digital media and computational technologies was prone to powerfully affect capitalist economy and neoliberal governance, matters surely as relevant to the social sciences as to the humanities. Already there was a development of interdisciplines around programming, code, platforms, and algorithms in science studies, digital humanities, and media studies. There also was a turn to rethink economy, governance, and sociality in terms of networks and big data. In these years of the second decade of the twenty-first century, I would continue to trace the relationship of measure, digital media, and computational technologies to population, economy, and governance.

NETWORKS, DERIVATIVES, AND THE DATALOGICAL TURN

While Massumi had argued that ontopower was "beyond biopolitics" in a joining of neoliberal economy and neoconservative governance, the turn to algorithms and big data in critical theory and media studies would point to the ways in which a beyond biopolitics is dependent on digital media and computational technologies. Further, these media and technologies were understood to have enabled networks to undo a system's thinking about the fixed relation of parts and whole or parts as constituting the whole. Networks, imaginatively, discursively, and perhaps actually, were displacing what long had been referred to as the two levels of the social system: structure and individual, or macro and micro. Bruno Latour and his colleagues would propose that structure and individual and macro and micro levels of the system are "not essential realities but provisional terms," a "consequence of technologies used for navigating inside datasets."[23]

With massive amounts of data and the technologies to parse them, they went on to argue, the two-level standpoint (2-LS) that distinguishes the individual and structure has been displaced by the one-level standpoint of the network (1-LS). In the latter, the access to data about the individual or the collective is always the same: they are both nodes of a network, no matter the difference in their strengths of affiliations. That is to say, in terms of accessing a node in a network of circulating forces, there is no need for a predetermined ontological distinction between nodes. It is no longer necessary to conceive the whole as constituted by its parts; there may be more complexity in the parts than the whole. To dramatize their point, Latour and his colleagues claimed that "the whole is always smaller than its parts."[24]

This provocative proposal not only echoed my understanding of algorithms—that, in their operation, simple algorithms do not evolve into one totalizing algorithm and that the parts are not dedicated to operate within the parameters of the whole—it also allowed me to link my understanding of algorithms to what Randy Martin described as the displacement of "the system metaphysic" by what he called the "social logic of the derivative."[25] Taking up the derivative in relationship to financialization, Martin offered a political economic accompaniment to Latour's and his colleagues' treatment of networks and reset the framework for rethinking subjectivity and sociality in relationship to the measure of value. Writing in the wake of the financial crisis of 2008, Martin reminded us that structure and individual, sociality and subjectivity, in the first formulations by nineteenth-century sociologists, were features of the neoclassical configuration that separated the economy from politics or the state and the public sphere from the private sphere while, however, serving to include a national population. While producing excluded groups of people along lines of race, gender, sexuality, class, and ability that, at the same time, are constitutive of a national population, the neoclassical configuration proposed that the economy was to offer a measure of the social good for a national population, "making claims to integrate the wealthiest and the poorest through common principles of rationality and a shared promise of prosperity" (84). But, as the financialized economy finds its own self-regulation through derivative trading without concern for the market's equilibrium, and as politics is all but folded into economy, these claims for a national population have come undone along with the system-metaphysic. Instead, derivatives convert what was containable to what is dispersed; they connect only the derived aspects of things and open these to risk "without first or ultimately needing to appear as a single whole or unity of practice or perspective" (87). They gather the disparate together only to endlessly contest fundamental value in pricing derivatives through trading.

Martin even connected the derivative logic of sociality with the decolonization of those very populations whose exclusion on the basis of race, gender, sexuality, class, or ability had been constituent of national populations in the neoclassical configuration. This is so because the derivative acts for and with an "undoing of imposed unities and alignments of persons and places—a movement away from encapsulating forms of nation, selfhood, mass that pose as terms of autonomy and freedom" (100–101). The derivative references these undone unities as it "entangles them in relations that operate beyond their local manifestations " (101). Even capital, Martin proposed, undergoes the derivative logic: "By abstracting capital from its own body, carving it up into more and less productive aspects that can be applied toward gain, aggregates of wealth making or terms of exchange (like currency exchange or interest rates), derivatives do to capital what capital itself has been doing to concrete forms of money and productive conditions like labor, raw material, physical plants" (89). With all this, Martin nonetheless concluded that the derivative does not represent a disconnection of financial capital from the real or from the real economy of production. It is simply that the real economy of production has become a matter of circulation, which, however, changes the relationship of the social and the measure of value and populations.

While Martin's descriptions of the derivative were meant to treat the matter of debt and risk as central to financial capitalism, they also offered a provocative perspective on measure, especially probabilistic measure. As the pricing of the derivative happens through trading, Martin suggested that the derivative is a volatile value, or the value of a nonlinear, nondirectional volatility, a self-generating volatility that brings neither equilibrium nor stable prices to the market. Pricing through trading, he suggested, is "a nonprobabilistic measure": "a point of reference after the fact that is treated as an intent, a target to be hit based upon something that has already occurred, hence a momentary conversion of an unknown into a measure that cannot hold" (91). While the derivative is oriented to the future, the future is used only to define the present moment of pricing, moment after moment after moment.

Here Martin's language points to a link between a nonprobabilistic measure in the derivative's probing for volatility or the improbable and a scrambling of past, present, and future that befits a prehensive logic. Like the turn to a prehensive logic that Parisi made in her shifting focus from ontopower's preemptive monitoring of the environment's affect to, instead, the indeterminacy immanent to the algorithm itself, Martin's derivative logic of sociality shifts focus from an affective economy, as Thrift had described it, to an indeterminacy that is immanent to the working of measure in a financialized market economy. It was becoming more apparent that the ongoing ontological transformation of measure to affective measuring comes with a profound change in the relationship of governance, economy, and demography that would turn critical theory and media studies to the datalogical.

It is this changing relationship of governance, economy, and demography that was the focus of my 2015 publication "The Datalogical Turn" (included in this collection), in which my graduate-student coauthors and I turned our attention to the relationship of big data to the discipline of sociology, especially its vocational adherence to demographic research. Whereas demographics (of a nation, if we follow Martin) produce populations for statistical analyses and makes them visible for ongoing measurement and governmental control, with the datalogical turn, this relationship between demographics and statistical analysis breaks down. Instead, there is ongoing analysis across a wide range of datasets in real time without concern to articulate a preestablished demographic. While we recognized that sociology's "epistemological unconscious," as George Steinmetz had referred to sociology's often unconscious allegiance to empiricism, scientism, and positivism,[26] always has been oriented to the datalogical, we also proposed that sociology currently found itself out-flanked by datafication or computational technologies operating beyond the academy generally. As we put it: "Sociology's statistical production of populations in relation to systems of human behavior is being disassembled and distributed in derivative and recombinable forms operating in the multiple time-spaces of capital."[27]

In "The Datalogical Turn," we drew on Martin's postsystem derivative logic of sociality, linking it to Parisi's treatment of algorithms not as mere channels for data, but as themselves spatiotemporal data structures, where parts can be bigger than the whole, even undoing the whole, changing parameters in real time. As we saw it, the postsystem orientation of the algorithm itself meant that the algorithm's ontology is dynamic or mediatic and that algorithms can learn from what they do, operating as they do on the indeterminacy of incomputable data. In this, "The Datalogical Turn" urged a further exploration of the relationship of digital media, computational technologies, and the other-than-human agencies operating in governance beyond biopolitics for a postnational capitalism.

All through the first two decades of the twenty-first century, in critical theory, philosophy, and media studies, there would be an ongoing shift from focus on media centered on and attuned to human experience to focus on other-than-human agencies operating in protocols, code, interfaces, platforms, programming, and algorithms. Mark Hansen would refer to the "datafication of twenty-first-century media" in order to describe the analytic capacities of digital media and computational technologies linked to data mining of internet use, mobile tracking devices, biometric and environmental passive microsensors, drones, and more.[28] In his view, not only do these digital media and computational technologies operate with other-than-human actants; these actants enable digital media and computational technologies to access, register, and disseminate data of the environment, including data about our own implication in it.

In offering "a wide swathe of environmental data," datafication, Hansen argued, offers the "pre-affectivity" of "a self-sensing world," a "worldly sensibility" or "the environmentality of the world itself," but not as a virtual remainder or an excess of affective responses. For Hansen, potentiality is "extremely concrete and empirical, though not in the traditional philosophical sense of being directly available for the experience of human perceivers" (70). That is to say, while the datafication of twenty-first-century media displaces human consciousness and bodily-based perception as "the stable, substantial hub of experience," revealing that these are not fundamentals, but rather accomplishments that involve "the coexistence of multiple experiential presents—multiple, partially overlapping presents from different time frames and scales" (45), it also calls into being "a 'new' (or, more exactly, a dormant and as yet untapped) potential for directly experiencing worldly sensibility" (117–18).

This leads Hansen to rethink the indeterminacy of datafication and the potentiality of worldly sensibility in terms of a rereading of Whitehead in which he refuses to take *concrescence* as the sole source of potentiality in the process of creativity, as a number of readers of Whitehead, including Parisi, have done.[29] Instead, Hansen proposed that what is speculative—the potentiality of concrescence—also is to be conceived as a matter of the potentiality of existing actualities or entities. Turning to material processes of constitution and transition, Hansen argued that, in its constitution (that is, in its concrescence), the entity is actualized in its passive receptivity to the potentiality of other entities, while in its transition to being an existing actuality or entity, the potentiality of concrescence is carried over into the entity. As each entity or actuality is an "intensity," it can be both actualized and objectified, as well as be the potentiality for the concrescence of another entity.[30] There is no sharp distinction between the potentiality of concrescence and the potentiality of actually existing entities. Potentiality is understood to be "of the settled universe that informs the genesis of every new actuality," while incessantly renewing the world's materiality or worldly sensibility. More specifically, potentiality is in "the contrast among already existing actualities, . . . the real potentiality of the settled world at each moment of its becoming," becoming different with each new actuality, or what Whitehead refers to as "data."[31]

Rethinking concrescence and the potentiality or indeterminacy of the settled world, Hansen further follows Whitehead in his reconsideration of probabilities. For Hansen, Whitehead's unique sense of probabilities not only befits the massive amounts of data circulated with the datafication of twenty-first-century media; it also invites a transformation of causality. As massive amounts of data cannot ever be finalized or finally captured, Hansen argued, probability ceases to function either as an "a priori calculus of probability" or as "empirical probabilistic systems"— that is to say, when probability is in relationship to the number of possible outcomes that can be considered equiprobable (121). Quoting Whitehead, Hansen proposed instead that "probabilities are expressions of real forces, of actual propensities rather than empty statistical likelihoods" (ibid.). Causality, rather than a matter of the "acts of discrete agents," is a matter of tendencies drawing on the continual becoming of the worldly sensibility that datafication realizes.

No matter the precision of the "predictive analytics" of twenty-first-century media or the measures of datafication, Hansen concluded that there is always a "surplus of sensibility" (119, 121). But this surplus is not virtual or an affective remainder; it is, rather, an effect of the ontological indeterminacy of measure, the productivity of measure as a matter of actual propensities in a lively world. In this sense, Hansen's take on measure is a reformulation of the relationship of temporalilty and a prehensive logic's probe for the improbable. Indeterminacy or the improbable are located in the present not as a capture of the future as in preemption but as a futurity immanent to the present that is the preaffectivity of a worldly sensibility that datafication realizes. Again following Whitehead, Hansen argued that "every actuality includes in its present feeling, *its* potential to impact future actualities *but also* . . . that it feels the potentiality for the future in its present and indeed as part of what constitutes the causal force of the present" (210).

To my mind, the feeding forward of data to consciousness and bodily-based perception and the causality of propensities in the present lent to a reformulation of probability in Hansen's, Parisi's, and Martin's works and was resonant with the indeterminacy that critical theory, media studies, and philosophy had begun to locate as immanent to digital media and computational technologies. All of this informed what was becoming a postsystem arrangement of power beyond the separation of the micro and macro scales of individual and society in the networking of governance and economy. In this context, the question would again arise as to the status of a "beyond biopolitics" and the undoing of national capitalism in efforts to globalize neoliberalism, a question too about population racism in relation to the intensified datafication of the unequal distribution of life capacities along lines of region, race, gender, sexuality, religion, class, and debility.

In the 2016 publication "Rethinking Race, Calculation, Quantification, and Measure" (included in this collection), I would rethink population racism, datafication, media, and computational technologies.[32] I would address Roderick Ferguson's argument that the entrance into the academy in the 1960s and 1970s of ethnic studies, Black studies, Puerto Rican studies, women's studies, queer studies, and postcolonial studies, while subverting the sovereign subject, nonetheless only deepened the relationship of race to calculation, quantification, and measure. In factoring in minority difference in a regime of calculation that betrayed the kinship this regime had "to prior and emerging regimes of calculation and alienation," the academy served to make minorities biopolitical subjects, subjects of calculation, self-calculating, and competitive.[33] As the intended subversion of the sovereign subject was itself subverted, unable to wield much power, the relationship between racism and biopolitics would again need to be rethought.

In "Rethinking Race, Calculation, Quantification, and Measure," I also would point to the debates around Foucault's periodization of racism in relationship to colonialism, especially noting Jasbir K. Puar's insistence on distinguishing colonial and settler colonial racisms, proposing that, in the latter, biopolitics no longer needs to contain illness, limiting it to some populations in order to create the health of the nation.[34] Taking as an example Israel's occupation of Palestine, especially its 2014 *Operation Protective Edge* in Gaza, Puar argued for a move from disability linked to identity to debilitation of the life capacities or the affective capacities of populations, where environments are made uninhabitable and populations are sick or slowly dying but do not necessarily think of themselves as disabled. There is instead a generalization of precarity and debilitation. In contrast to the "make live" of biopolitics, Puar argued that there is a "'will not let die' and, its supposed humanitarian complement, 'will not make die,'" in which "maiming" a population targets their capacity to live well, well enough to resist (8).

The Palestinians are a case in point of a population's labor no longer being needed to produce a surplus value that, in "Notes toward a Theory of Affect-Itself," my coauthors and I argued was becoming the motivating force of an affective economy, along with what I would later call its accompanying aestheticizing of population racism. The violence of what Puar called an "inhuman biopolitics" becomes economically productive in both the technologized destruction of affective capacities of population and environment and the ongoing investment in technologizing their rehabilitation. At the same time, the aesthetic of population racism becomes a matter of a prehensive scramble of temporality in the projective calculations aimed to shape the indeterminacy of the present to fit a selected future. Pointing to the "unfettered access to futurity" that computational technologies can give, Puar argued that, beyond the biopolitics of an inhuman biopolitics, populations "are not only living human time, and 'population time,' but also versions of inhuman time" (15).

From this perspective, the turns in philosophy, media studies, and critical theory to the posthuman, the nonhuman, and the ahuman befit both a postnational capitalism and a beyond biopolitics, treading a fine line between inhuman biopolitics and the recognition of other-than-human agencies of nonhuman animals and all things, including the agencies of digital media and computational technologies. In this sense, critical theory, philosophy, and media studies can be seen to have presaged a postsystem arrangement of power beyond the micro and macro scales of individuality and sociality that will bring ongoing threats, as well as potentialities for resistance. In his recent work, Benjamin Bratton has described such an arrangement, what he calls "The Stack," as an "accidental megastructure" of planetary computing.[35] Vertically stacking layers of cloud computing, ubiquitous computing, massive addressing systems, human and other-than-human users that are actants in data processing at its every layer, The Stack is not the result of a "master plan, revolutionary event or constitutional order" (8). It is, rather, an "accumulation" of all other attempts, successful and failed, to solve problems faced by computational technologies: accidents that are productive of other technological developments. While, for Bratton, The Stack is a design model for thinking about the technical arrangement of all the layers of computing as a totality, it also is a conceptual model for thinking the contradictory and complex spaces that have been produced in its image, assemblaging human and other-than-human agencies, or what he calls *Users*.

SUBJECTIVITY AND SOCIALITY / THE PERSONAL AND THE NETWORKED: WRITING THE USER UNCONSCIOUS

Although The Stack is doing the work of synthesizing many layers of computing, what it synthesizes is so complex that its totality surely is speculative as well as empirical. It is speculative because it is always about to change, if not possibly be completely redacted, for one, because it might not prove to work or work well enough; after all, The Stack produces and is produced through accidents. What Bratton calls accident, however, might be better understood in terms of the operation of indeterminacy immanent to computation, which, while beyond human consciousness, cognition, and body-based perception, is not merely accidental. After all, The Stack, as Bratton has argued, also is an empirical mapping of a "political geography" and the technologies that are making it, such that its computational sovereignty challenges the political geography of nation-states. By no means simply marking the demise of the nation-state, The Stack arises at a time when the state has never been "more entrenched and ubiquitous and never more obsolete and brittle," a situation that will continue to face us in the near future both politically and technologically (6).

What is at issue, in any case, is the many layers of computing that The Stack interiorizes and vertically arranges that allow it to take over some of the functions of the state and the work of governance. The state and governance are being redesigned in the image of The Stack as the identity of the user is becoming central to its operation at every layer of computing. As various layers of computing bind polities to themselves, let us say a school, a city, a police force, or molecules of energy, these address every agency as users, making being a user what counts (10).

While Bratton recognized The Stack's displacement of the micro and macro levels of sociality, of individual and society, which Latour and his colleagues also discussed in their treatment of the network, he also would complicate their view of the user as simply a profile of its interactions with various platforms. Instead, Bratton argued for a recursion in the profile of the user's traces, recognizing that it is the medium of ongoing interfacing and an ongoing redesign of the user (266). This recursion points to "the identification and measurement of Users that already organize themselves with the very mechanisms that are used to do the measuring" (267). In this sense, Users' profiles are both "more and less than the whole that sums their sums"! (ibid.). In contrast to Latour and his colleagues, Bratton argued that, while users can be more complex than The Stack as a whole, they are always feeding data back to The Stack as The Stack feeds data forward to them. In this sense, The Stack does not put technology into sociality; rather, Bratton claims, The Stack is "the armature of the social, itself" (xviii).

In all this, not only are human users not the only users, but it is the other-than-human users that have made users what count in The Stack. For Bratton, this does not mean that human users and the other-than-human users are the same, a point on which critical theorists, object-oriented philosophers, and media studies scholars also have insisted. What it does mean is that the human user and human-user-centered design have been displaced by a focus on the other-than-human users of The Stack. That is to say, human users have been decentered and deprivileged and, for Bratton, this deprivileged human subject does not offer the best perspective on The Stack. He hopes instead that the other-than-human users can show "a different way for us to be both human and not" (374).

As The Stack throws an "autophenomenology" off its axis, another view of the user than the "psychologized single serving human" is put forward (262). Assuming, as Hansen does, that the human user is implicated in the wider field of environmental or planetary data, a worldly sensibility, Bratton would warn against a geopolitics of computation predicated on the biopolitics of privacy or increased surveillance. This, he argued, results only in the "preparanoia of withdrawal into an atomic and anomic dream of self-mastery that elsewhere one might call 'neoliberal subject'" (360). Although not disagreeing with Bratton about the user or about calling for more privacy and more surveillance as derivative of a neoliberal logic, Wendy Hui Kyong Chun has taken another look at the human user in relationship to social media.[36]

Chun would treat the human user as a "YOU," a figure that collapses the "I" and its cloud of data traces into a node in a network or the many networks of The Stack that includes the planetary data of a worldly sensibility. As Chun sees it, what is most notable about the YOUs is that they are subjected to and subjects of a sociality in which the separation of the private and the public spheres of the neoclassical configuration has been displaced by the separation of "the personal and the networked" in the wake of neoliberalism's contraction and massive dissemination of privacy. However, as the separation of the personal and the networked is more imagined than actual, even as it is extended only to some as their privilege, YOUs' privacy actually has become entangled with publicity, where YOUs are prone, if not invited, to be caught in public acting privately. In embracing and denying the networks of data from which the I is inextricable, the YOUs of social media, Chun proposed, become the shame-able and hate-able/love-able subjects of sociality.

Chun gives the example of Amanda Todd, the fifteen-year-old who had flashed for an admirer online and then was online blackmailed—that is, the exposing photograph was sent to a porn site and then to classmates and more (135–65). After becoming depressed, having panic attacks and using drugs and alcohol, Todd committed suicide. But long before doing so, she took to YouTube and, using handwritten notecards as her means of communicating, gave witness to her self-abuse caused by the blackmailer's abuse, but also the abuse of those who blamed her for having become a victim in the first place, although some responded positively, even sanctifying Todd as an angel. This way of communicating on social media is not new and for some time has been linked to the template of various coming out stories, as an epistemology of the closet became an epistemology of outing, even self-outing, that either idealizes or blames and shames the closeted victim and, increasingly, the outed/self-outing victim as well.

But Chun would explain that the love and hate that users of multiple networks communicate to users like Todd points not so much to sexuality being confessed (although sexuality plays a part). Rather, the user is loved and hated because of confessing to shameful self-abuse in response to others' abuse: "What is sought is a release from shame by admitting to shame" (155). The confessing user, however, is treated more often than not as an attention seeker, if not worse. No matter what abuse has been suffered, it is in confessing to self-abuse that the user is seen to have transgressed the imagined boundaries of the personal and the networked. As the user is more often than not a female, the transgression is made a matter of a racialized heteronormative application of gendered sexuality, since the female's privacy supposedly is protected, at least for some, mostly white women, in order that the boundary of privacy be held by her for mostly white males. But for Chun, the racialized heteronormative application of gendered sexuality operates not only to make the user the figure of a victimized subject or a traumatized subjectivity. In shamelessly communicating shame, the user, although a wounded subject, more importantly becomes the scapegoat for the leakiness of social media, not as "an unfortunate aspect of new media and digital culture, but the point" (13). As Chun put it, "the user and her habits of leaking are blamed for systemic vulnerabilities, glossing over the ways in which our promiscuous machines routinely work through an alleged leaking that undermines the separation of the personal from the networked" (14).

In taking up users' habits of leaking, Chun has drawn on her larger argument that users' relationships to social media have become a matter of habit. As habit transforms a receptivity to change into an unreflective spontaneity beneath conscious awareness, it links users to other human users, as well as other-than-human users; habit is "the productive non-conscious" of digital media (7). In this claim, Chun has offered another layer of commentary to what I have called "unconscious thought in the age of teletechnology," which Thrift referenced in his conceptualization of the "technological unconscious," which then Katherine Hayles reconceived as "the technological nonconscious."[37] Like my elaboration of unconscious thought in the age of teletechnology, Thrift's technological unconscious, was meant to propose that different technologies have differently informed conscious and unconscious thought; going further, Thrift suggested that, with digital media, the unconscious was operating at "a prepersonal substrate . . . of unconsidered anticipations" that connects us to digital media and other users.[38] Hayles would adjust Thrift's phrasing only to emphasize the way in which digital media operate "through somatic responses, haptic feedback, gestural interactions, and a wide variety of other cognitive activities that are habitual and repetitive and that, therefore, fall below the threshold of conscious awareness," what can be described as a matter of nonconscious affect.[39] Focusing especially on the way code dissociates affect from consciousness, black-boxing its operation, Hayles concluded that we are suffering "the traumas of code," by which she meant the traumas of what is felt but not known, even as code makes it possible for us to reconnect digitally to the nonconscious.

While, in *Autoaffection*, I, unlike Hayles, Thrift, or Chun, treated unconscious or nonconscious processes in terms of an originary technicity, I had not fully developed its relationship to affect and the human body as Hansen would in his discussion of the skin as the infant's first medium, as an originary technicity.[40] Drawing on Maurice Merleau-Ponty, psychoanalyst Didier Anzieu, and other digital media artists and scholars, Hansen argued that, as the infant's touching itself meets its touched skin, there is a gap of temporality that the skin materializes or concretizes as a border and a medium between a containment within and an environment without, subjectivity and sociality, individual and structure.[41] Not only is there no fall from nature into technicity or sociality, but vision or the Lacanian mirror is displaced by the skin as the first medium, as "the cusp between the biological and the psychic."[42] Thinking about the skin as a medium of a temporal passage seems especially relevant to thinking about digital media that operate, as Hayles put it, through somatic responses, haptic feedback, and so on; that is to say, operate affectively.

However, as digital media and computational technologies increasingly operate with other-than-human agencies to give access to a worldly sensibility or to environmental or planetary data that pre-affectively condition human consciousness and bodily-based perception, Hansen would turn to a discussion of "worldskin," arguing, "we can no longer constrain embodiment to the body, can no longer contain it within the (organic) skin."[43] That said, it may be necessary to interrogate the skinned body as the container of inner or unconscious processes when affectivity, liveliness, or consciousness has been extended to other-than-human agencies or users. This is not merely a matter of conceiving unconscious processes beyond the human subject or its body, but rather of reconceiving the relationship of the psyche to the other-than-human or "the nonhuman," as the psychoanalyst Harold Searles described it, in recognition that the human's early relationship to the liveliness of the nonhuman never fully comes to an end.[44]

Drawing on Searles, psychoanalyst Sue Grand even proposed that "there is a nonhuman stratum to early self experience and thus, the self can accrue a nonhuman physical form" as an ongoing resource of attachment.[45] As Grand put it: "If the psyche comes into being in relation to human others, so it comes into being in relation to the nonhuman world. Perhaps we all have a nascent thing-self."[46] For Grand, the "thing-self," often linked to traumatic experience, can also be a resource for positive, cosmological, and even ecstatic experience (337). Even when she does treat traumatic experience, particularly in relation to sexual abuse, Grand, while proposing that abuse undoes "the psychic skin," nonetheless refuses to equate the skinned body with sanity. Instead, she pointed to the contingency of the body's being there or not in relationship to the "I" and goes on to speculate that: "Perhaps the 'I' feeling can contract and expand to include or exclude the body and thus is not simply derived from bodily states. Perhaps we have something like a nonhuman mental ego, contracted in relation to nonhuman 'culture,' and generative of both anxiety *and* 'centeredness'" (ibid.).

Adjusting Grand's speculation to include a recognition of the liveliness of the other-than-human or thing, I would propose that digital media and computational technologies may well be eliciting the human user's thing-self, giving shape to what I am calling the user unconscious in order to point to the activity of the unconscious in relationship to the collapse into the YOU, of the I and the cloud of digital traces, including the data of a worldly sensibility. These, no matter how disavowed, are becoming an intimate part of the I, evoking a thing-self that opens the unconscious both to the liveliness of other-than-human actants and to the reformulation of embodiment in the YOU. That is to say, the YOU refers to that part of the I that is not humanly embodied, not so much a digital disembodiment, but an other-than-human embodiment. The I is not simply humanly embodied and, as such, is not one with the organism. Embodiment cannot be contained within the organic skin.

In this way, digital media and computational technologies also may be transforming the meaning of trauma, pointing not only to the traumas of code but also to the traumas of abuse and violence when the I is not only humanly embodied and not one with the organism. In the latter case, it might be considered that there has been a collapse of the differentiation of "organic trauma and sociopolitical trauma," as Catherine Malabou has put it in her discussion of extreme relational violence as is prevalent in an inhuman biopolitics.[47] For Malabou, this means that, in its effects, sociopolitical trauma increasingly looks like organic trauma. But I would adjust Malabou's proposal by pointing to a more general condition in which the distinction between the organic and the sociopolitical is being transformed by an embodiment beyond the body or organic skin and in which the transgression of the separation of the personal and the networked is becoming the normative edge-defining sociality. Here the ends of humanity may well be its own inhumanity, but still not without potentiality or a chance for another "genre of humanity" to come forth, as Silvia Wynter would put it.[48] After all, the thing-self, as Grand reminded us, can also be a source of positive, cosmological, and even ecstatic experience, pointing to "a different way for us to be both human and not."

In seeing the YOU as a wounded subject who also is the scapegoat for the leakiness of digital media, Chun wants to recognize the potential in the YOU's desire, expressed in the notecard videos, to become part of a community, albeit one of the shamed. This potential, Chun has proposed, is in the reminder that the YOU offers that the individual is a "singular/

plural," to use the terms Chun has borrowed from Jean-Luc Nancy.[49] As subjects are constituted as singular through a plurality of others, including other-than-human others, the community that might be realized among YOUs, which would not be based only in shame, is what Chun described as an "originary multiplicity," which is "not represented by society but rather through writing."[50] Again drawing on Nancy and slanting writing toward digital media, Chun proposed that writing is not so much about meaning as about communication, seeking nothing but "an originary multiplicity," an "inoperative" we.[51]

Like the notecard videos, the experimental compositions that appear in this collection were written while I was seeking an addressee, a we, not, however, through social media, but through a long-term psychoanalysis, during which time I also went back to spend time in the community where I grew up, Corona in Queens, New York. In "Ecstatic Corona: From Ethnography to Performance" (included in this collection), I have written about the overlap of years spent visiting Corona and years in psychoanalysis and about my engagement with a number of young adults whom I met during the visits to Corona and with whom I would produce and perform multimedia events about our experiences together.[52] However, while my experimental compositions, those that appear in this collection, also have drawn on my recent and childhood experiences of Corona, they were more specifically meant to evoke unconscious processes in engaging with twenty-first-century critical theory, philosophy, and media studies. In doing so, they gesture toward an unconscious of thought in the age of digital media and computational technologies, which is as well the user unconscious and its thing-self states.

The compositions turn unconscious processes into a poetic mode of writing evoking what can never become fully conscious, but which allows placing a subjectivity inside twenty-first-century critical theory, philosophy, and media studies, personalizing them. Or to put it another way, this subjectivity is not opposed to the YOU of digital media; digital media is its situation, while the traumas of my Corona and others' Corona involve self- and others-exposures that cross the separation of the personal and the networked. Like the notecard videos that Chun has described, the experimental compositions insist that the YOU and the

YOUs be recognized to be calling forth a rethinking of subjectivity and sociality in the criticism of digital media and computational technologies, as well as in revising twenty-first-century critical theory, philosophy, and media studies; that is to say, the experimental compositions offer a way of writing criticism that was meant to mitigate shame and modulate hating, turning its intensity to loving. And as Nancy would have it: "There is a need to *write* it, because the communication that is community exceeds the horizon of signification."[53]

Writing in this sense decenters the psychoanalytic theory that often has been privileged in past critical theory, philosophy, and media studies and, instead, mines more fully unconscious processes produced in the sessions of an analytic practice, in the relationship of transference and countertransference between analyst and analysand. Freed to a great degree from any urtext or narrative constraints, the unconscious processes produced in the practice of psychoanalysis are more like what Christopher Bollas has described as "lines of thought emerging from different sources, converging now and then, and then radiating out to infinite space."[54] The experimental compositions in this collection sought to engage unconscious processes in a poetic form that cuts away from and to the autobiographical, the theoretical, the human, the other-than-human, the YOU and the I, the YOUs and the we, while attending to the musicality, the rhythmicity of the strike of the cuts themselves.

THE RECENT PAST AND THE NEAR FUTURE OF THE PRESENT

The essays that were collected in the 2011 publication *Beyond Biopolitics* originally were presented at a conference I organized in 2006. By the time Willse and I would write the Introduction to the collection, Barack Obama had been elected president and we were engaged with the ongoing debate over torture.[55] In his confirmation hearings, Eric Holder had commented that waterboarding is torture, and in a 2009 executive order, the so-called torture memos, Obama had banned harsh interrogation tactics. As Willse and I saw it, this take on torture distinguished the Obama administration from the Bush administration while, at the same time, legitimating a war on terror by other means, those practices now renormalized as "not torture."

After all, in the very first months of his administration, Obama deployed more U.S. troops to Afghanistan, committed airstrikes in Pakistan, and maintained a U.S. military presence, along with mercenary troops, in Iraq. This doubled view of torture was emblematic of what Willse and I described, drawing on Foucault, as the preeminence in governance of administrative functions of compliance and efficiency. These administrative functions inform a legalistic and formalistic (in)equality served by calculative tactics that, as Nasser Hussain put it, carry the "legal decimation of personhood that began with slavery," well preparing the way for terror and torture.[56]

Reopening the debate over torture in what were the first days of his presidency, Donald Trump's comments, claiming its necessity and effectiveness, were a sharp reminder of what Willse and I wrote in the conclusion to the introduction of *Beyond Biopolitics*. We argued that, "if the Obama administration promoted itself as an end, as a break with the past, even as it acknowledged its own miredness in the ghosts of the past," already in the early years of his administration, Obama's actions and failures to act would prove otherwise, characterized as they were by "the mutation and extension of the prison industrial complex, the detention and deportation of immigrant populations, the violent militia and military border control, the mass death and the abandonment of thousands . . . after Hurricane Katrina."[57] Nonetheless, we also argued that "the attempt to critically engage the present and the near future of neoliberalism and its governance of populations, its investments in the proliferation of risk and its production and circulation of death, is inevitably drawn to indeterminacy and emergence as the sources of change."[58]

In the years that followed, probing for the indeterminate would come to characterize not only the operation of the digital in the biopolitics of capitalist economy and neoliberal governance. It became central also to the turns in thought of twenty-first-century critical theory, philosophy, and media studies as computation took center stage, upstaging language and meaning. If critical theory, philosophy, and media studies recognized the undecidability of the political leanings of indeterminacy, it nonetheless was seen to carry a hope, an offer of a possibility for change, or better, a chance for modulating affect, entangled with digital media and computational technologies, toward a desired politics. Even now, this still is the hope. It is the hope of an affective politics that, as Martin argued, must veer from the question of representation and identity, rethinking these at a slant, as a matter of mobilization: "to see how we move together but not as one"; to see "what we are in the midst of or what is in our midst."[59]

As we live with the effects of the Trump presidency that has added to the histories and rhetoric of racism, sexism, xenophobia, and what might be called prefascist populism, we are faced with the license that has been given to support these in public, or rather, to make them affectively circulate in public as something more like personal opinion. Trump's tweets not only disavow their networked condition of dissemination; in doing so, they also manipulate that condition, transgressing the separation of the personal and the networked. So, even as a nationalistic candidacy was announced, the networks that made the Trump presidency possible and continue to inform its affective tone were and are, among other networks, the global networks of social media. Surely digital media and computational technologies will continue to be important objects of study and criticism, especially as computation is interiorized in a structure like The Stack and as social media incites unconscious processes of the YOU and the thing-self of the user unconscious.

Notes toward a Theory of Affect-Itself

Patricia Ticineto Clough, Greg Goldberg, Rachel Schiff,
Aaron Weeks, and Craig Willse

In this essay, we offer a series of notes toward a rethinking of affect in response to recent debates about the (im)measurability of value of affective labor. We propose shifting from a perspective that views affect as a property of the laborer to a conceptualization of what we call "affect-itself." We make this move by following recent rearticulations of matter, energy, and information in the life sciences and quantum physics. Recent thinking in science points us to ways in which the value and measure of affect depend upon investments by both science and capital in dynamic matter's capacities for self-forming. Far from rendering the measure of value irrelevant, an economy of affect-itself suggests that, while measures had previously provided representations of value, affectivity itself has now become a means of measuring value that is itself productive of value. Finally, looking toward theorizations of neoliberal governmentality and politics of "preemption" in relation to an economy of affect-itself, we offer a consideration of what politics might be, and could be, in such a context.

Theorists have recently debated the ability of the labor theory of value to explain forms of "affective" labor. Considered to be "immaterial labor" or labor of "the general intellect," affective labor has raised questions for theorists about the very possibility of measuring value.[1] In his critique of Michael Hardt and Antonio Negri's treatment of the immeasurability of the value of immaterial or affective labor, George Caffentzis has taken the position that value is still measurable, and that its measurability is central to anticapitalist projects. Caffentzis not only proposes that measuring exploitation depends on being able to measure the value of labor. He also argues that capitalism "imposes an extremely quantified form of life on its constituents, so that those who would resist capitalism must have quantitative capacity to deal with such an obvious feature of its antagonist."[2] Caffentzis goes further and underscores the precariousness of claims of immeasurability, pointing to the ways in which mathematics has again and again met the challenge of developing measures for what is at first thought immeasurable.

Exploring the mathematics and sciences of measure has been important to Caffentzis's analysis of labor, energy, and value; noteworthy is his treatment of the oil crisis of the early 1970s as a work-energy crisis, in which he returns to late-nineteenth-century thermodynamics. Caffentzis argues that thermodynamics was *the* science informing Marx's theorization of abstract labor power as the potential energies of workers abstracted to hours of expended energy in the production of surplus value.[3] About thermodynamics, Caffentzis concludes: "physics . . . provides definite analyses of work and new plans for its organization. Its models may appear abstract, but they are directly related to the labor process."[4] In underscoring the relationship of measure, value, and science, Caffentzis inspires us to rethink affective labor in terms of the sciences that have informed contemporary understandings of affect.

Following Caffentzis's turn to the science of thermodynamics for an understanding of the processes of generating and measuring value, we offer a set of notes about value, labor, measurement, and affect in relationship to information theory being developed in physics and the life sciences (especially biology). In these sciences, information is understood as a capacity of matter to self-form and to engage in self-measurement; information is itself, along with matter and energy, presumed to be physical. As such, thermodynamics is now proposed to be a special case of information theory.[5] In addressing value, labor, measurement, and affect in terms of the subsumption of thermodynamics into information, we aim to rethink the assumptions of the labor theory of value inherited fromMarx.[6]

We are proposing that the assumptions of the labor theory of value must be problematized even more than they have been in discussions of affective labor, which move beyond the individual laborer in favor of a "general potentiality" of humanness but do not question the embodiment of this potentiality, its form of mattering.[7] We attempt to do so in order to reconceptualize labor power in relation to affectivity, or pre-individual capacities to affect and to be affected. In contrast to discussions of affective labor, our discussion situates affect at all scales of matter, such that the distinction between organic and nonorganic matter is dissolved.

We are moving beyond the laborer's body assumed in the labor theory of value—what we will refer to as the body-as-organism—in order to speculate about the ways in which capital is setting out a domain of investment and accumulation by generalizing or abstracting affect to affect-itself. We are questioning the assumption of the body-as-organism neither to dismiss human labor nor to propose alternatively that machines, let us say, produce surplus value, but rather to suggest that, if the distinction between organic and nonorganic matter is dissolving in relationship to information, as we are suggesting it is, then labor power must be treated in terms of an abstraction that would befit not only organic and nonorganic bodies, but also bodies that are beyond the distinction altogether—that is, bodies that are conceived as arising out of dynamic matter or matter as informational. Affect-itself is admittedly an underspecified concept because it is meant to address the becoming abstract, and therefore becoming subject to measure, of that which is seemingly disparate—that is, pre-individual capacities ranging from preconscious human bodily capacities, to human genetic materials functioning outside the human body, to the capacities of computer programs to elaborate scales of complexity beyond the specifications of the program, to the capacities of bacteria to cross species now lending to a reconceptualization of evolution, as well as becoming a model of bioterrorism.

As we shift focus from affective labor to affect-itself, then, we follow theorists whose conceptualizations of affect draw on the life sciences and physics. These theorists, whom we take up below, have opened the human body to matter's informational substrate, drawing on the bioinformatics of DNA in biology, or quantum theory's positing of information as a form of measure. We explore the ways in which these sciences have enabled theorists of affect to conceptualize it as a matter of virtuality, indeterminacy, potentiality, emergence, and mutation. Like these theorists of affect upon whom we draw, we do not mean our engagement with the sciences to be a full explication of particular scientific fields, theories, or propositions. Not only are the scientific theories to which we turn themselves debated in their respective fields, but our purpose is not an application of scientific theories to social criticism. It is rather to recognize that these scientific theories have contributed ideas about affect that have made it a nodal point for the shifting direction of social criticism. There are philosophical resonances between the ongoing elaboration of information theory in developments of the life sciences and physics and recent social, political, and economic transformations. The scientific conceptualization of affect has led social criticism to rethink matter, energy, measurability, value, and information, on one hand, and on the other, labor power, capitalist productivity, and governance.

We are not, however, merely making metaphorical use of certain scientific borrowings. For one, we assume that the sciences employed by theorists of affect are sciences with which capital is also entangled. That is to say, scientific discourse and capital participate together in setting a field of investment by abstracting affect to affect-itself and engaging information as measure. Caffentzis reminds us that, from the beginning, capital has been implicated in the sciences because of its engagement with the abstract potential of labor power. If, in the nineteenth century, science and capital were engaged in efforts to manage workers' bodies as a thermodynamic control of entropic energy, we propose that, now, science and capital are engaged in efforts to directly modulate the pre-individual or the potentiality of the indeterminate, emergent creativity of affect-itself.[8] This means that we are rethinking the relationship of science, governance, and productivity, speculating that a tension between control, on one hand, and indeterminate emergence, on the other, constitutes the problematic at the heart of a radical neoliberal governance of productivity.

We will propose that governance is now a matter of preemption, but not only to anticipate and control the emergent, but rather to precipitate emergence and, thereby, act on a future that has not yet and may not ever arrive. As our notes conclude with the discussion of affectivity and radical neoliberal governance, we want to recognize the ambivalence embedded in our conceptualization of affect-itself, as our treatment of it moves back and forth between preconscious human bodily capacities and affective capacities at all scales of matter. This ambivalence is part of the ongoing process of the abstraction of affect to affect-itself; it also is part of the effort of a radical neoliberal governance to modulate potential and emergence.

NOTE 1: We conceptualize affect somewhat differently from a number of theorists of affective labor, leading us to speculate about affect-itself.

By the 1990s, theorists used the concept of affective labor as part of an effort to account for what they saw as important shifts taking place in capitalism and its organization of labor. Building on debates that had primarily been taking place within the Italian Marxist tradition of *Operaismo,* some theorists went on to examine kinds of labor that have not typically been thought of as work and that involve the production of activities rather than consumable commodities, for example, "defining and fixing cultural and artistic standards, fashions, tastes, consumer norms and, more strategically, public opinion": in short, the labor of communication and cooperation.[9] Some theorists have treated the work of communication and cooperation more broadly, defining affective labor in a way that highlights certain capacities of laborers, those linked to "thinking and abstract knowledge," or "the general intellect," to use Marx's terms.[10]

Akseli Virtanen, for one, argues that affective labor "is neither direct human labour the worker performs (shaping materials of nature, producing new objects, etc.) nor the time he or she expends," but rather "the appropriation of his own general productive power, his understanding of nature and his mastery over it by virtue of his presence as a social body . . .—it is, in a word, the development of the social individual which appears as the great foundation-stone of production and of wealth."[11] Similarly, Paolo Virno argues that the "primary productive resources of contemporary capitalism" lie in the "linguistic-relationship abilities of humankind . . . ," that is, "the complex of communicative and cognitive faculties (*dynameis,* powers) which distinguish humans."[12] For Virno, the general intellect is the foundation of a social cooperation that exceeds the cooperation of laboring. This cooperation moves from a "preliminary sharing of communicative and cognitive abilities" to "the life of the mind," which is in excess of the individual in that these capacities are heterogeneous (67).

These heterogeneous capacities, Virno argues, are an "interweaving" of pre-individual elements and individuated characteristics. Drawing here on Gilbert Simondon to elaborate what Marx referred to as "the social individual," Virno goes on to propose that the labor power of the social individual is pure potential, something "non-present," "non- real" (82). Yet, this potential is bought by capitalists under the law of supply and demand; it is here that Virno locates "the genesis of surplus value . . . the mystery of capitalistic accumulation" (82). For Virno, then, labor power is productive because it "incarnates potential; it actualizes it" (82).

But how is this incarnation conceived? Is potential actualized only through the work of human laborers? While Virno's and Virtanen's analyses of affective labor imply that abstract labor-power is in excess of any one laborer's body, our question is: is it in excess of the body conceived as human organism? As Virno and Virtanen move us into a realm of affect that supercedes the individual, they begin to problematize the dominant conception of the laboring body as a self-enclosed, bodily totality possessed by a human subject to whom affect belongs, what we are calling the body-as-organism. The point we want to make is that the objective existence of bodies whose energies can be measured and administered under capitalism should be understood in the context of the effects of historically specific modes of administration and measurement. This is not to say that the body is simply a construction, but rather that bodies and techniques of administration and measure all arise out of dynamic matter as parts of a network of capital and scientific discourse. Given this, we are proposing that the body-as-organism is generated by a system of measurement and administration that does not adequately characterize the workings of capitalist economy and governance at this time.

Instead of looking to the body-as-organism to actualize labor-power, we are proposing that a dynamic, indeterminate matter is presently being configured in capitalism with corresponding techniques of administration and measurement aimed at scales below, above, or perhaps beyond that of the bounded body-as-organism. Therefore, while we are also concerned with the "dynamic powers" to which Virno refers (98), we conceive them not as a matter of general intellect, a disembodied matter, but as a generalized matter beyond the laborer's body, a matter of affect-itself. We are proposing that there is an abstracting of affect to affect-itself, which disregards the bounded-ness of the human body, thus troubling the conceptualization of the body as the body-as-organism.

NOTE 2: We are proposing that the conceptualization of affect-itself troubles the conceptualization of the body assumed in the labor theory of value, the body-as-organism, defined as autopoietic. We are thus led to speculate about the connections between different scales of matter.

What is the bounded human body that affect-itself bypasses or disregards? Recalling Umberto Maturana and Francisco Varela's notion of autopoiesis, we can describe the bounded human body as a closed system; it is closed to information that would compromise the body's organizational integrity while remaining open to energy needed to maintain the body's drive to homeostasis and equilibrium.[13] As Maturana and Varela describe it, the autopoietic organism is a complex relation of parts, structures, and functions—genes, organelles, cells, tissue, bodily fluids, organs, and organ systems—all working together to reproduce the life of the body by preserving the functional relationship of the organism's parts to its environment. The organism selects its environment with the aim of maintaining its internal equilibrium, such that chance occurrence, mutation, or the creative transmission of information across species boundaries can be only destructive or threatening to life.

The autopoietic body is strictly confined to the laws of classical thermodynamics, which connect human finitude to a conception of the human body as driven by equilibrium and homeostasis. It is a body organized for production and reproduction within a thermodynamic cycle of energy accumulation and expenditure. However, moving beyond the closure of the body-as-organism and its drive to maintain equilibrium and homeostasis, our conception of affect-itself points to a mode of production and reproduction for which affect need not be confined to the body-as-organism, but rather may be described as a property of matter generally, disregarding distinctions between the organic and the nonorganic, the open and the closed, the biological and the physical, even the simple and the complex.[14] In conceptualizing affect-itself, we situate a body "within a wider field of forces, intensities and duration that give rise to it and which do not cease to involve a play between non-organic and organic life," as Keith Ansell Pearson argues.[15] Our conceptualizing of affect-itself follows theorists of affect who, in defining it as the pre-individual capacity to affect and to be affected, attribute to affect the ontological dynamism of matter generally.

Theorizing affect as the pre-individual capacity to affect and to be affected, Brian Massumi, for one, takes as an example of affect those bodily responses, autonomic responses, that have been defined as in-excess of conscious states of perception and, therefore, point to a "visceral perception" preceding perception.[16] If this reference to autonomic responses seems to make affect the equivalent of the empirical measure of bodily effects registered in activity, such as dilation of pupils, intestinal peristalsis, gland secretion, and galvanic skin responses, Massumi goes on to use such measures as a philosophical flight to think affect in terms of the virtual as the realm of potential, unlivable as tendencies or incipient acts, indeterminate and emergent.

For Massumi, the turn to affect is about opening the human body to its indeterminacy, for example, the indeterminacy of autonomic responses. It is therefore necessary for Massumi to define affect in terms of its autonomy from conscious perception and language, as well as emotion. He proposes that, if conscious perception is to be understood as the narration of affect—as it is in the case of emotion—there is nonetheless always "a never-to-be-conscious autonomic remainder," "a virtual remainder," or what we would describe as an excess that pertains to the virtuality of affect itself.[17] Massumi's turn to the body's indeterminacy, then, is not a return to the "pre-social." Arguing that affect is not to be misunderstood as pre-social, Massumi proposes that it is "open-endedly social," "social in a manner 'prior to' the separating out of individuals."[18] So, affect is pre-individual and remains so; with each actualization, there remains a virtual remainder of affective potential. It is in this sense that affect refers to the openness of bodily matter to its own unstable, pre-individual capacities, which relate to it in a nonlinear, nondeterministic way. Affect is to be understood in terms of potentiality, indeterminate emergence, and creative mutation—that is to say, in terms of the ontologically real virtual remainder that enfolds and unfolds space-times implicated in matter.[19]

If thermodynamics enables the articulation of the human body as an autopoietic, equilibrium-seeking organism, then what science speaks to the virtuality of affect as it escapes this body? Following Massumi, we are drawn to David Bohm's discussion of quantum physics and "the implicate order."[20] As the essential feature of the implicate order is its "undivided wholeness," where everything is enfolded in everything else and as well enfolded in the whole, Timothy Murphy argues that quantum phenomena are real even though they have no "continuous material existence"; quantum phenomena "themselves do not so much exist as *insist* or *subsist* in an enfolded form of space-time that is real despite its apparent ideality or abstraction."[21] All things unfolded in what Bohm calls "the explicate order" emerge from the implicate order and return to it. While they exist, they are in a constant process of unfoldment and re-enfoldment. Bohm refers to "active information" as a way to understand the potential of enfoldment—the potential of any thing to affect itself and to be affected by its quantum field—what he refers to as "quantum potential." In our conceptualizing affect in terms of the implicate order, we are proposing to attribute to affect what Murphy describes as "quantum" or "virtual ontology."[22] We are proposing to think affect as inhering not only in the human body but also in matter generally, at every scale of matter as that which is potentiating or informational.[23]

NOTE 3: Theories of information are crossing from thermodynamics to bioinformatics to quantum theory. Quantum theory's treatment of information leads us to propose that affect-itself is not beyond measure because it is involved in the process by which dynamic matter informs and measures itself.

Bohm's conception of information differs from the conception of information as a representation, proposed by theorists such as Niels Bohr and Werner Heisenberg. For these theorists, quantum phenomena are *known* only through experimental frameworks and are, thus, inseparable from the apparatuses of measure (or representation).[24] The phenomena are endowed with real existence only through the measuring apparatuses that represent them; they have no ontological status apart from these representations, which can describe them only "analogically by probability."[25] Murphy notes that theorists like Bohr and Heisenberg argue that, at the quantum scale, "a mathematical representation is all that remains of the physical world."[26] In this argument, any ontological attribution of physicality to what is below the threshold of probability is thought to be merely metaphysical. While Bohm argues that the measuring and the measured "participate irreducibly in each other," it is not a matter of epistemology, of how things are known, but a matter of ontology. As such, measuring, for Bohm, is a question of matter informing itself, where information is to be understood as physical. While quantum phenomena are indeterminate, they are real and their existence does not depend on their relationship to representations or measuring apparatuses. Rather, quantum phenomena are ontologically indeterminate in relationship to all that they are determinately implicated with.

In refusing a phenomenology that reduces quantum phenomena to consciousness or a measuring apparatus, Bohm instead points to "the existence of subquantum factors that affect events . . . that requires the assumption of an infinitesimal wave pattern that simultaneously links all aspects of an extended field of forces."[27] Therefore, all things affect each other through the quantum potential of the quantum field, even when the elements are separated by long distances, a feature of the implicate order that Bohm refers to as "non-locality." This action at a distance points to a common pool of information belonging to the quantum field as a whole, what Bohm calls "active information."[28]

Active information is measure in matter, an in-forming in which the measuring and the measured constitute a specific case of the undivided wholeness of the implicate order. Given nonlocality (or action at a distance), the effects of measure do not depend upon the strength of the quantum potential of the field but only on its form. Matter is a process of self-informing raw energy, an explication of the implicit with a remainder.

As Bohm puts it: "One may think of the electron as moving under its own energy. The quantum potential then acts to put form into its motion, and this form is related to the form of the wave from which the quantum potential is derived."[29] A form, having very little energy, "enters into and directs a much greater energy. The activity of the latter is in this way given a form similar to that of the smaller energy."[30] Bohm also sees this in the action of the DNA molecule that acts in the living cell to give form to the synthesis of proteins such that only the form of the DNA molecule counts, "while energy is supplied by the rest of the cell and indeed ultimately by the environment as a whole."[31] Bohm concludes that: "At any moment, only a part of the DNA molecule is being 'read' and giving rise to activity. The rest is potentially active and may become actually active according to the total situation in which the cell finds itself."[32]

In relationship to in-forming, Bohm proposes that it is inappropriate "to say that we are simply measuring an intrinsic property" of the measured. What actually happens is a participation of the measuring and the measured that "reveal[s] a property that involves the whole context (of measuring or informing) in an inseparable way" (6). Indeed, Bohm proposes that "the ordinary classical and common sense idea of measurement is no longer relevant" (ibid.). Rather, the participation of measuring and measured in one another is affective; that is, it produces a multiplier-effect, with quantum effects feeding forward and back through all scales of matter.[33] In-forming or measuring, as Murphy might put it, "registers the whole configuration of field becomings and interactions and communicates this constantly shifting configuration to all of the constituent fields and singularities."[34] Drawing on the thought of the implicate order, active information, and quantum potential, our conceptualization of affect signals an investment in the emergent at every scale of matter and as such, a dissolution of the distinction between organic and nonorganic life. It is not surprising, then, that the conceptualization of affect has drawn to it, along with the discourse of physics, the discourses of the life sciences and genetic engineering technologies as well.

In her treatment of affect, Luciana Parisi draws on the discourses of genetic engineering and theories of evolution.[35] She shows how genetic engineering works in ways reminiscent of what evolutionary theorists describe as the informational work of mitochondrial DNA, an informational relic originating from a virus billions of years ago but that now replicates without the body of the virus. Drawing on Lynn Margulis and Dorion Sagan, Parisi engages their treatment of the replication of mitochondria in a process called endosymbiosis.[36] In this process, mitochondria take up residence in a cell body of another organism without changing their own method of informing. Like bacteria, mitochondria have no immune system, so they assemble across phyla without fidelity to relations of genus and species; they communicate horizontally, assembling through contact or contagion rather than through a linear transmission respectful of species and genus. Parisi argues that endosymbiosis therefore adds "microbial memories and cellular parasitism" to reproduction through nucleic DNA.[37] Endosymbiosis models a process of precipitating an uncertain future by proliferating mutation, a process that is descriptive of genetic engineering as well.

Taking mammal cloning as an example of genetic engineering, Parisi proposes that what occurs in cloning is that the cell is "brought back to a virtual stage of growth also defined as zero degree of development."[38] However, while this suggests that the "ageing time of adult cells can be reversed and reprogrammed for new functions," Parisi goes on to argue that this does not mean that molecular time is either progressive or regressive, where "a return to zero is a return to . . . ground zero out of which life grows" (157). Rather, Parisi sees in cloning an example of the nonlinear relationship of causes and effects that "indicates the proliferation of unpredictable differentiation, the actual becoming of cells whose implications are yet to be realized" (ibid.).

Usually meant to control mutation, the genetic engineering of cloning instead "triggers an unexpected cellular becoming rather than engendering a mere copy of an original" (ibid.). This kind of replication, "the contagious fabrication of life and ultimately the continual variation of matter," is descriptive of genetic engineering that is provoking or precipitating emergence, rather than only preventing it (159). In light of Bohm's formulation of active information, Parisi's treatment of genetic engineering suggests that it is a measuring in matter, an in-forming that

actualizes what was only potentially active in the form
It is a manipulation of the time-spaces implicated in matt
of capacity or affect that might be described in terms of w
Steven Goodman, calls "mnemonic control."[39]

*NOTE 4: We are proposing that affect-itself works along
with power through mnemonic control, a manipulation of
the unfolding and re-enfolding of space-times implicated
in matter. Critical engagements with this power, what we
will refer to as "preemptive power," necessarily engage the
reconfiguration of matter, energy, affect, and information
that is presently being invested by science and capital.*

By mnemonic control, Parisi and Goodman mean to rethink the relationship of memory and power in the context of the ubiquitous computing of
a distributed system of memory storage devices across the planet. They
argue that: "Power no longer leaves the future unoccupied and open. It
doesn't merely operate on probabilities, i.e. actual forms of living that
already exist in the present-past."[40] Rather, they propose that power is
now engaged with memory and its working at the informational scale of
matter and, therefore, that power "engages . . . the virtual entities and
their active agency within actual, living processes" (2).

   In pointing to the technological context of memory, Parisi and Goodman mean to emphasize the use of control technologies to both anticipate
and precipitate contagion that Parisi considered in her treatment of mitochondria. She and Goodman point to "the contagious virtual residue of
memory," potentials of the affective or the informational to be actualized
in a deployment of what they call "preemptive power" (3). As Parisi and
Goodman see it, the aim of preemptive power is to manipulate memory
by bringing the future into the present. Taking as an example genetically
engineered manipulation of space-times as in cloning, Parisi and Goodman argue that preemptive power actualizes the future by foreclosing
creative mutation, seeking to anticipate or control emergence; but it
also therefore precipitates emergence and produces more uncertainty.

reemptive power "tackles a universe of micro temporalities enabling the future not to be predicted by means of probabilities but to actively occupy the present by means of immediacy"—that is, affectively. "Such a sense of present futurity entails how uncertainties cannot be calculated in advance" (6). Uncertainty is made an experience of futurity in the present. "The future yet to be formed is actively populating the sensations of the present anticipating what is to come, the feeling of what happens before its actualization" (3). This is in order to be able to trade on uncertainty, to trade on a future at its most unpredictable, at the limit of the calculable— to trade on emergence.

Preemptive power means to foreclose the potential of "mnemonic mutation" by making uncertainty a means of controlling the present with an affective experience of the future. In that preemptive power drives itself to time-spaces beyond the measure of probability, mnemonic control also allows for mnemonic mutation, a production of affect, the in-forming of quantum potential. Thus, preemptive power aims at the not-yet-actualized, or affect-itself, to find a resource for energy in the virtuality of the implicate order. Since the implicate order is an "an-entropic order," where the entropy produced in the energy expended by active information is profoundly deferred throughout the various scales of matter, the investment of capital and science in the virtual or affect-itself may be understood as a strategy for meeting the work-energy crisis of contemporary capitalism. It may well be the dream of capitalists to be able to apply small amounts of energy in the expectation of a multiplier-effect in the reverberations of active information across all scales of matter.

Such a dream may already be giving productivity a different measure, the one we have been exploring as information immanent to matter, which, when taken as a measure of value, proposes that the imperative of capitalism to extract value from human laborers is reaching a threshold beyond which preemptive power is realized as a way of governing life or affect-itself, where, as Massumi puts it: "Productive powers shade into powers of existence.... Productive powers are now growth factors, power to be, becoming."[41] As such, affect has become an economic factor, an action on the future whose value is measured affectively, "not in labor time but in life-time."[42]

NOTE 5: While affective labor has been theorized in terms of changes in capitalism in the early 1970s, our conceptualization of affect-itself is befitting to conditions of productivity and its governance in the early twenty-first century when practices of speculation dominate not only for anticipating the future, but for precipitating it as well.

The conditions of possibility of affective labor set out in the early 1970s are usually described in terms of a shift to a service economy, as well as a globalization of financialization that follows on the formal subsumption of the reproduction of the laborer into capital in the post–World War II economy of mass production and mass consumption. As reproduction becomes a matter of market exchange, the reproduction of labor becomes a force of production. There is the resulting collapse of the distinction between production and consumption and an intensification of capital circulation. The development of digital technologies serves to replace workers and also to help augment the networking that becomes necessary for a globalized circulation. There is increased investment in the capital-intensive industries of technoscience and communication technologies that necessitate and make possible the transfer of surplus value extracted from the low-investment sector of the service industry to the high-investment sector, for example, the capital-intensive industries of information and communication. Under these conditions, usually analyzed as effects of the breakup of the Fordist-Keynesian regime of capital accumulation, laboring is more readily described as affective, a matter of linguistic, communicative, or intellectual capacities.

This transfer of surplus value from labor-intensive to capital-intensive sectors, and usually from one part of the globe to another, was to be protected or secured by what would come to be called neoliberal policies of institutions like the World Bank and the International Monetary Fund. This included the structural adjustment of debt, privatization or the decline of government-supported security nets for populations, the manipulation of worldwide fiscal and monetary policies meant to create and manage crises, and, finally, a redistribution of populations through immigration and forced migration. While these characteristics continue to describe the global economy, we are proposing that capitalist productivity is not just in the state of a flexible "accumulation by dispossession," as David Harvey would have it.[43] Along with financialization, privatization, and the management and manipulation of economic crises, capitalism meets a threshold beyond which a plane of investment and accumulation is laid out in the domain of affect-itself, along with what is referred to as the real subsumption of life itself, for which the relationship of governance and economy is reenvisioned in what can be referred to as a radical neoliberalism.

In taking up a radical neoliberalism, we are following conceptions of the relationship of governance and economy that build on Michel Foucault's treatment of biopolitics and governmentality and address affect and power of a radical neoliberalism.[44] Massumi, for one, sees the early elaboration of a radical neoliberalism in present conditions brought on by crises of governing capitalist productivity such as Hurricane Katrina, the war in Iraq, and the war on terrorism. Exemplified by these events, a radical neoliberalism is characterized by a strategic oscillation in governing between regulation, which exerts a downward pressure on the productivity of life, and sovereign command, which moves in when there is catastrophe or crisis. But when it does, it does so in order to provoke life, urging it to intensify its own productivity.

Command is better understood as "negative command," a command that withdraws after life systems are restarted. Negative command, therefore, must necessarily operate in adjacency with the self-organizing processes of technical systems, where the technical is engaged with the informational substrate immanent to matter. While regulation and command work in oscillation with each other, both command and regulation are to leave the field once life is "normal" again or when life has been jump-started again. Once government has guaranteed economic activity in the productivity of life, then it is passed back over to the business of capitalism so that capital might make more out of life. At least, that is what is expected.[45]

Others have described neoliberalism as the extension of an economic rationality to all aspects of society, including life-itself, where indeed the market is the organizing and regulative principle of the state and where the state legitimizes itself by behaving "like a market actor."[46] But what Massumi argues is that life-itself is involved in this political economic process in the sense that the rationality characterizing the turn from neoliberalism to radical neoliberalism is a rationality of affectivity. He refers to the political production of "affective facts," when public fear and anxiety are stimulated by the state, and these affects begin to operate on their own, as when airports are closed because of a threat that may later be proven to be unfounded. In this case: "Threat triggers fear. The fear is of disruption. The fear is a disruption."[47]

The affective fact displaces empirical facticity and prompts the "breakdown of logico-discursive reasoning" (7). While neoliberalism made use of indexes to prevent what was forecasted as coming from the future, reading the past as harbinger of the future, radical neoliberalism, by contrast, does not rely on prevention. It means to effect: for example, when fear of the future is stimulated in the present, the fear brings the future into the present in the form of an affective fact (8). Massumi, like Parisi and Goodman, treats this affective modulation of futurity as a deployment of preemptive power (ibid.).

In a radical neoliberalism, affectivity functions beside command as "a component of passage between mechanisms, orders of phenomena, and modes of power."[48] Affectivity fuses the formerly separate spheres of so-called liberal democracy, causing them to function as one, "woven into the economy, making a directly economic mode of power the motor of the process as a whole: the ontogenetic power productive of becoming."[49] Affect holds together disciplinary and biopolitical regulatory mechanisms, along with command in its sudden flashes of sovereign power. It does so to modulate futurity and operate on what Foucault referred to as populations, a heterogeneous massification of singularity, which differ from historically constituted agents such as classes. Populations are subject to the management of the social, biological, and economic conditions of the reproduction of life. But they are not simply populations of individual subjects, but more populations of capacities appearing as data in touch with the informational substrate of matter. These are populations referring to affect-itself and the way in which data is autoaffective, stirring up matter in the measure of exploitation, domination, and mistreatment.

The challenge for theories of affect, then, becomes how to articulate a politics in the present when what constitutes the present is set in relation to a preemptive modulation of futurity. We offer some initial thoughts on this challenge in our conclusion.

CONCLUSION

We have situated the questions of measure and value in the context of those sciences that, along with capital, have brought forth affect as an economic factor central to a radical neoliberal governing of productivity. We have been mindful that science and capital have always been bound up in an effort to make the expenditure of energy more productive, more valuable. In other words, there can be no measure or value, and therefore no capitalist productivity, without science. Modes of evaluation and measurement necessary to capitalist productivity depend on the intelligibility that science brings forth in the world, constituting the world.

In focusing on affect-itself in relationship to information, we have been engaged in rethinking value and measure in the context of a shift in governance. We consider this to be a shift away from a state project to temper, direct, and regulate the economy through consciously calculated intentionality (as in Keynesian economics) and toward a radical neoliberal governance of economy where the value of productive activity is no longer found in conscious and calculated intention, but rather in the play of uncertainty and the direct manipulation of affectivity. Whereas a post–World War II economy was subordinated to the calculations, goals, and intentions of the state, a radical neoliberal governmentality now subordinates its activities to the logic of a market economy and a rationality of affectivity. Here, the value of affect emerges adjacent to the production of use values for exchange and where the distinction between laboring and activity can no longer be maintained.

Thus, the economy is no longer directed and regulated with regard to the particular social goals of the state that would necessitate the disciplining of laborers on behalf of social cohesion. It is no longer taken for granted that such activity will cause in any determinate way the achievement of a state plan of calculated intentionality. Rather, a radical neoliberalism submits social life to the imperatives of a market economy, which are uncertain. If value still refers to activity that might be described as "socially necessary," this is only under conditions in which the socially necessary is a variable to be determined after the activity can be deemed productive; thus, what is of value is always uncertain or deferred.

We have argued that this does not mean that there is no measurement or that questions of measure are irrelevant in contemporary capitalism. Rather, we have been engaged in a rearticulation of measure and its relationship to value. We have offered notes toward exploring this changed relationship in which we have proposed that affectivity is central to the present relationship of measure and value. Whereas measure had previously provided a representation of value, now affectivity has become a means of measuring value that is itself autoaffective, producing affect in a multiplier effect across metastable scales of matter. This is to think in terms of affective measure, to understand measure and affect not simply as related, but as occurring simultaneously in relations of metastability. Focusing on the affective circuit of fear and (in)security in the deployment of preemptive power, we have proposed that there is a measure of affectivity produced in the uncertainty or deferral of value. Rather than economic indicators establishing confidence in economic futures, the affective production of (in)security has become itself an economic indicator. That is to say, an increased sense of security or insecurity becomes a prospective evaluation of the economy's future behavior. As such, the value of an action or commodity is affective, rather than its being a matter of known effects of a calculated intentionality. In an economy of affect-itself, value is that which endlessly unfolds from all action and this is the nature of its measure: it feeds forward and backward across all scales of matter—what we have described as matter measuring itself.

If, for Caffentzis, the politics of measure involve the estimation of the exploitation of laborers in the production of surplus value, we have been arguing that rethinking measure in relationship to value at this time also speaks to questions of the political. While the measure of value still can be said to provide estimations of exploitation, it is not in terms of hours of energy expended by laborers in activity that is distinguishable from living. Rather, exploitation must be measured along with oppression, domination, mistreatment, and misrecognition as matters of affective capacity, a politics of the differential distribution among populations of capacities for living. These are not simply populations of individual subjects but also populations of capacities appearing as data or information without reference to individual subjects. Thus, in an economy of affect-itself, data of disease, terror, poverty, illiteracy, and criminality all become players in a politics of affect, a matter of information, an in-forming in matter. For us, politics within a radical neoliberal governance of affect-itself must engage with the modulation of futurity at all scales of matter. How data about capacities for living feeds back across all those scales (genetic, human, populational, and otherwise), or how the measure of capacity sets off multiplier effects that precipitate future life capacities and their value, are the questions that remain for developing a political ground adequate for responses to capitalism today.

War by Other Means

WHAT DIFFERENCE DO(ES) THE GRAPHIC(S) MAKE?

How is one to feel about war?
About a world map of hot spots,
laid out again and again before you?
Zones of conflagration, burning, burning
burning the ground
up into those lives
that the ground once supported.
What does it feel like to be asked to do good in a world,
war-torn and burning still,
when there is war in hot spots all around us
but where we do not live. Where do we live?

What follows is a series of reflections on the graphic display of the horrible effects of unending war appearing in *I Live Here,*[1] a boxed collection of four books published in 2008 by Random House with the support of Amnesty International USA.[2] *I Live Here* was produced by Mia Kirshner, an actress, J. B. MacKinnon, a writer, and creative directors Paul Shoebridge and Michael Simmons. The work of twenty-two other artists, writers, and researches also appears in the boxed collection of the four books of *I Live Here* and the later developed website. Each is a collage-like composition of journal entries, stories, photographs, and graphic novellas about the war in Chechnya, the ethnic cleansing at the Burmese border, the disappearance and death of women around the maquiladoras near the Mexican border, and the AIDS epidemic in Malawi, Africa.

I Live Here means to address violence and abuse in four corners of the world by telling the stories of the silenced and the overlooked, making "the lives of refuges and displaced people" speak both "the personal and the global," to use the words printed on the back of the box of books. Promising "a raw and intimate journey to crises" around the world, *I Live Here* is meant to graphically stir shame, pity, and sympathy, if not disgust and horror, in those of us who are not there and who, it is hoped, will bear some sort of responsibility and, thus, be incited to action in the local and global spheres.

But, I wonder. These stories of children-soldiers, prisoners, sex workers, orphans left by parents dead of AIDS, those abandoned, depressed, near-suicidal, confronted by the hatred of neighbors of different ethnicities, if not the same ethnicities, communities, and families, these stories really are not unheard of or overlooked stories. These are the stories that often accompany demands for humanitarian response to crisis, increasingly criticized, however, for the political economic circuit that these demands have enabled, the moral posturing that can lead to economic sanctions, as well as covert and overt war, which sometimes has been the case with the demand for human rights, for example. The particulars of these stories, it would seem, cannot but be remembered, forgotten, and remembered again and again until there is little else but the stories' appeal, an appeal that has been made just as often in the branding of war, a branding that is meant to draw support for war's tactics and strategies: branding war as interested in the protection and/or the liberation of victims, women and children especially, and therefore as modern, progressive, civil, and democratic, as the wars in Iraq or Afghanistan at times have been branded by the U.S. government.

I am proposing that the branding of war is the same sort of branding that *I Live Here* uses in order to urge a humanitarian response to war. As the traumatic effects of war keep piling up, the appeal for a humanitarian response to war's effects cannot come to an end, cannot be meant to end war, but rather to be ever engaged in alleviating the effects of war, to ever be engaged in war by other means: endlessly moving us within an affective circuit that gives us the sense of being both victimizing and victimized, accusing and being accused, shaming and being shamed, claiming innocence and feeling guilty, like the music on the website of *I Live Here,* looping through a sound again and again of a child's music box as if broken, turning the sound again and again from child-innocent to perverse-eerie (see http://www.i-live-here.com/).[3]

I turn onto a page and before me is a collage of photographs taken at the Don Ban Yang Camp at the Burmese border. My eye moves quickly around the center photograph with just a vagina miserably exposed with a finger stabbing a stick inside to bring about an abortion by bleeding out the fetus from this anonymous uterus. The photos all around show parts of children's bodies, a back of a young person with bones jutting out of its starved body, and sites of abandon and squalor.

In her discussion of what she calls "aesthetic capitalism," Christine Harold points to a shift in the functioning of brand from its being about representation or the auratics of the circulating sign to designing objects that themselves can stir affect.[4] Here, "affect" refers not to emotion but to a bodily capacity to affect or be affected. Affect is a bodily readiness, a trigger to action, including the action of feeling an emotion, or its repetition. While emotions are commensurate with a subject, affect is a nonconscious, a-subjective potentiality. Affect is a vector of unqualified intensity opening to future actualization. Harold asks us to think of the affectively branded objects that commodities have become: how by design they can affectively stir anticipation of future activity. They can give the feel of participation in a future. Affectively branded commodities carry in their design the value of users' future manipulation, implying an untimely future, a future out of place. While affective branding can lead to the inventive recasting of commodities toward a consumer hacking or do-it-yourself aesthetic, there often are darker implications of affective branding seen in its political use.

As Luciana Parisi and Steven Goodman argue, affective branding actually works not by giving one future possibilities, but by preempting the future.[5] For Parisi and Goodman, the preemptive logic of branding is a "mnemonic control" that means to remodel long-term memory through an occupation of or the "parasiting" on the dynamics of affective potentiality in the neurophysiological plasticity of the body-brain. Mnemonic control is something like "a distribution of memory implants" that provides one with the bodily or affective memory of an actual experience that one actually has not had while, nonetheless, giving a base for future activation in a repetition of anticipatory response.[6] Mnemonic control is an activation of affective potential that means to foreclose actualization, turning anticipation back on itself so that there is a production of a surplus of affect that keeps the rise of affect repeating. Thus, the power of mnemonic control is in this turn to affect as life's non-lived or not-yet-lived potential. It brings life back to a non-lived potential in order to direct affect's emergent effects. Brian Massumi calls this power "ontopower," a preemptive power beyond the biopolitical control of life.[7] Tiziana Terranova, following Maurizio Lazzarato, describes this power as "the ontological powers of time-memory."[8]

It is hard to look and not to look again at the series of scenes of violence at the border between Mexico and the United States. Here are a series of photographs that recreate scenes of passionate murders composed of dolls in miniaturized rooms or back alleyways. In one, blood is splattered over women doll bodies thrown on beds and floors, ripped apart and left with breasts exposed, legs severed from torsos. The dollhouse furniture in pieces is thrown about the room. In other photographs in the series, there are women dolls who, having prostituted themselves, now lay with little clothing to cover them. One has the heel of her foot ripped open and her hands are swollen from the rope tied around them. Dead. I cannot see her face: no eyes, no mouth, no nose. Senseless doll. The series of photographs ends with a man propped up against a wall. His pants zipper is opened and there is a doll between his out of proportioned legs. She is wearing a knitted outfit with baby shoes on her feet and a teddy bear at her side. Her face is lost in his crotch as he smokes a cigarette. I go back to previous pages and pages of women's names, missing from the border between Mexico and the United States. It is difficult to read them. There are no spaces between the names; they become a sea of letters.

To point to the foreclosure of actualization in relation to the overproduction of affect and bodily memory is suggestive of the psychoanalytic conceptualization of trauma. In psychoanalytic terms, trauma points to a repetitive suffering without the accompaniment of a conscious or even an unconscious memory or representation of the traumatic event. The traumatic event is an unsymbolizable event and, being severed from language, becomes a bodily memory. However, the mnemonic control of a preemptive logic does not function traumatically as an unsymbolizable event leaving traces as bodily memory. Rather, it functions to produce memory of bodily sensation of an experience that one actually has not had. This preemptive parasiting on the non-lived or the not-yet-lived, I want to suggest, instigates a reconceptualization of bodily memory and language, specifically in the context of a change in governance toward the deployment of ontopower, the governance of affect with new technologies of time-memory: new media technologies and biotechnologies as well.

Thus, rather than conceiving the relationship of bodily memory and language in terms of the disciplining of the organism where body parts and their affective intensities are expected to take the shape of a racialized, hetero/homonormative unified body bound to the subject of language, the subject of conscious and unconscious representation, I am proposing instead that we think the body differently. I am proposing that we think body parts and affective intensities without presuming their disciplinary enclosure in the organism. Language too might be thought to operate differently from being the representing medium of the speaking subject. Language might be thought to function to intensify or mute affect above and below the speaking subject of conscious and unconscious representation, as for example in the language of formatting, performance, programming, or design. So, while racialized, hetero/homonormative formations still are operated to produce the disciplined organism as the unified body of the speaking subject, nonetheless, these formations are being subjected to a reformulation as the disciplining of the organism into the unified body of the speaking subject is underdetermined by a circulation of body parts and affective intensities assembled with technologies of time-memory.

> I cringe involuntarily, looking at the black ink drawings of Mi-su, who, at eleven, becomes a sex worker in Thailand. The drawings show the young body of this girl on her knees reaching out to the paper money thrown on the floor. The sex act is made explicit through a series of drawings of bodies entangled in various positions. The apparent calm of Mi-su's non-resistant body makes the scenes seem like those of ordinary love-making, although there is no kissing or caressing. In the last of the drawings, Mi-su stands in front of a full length mirror one leg drawn up and her head dropped down as she attends to the hose that flushes water over her vagina. The image in the mirror is more like a black smudge of a barely human body.

If I am proposing that we consider body parts and affective intensities to be open to assemblage with technologies of time-memory, it is to enable me to focus more directly on the graphic graphics displayed in *I Live Here* and their racialized sex appeal. More than the content of the graphics, the collage-like design or formatting of photographs, drawings, and texts throughout the four books, allows for affective modulation through an irrational or near-random cutting up of the page by different genres of graphics and a cutting between the graphic elements of each genre. For the most part, the cutting is without regard for narrative composition or the offer of identification that narrative usually carries. So, while *I Live Here* asks a reading/looking subject to identify with those suffering the terrors of unending war through the displacements and disavowals of racialized, hetero/homonormative formations,[9] there also is a disturbance in identification as the design of the graphic throws a reading/looking subject back to the black between visual elements, back to matter, to body parts and the affective potential these body parts excite.

For sure, an invitation to identify is offered by Mia Kirshner, whose thoughts are presented at the beginning of each of the four books in the boxed collection. Urging the reader/looker to join her in facing the horror she is about to recount and show, Kirshner offers her reactions to being there, where she is in someone else's memories, which mix, she tells us, with her memory of her family's memory of the experience of the holocaust, the archetype of the psychoanalytics of trauma. Yet, this invitation to identify is not easily realized as the graphic makes identification passing, short-circuiting any sustained dialectic of I and other, not least because the reading and looking are shame-filled, edged with disgust, revulsion, fear and excitement that is sexual and racial. The reading/looking subject can feel the shrinking away of attention and the impossibility of not attending, being moved back and forth from an ethical frenzy aimed at action to an enthrallment attended with a kind of passivity. All of this is in the graphic composition that allows perverse arrangements of bodies and body parts that is, as well, a becoming obscene of the social. That is, there is an undoing of the scene of the social, lost, as sociality is, to a fast circulation of affect and shifting moods, an engaging and disengaging of focus in the quick turning back and forth from the terrors of unending war and the humanitarian appeals to alleviate its effects.

As such, the graphic undoes the centrality of cinematic imaging and its narrative formatting that makes the eye dive into the depth of the image, offering the subject more than the surface upon which to realize itself, offering, that is, a depth of identification in recognition and resemblance. But, as Timothy Murray asks, "what if the colossal projection of cinema were no longer the guarantor of a culturally uniform memory," displaced by "the mnemonic supplements of something potently disparate, something traveling quickly across the neural networks of global communications?" What if the moving image, he continues, "were less a fading shadow of something higher than us," but rather, "a lively interiorized mark, a digital burn of densely packed media bits" where the perceptual paradigm "has shifted from the spectacular projection and riveted reception of cinema to miniaturized registration, temporal folds, memory theaters and playful interaction?"[10] Something that is quite cryptic. We also might think of what Thomas Lamarre calls "animetism" to point to the layering of images one on top of the other in the production of animation, in the production of an animated flat surface.[11] Animetism reveals a tendency in the moving image, the potentiality for the manipulation of the interval or gap between layers of images that, when flattened, returns the image to black again and again and the reading/looking subject to matter again and again, being affectively stirred again and again rather than being carried along by narrative to the end of the story.

The young boys, nearly half of them orphans, are held at Kachere, Malawi's juvenile prison, awaiting trial, many even awaiting charges. They have recently arrived from the adult prison, where rape is rampant. They are shown in primitive drawings, some of which they have produced themselves. Here is one of those: a crude line drawing of boys sleeping, crowded into cells, without even room to roll over. Their look-alike heads and an arm or two are all that is left to see; the rest of their bodies are drawn like sacks. The boys have written some words that make up several pages of collages meant to suggest that the boys still are hopeful. They, at least, are alive; the drawings of their bodies follow the pastel colored drawings of dead children, one lying so sweetly, with butterflies lighting upon it. One of the 550,000 orphans with AIDS, dead. One of Malawi's innocents, dead.

Affect is at work. It is at work in a biopolitical governance that is moving beyond biopolitics, a governance where subject-formation through identification becomes light or where governance is not so much a matter of disciplining the subject or inducing a socialized adherence to the ideologies of the nation-state. This, what Michel Foucault described as discipline, is one form of biopower. For Foucault, there is another form of biopower, what he calls biopolitics, which focuses less on the disciplining of the subject and no longer takes the family as the model of good governance, the sovereign as a good father who will provide.[12] Biopolitical governance focuses more on species life, expressed in terms of the capacity for life across populations. While the sociologic of biopolitics is at first concerned with rates, averages, norms and deviations, where the individual is taken as a member of a group (the criminal, the insane, the poor), increasingly a sociologic has come to function where "classificatory and regulative mechanisms . . . are elaborated for every recognizable state of being . . . such that 'normal' no longer is the opposite and necessary complement of 'abnormal,' 'deviant,' or 'dysfunctional.'"[13] This sociologic, rather than place the individual in a group, complicates the individual in terms of his or her own propensities, his or her affective capacities, which are calculated by drawing on digitized databases from across institutional settings that carry the trace of the individual's behaviors to be read as tendencies. Rather than represent the individual as a member of a group, this sociologic is meant to evaluate the individual in terms of a statistical profile in order to assess his or her risk factors, or what his or her future might or might not come to be. That is, the individual increasingly is treated informatically or technically and, as such, is governed preemptively: evaluated or assessed in the present in terms of probable future outcomes.

The family, no longer serving as a model of good governance, serves instead as an instrument for obtaining data about the individual, as the disciplining of the organism gives way to the resetting of the limits of perversion in a redesign of the scene of the social. As such, governance is freed up to treat family violence, if not violence in general, as one risk measure of the life capacities of the individual and populations, where neither individual nor population refer to the subject of right or "the juridical-political notion of subject, but to a sort of technical political object of management and government . . . dependent on series of variables."[14] This deployment of population allows for a technicalization or socionormalization of violence that provides a vehicle for a "population racism," or the evaluative sorting of populations along a continuum of risk.[15] This sorting of populations in terms of risk, like the profiling of the individual's tendencies, makes things happen in the present based on what may or may not ever happen in the future: populations and individuals are made to live and let die.

Not surprisingly, population racism often needs to appear behind a human figure. Here, the imprisoned orphan, the prepubescent sex worker, the refugee, and the innocent toddler dying of AIDS are such figures, figures of an appeal, a sex appeal that is racial, that is meant to humanize and naturalize what otherwise functions merely as a calculation of risk. The ongoing graphic circulation of the horrible conditions of individual and populations is a political and economic resource of profitable information, even as the local settings of the terrors of endless war go on being economically and politically devastated.[16] As such, the humanitarian appeal is to attend to, to care for, an appeal that is entangled with the appeal for unending war. The appeal produces a surplus value of affect, available for reinvesting the political economy of aesthetic capitalism, which is entangled with the governing of affect or the not-yet-lived at the point of emergence, where ontopower is shadowed by necropolitics.

> In the camps, the women, cold, hungry and diseased, do most of the work. It is hard to tell their ages. The graphics make each of them look as if suddenly thrown into old age. I can imagine the sights that haunt their minds, of bodies exploded by missiles, and the horrid noises banging in their heads all but driving them mad. Their scarves are torn and their dresses no longer fit properly. I see the devastation all around them, but I am drawn to the women's eyes, again and again. Although blank, they still are transmitting exhaustion, disgust, terror—all edged with a dark despair. They have almost nothing. The Internally Displaced Persons of Chechnya, 320,000 of them, will not go back to their homes even when encouraged to do so. After a war that killed 30,000 to 80,000 persons, the displaced are literally war-torn, so they stay in the cramped and dangerous camps of Ingushetia.

Measuring affect is not easy. Indeed, in political economic terms, affect has been described as immeasurable, a description that comes by way of a comparison of measuring the value of a not-yet-lived potential to measuring value when it is surplus value produced through the exploited hours of workers' labor.[17] As the non-lived or not-yet-lived potentiality, affect works otherwise; it works presently in financial capitalism, where wealth is produced external to capital's organization of labor, or external to the accumulation of capital through production. What has been called the knowledge economy or the information economy, or most recently, the affect economy, of an aesthetic capitalism points to an accumulation of wealth through the working of a generalized intelligence brought about through past investment in the education and welfare of workers and the upgrading of technical management, which increasingly is not considered to be opposed to creativity and invention.[18] However, through the privatization and rarefication of education, health care, control of fertility, social security, and other social welfare provisions, and as the openness of digital networks continues to hold allure for giant corporations who wish to contain it, creativity and invention are being made scarce. It is in this political economic environment that a measure for affect is found, conceived as a measure other than or more than the measure of probability, which, as Foucault suggested, was the measure par excellence of biopolitics. Affective measure functions differently; it is a measure that probes for the improbable and more. It is a measure that generates enthrallment with measure, integrating words, numbers, images, and diagrams to turn measure into alluring evidence of an already present future. As such, affective measure is singular but productive, as it cannot but modulate and change the intensity of affect with each measure. Such measure not only produces a surplus value of affect but also makes it necessary that the scale of measure change with every measure. In this sense, it is an aesthetic measure, understanding aesthetic measure to be singular, nongeneralizable, particular to each event, or each capture of the not-yet. If this is the measure par excellence of ontopower, beyond biopolitics, it is because governance by mnemonic control is operating affectively and preemptively at a scale that is both above and/or below human consciousness, or even unconsciousness.[19]

Ontopower, it would seem, is yet another elaboration of liberalism in that it is accompanied by appeals to sympathy, pity, and compassion that have characterized liberal governance in the United States since its start, organized, as Lauren Berlant has put it, "mainly by the gap between its democratic promise and its historic class hierarchies, racial and sexual inequalities and the handling of immigrant populations."[20] More recently, in neoliberalism, a compassionate conservatism has given a particular cast to affective modulation as compassion is meant less for those who suffer structural inequality and more for the individual who is deemed to need relief from the state and given back dignity through work or tax cuts.[21] Humanitarian efforts also are carried along by a neoliberal ethos with an additional dose of cynicism circulating with terms like "compassion fatigue," "humanitarian militarism," and "humanitarian pornography." To resist cynicism while being wary of the economic and political business compassion has become, it is important to notice the demand made by this business of compassion to rethink governance and economy, bodies and populations, new media technologies and techniques for affectively measuring the value of affective modulation.

And still, there are the echoes of the cries for freedom and rights, as well as for alleviation from torture and economic inequality. These bid us to pay attention again to the way that a struggle against the horrific effects of violence and abuse and unending war may yet give shape to a new politics, to using technologies of affect to recast human suffering, torture, and abuse into social, political, and economic demand rather than a matter of response to humanitarian appeals.

Praying and Playing to the Beat of a Child's Metronome

He stood beside me.
We were praying.
I remember.

We were praying aloud,
his fingers
resting on the back of the pew
just in front of ours.
We bent our knees
and sinking down
into red leather cushions,
we knelt.

I remember
his fingers
on the back of the pew
just in front of ours.
And the organ music swelled
And the choir boys were singing.
In my head, the hymn repeating
again and again
like a musical ejaculation.

My soul doth magnify the lord.
My spirit rejoices in god my savior.
My soul doth magnify the lord.
My spirit, my spirit
My spirit rejoices.[1]

Ejaculations. That is what they are called, short prayers to be said over
and over again, all day long. "Pray unceasingly," says Saint Paul.

The philosophers are writing again about Saint Paul: the philosophers who refuse the one and only one.[2] Instead, they insist on "the inconsistent multiplicity" out of which "a consistent multiplicity" comes to be—as the accounted for.[3]

It is the counting that names
what can not be but be represented.
One, two, *and* three, one, two, *and* three.
One Two Three

The metronome is wound tight
and its swing arm set free.
He pushes his hand
against my drawn up leg,
bent at the knee,
and I learn right then to pray incessantly.
Rhythmicity catching the pleasure inside the pain
with the piano accompanying me.

Only the counted can be represented and not be.
Like my memories
Of my father
who made a living as an accountant
providing well enough
for my mother, my sister and me.

I can see his fingers.
I can see them at the adding machine.
I can see his fingers, my eyes fixed on them.
Moving quickly and then slowing,
Over and across, up and down.
The wedding band, by chance, hits
and there is quick tick of sound
like the metal bit catching
leather on the way down
to flesh.

The nuns had stopped requiring the novices to use the switch, a whip with medal bits on the edge of leather bands. But there were some switches to be found in the closet on a high-up shelf. In early morning light, before going to chapel, some novices used to make use of the switch. In the steady rhythm of leather hitting, metal finds the flesh releasing spirit buried deep within.

My spirit rejoices in God my savior.
My soul magnifies the lord.

In the thirteenth century, self-flagellation still was praised. As part of the daily ritual of nuns, whipping was considered another way of communicating with and becoming closer to God. The act was often done naked alone or with others, making a theater for God, but maybe not for God alone. By the fifteenth century, the Spanish Inquisition had declared self-flagellation to be pagan, heresy, idolatrous in the flagellant's identification with the crucified body of Christ. But, by the Enlightenment, whipping was thought to be a matter of nature opposed to reason. The nun's obsession with whipping, then, was to be explained in terms of her repressed sexual desires, and this reinterpretation provided a bridge sending the nun convulsing, in ecstasy, as if possessed, from the religious authorities to those of the medical sciences, from matters of sanctity to those of sanity.[4]

> In the church's transfer of power to medicine, the counter-pastoral acts
>   of flagellation,
> mysticism, and convulsion were reevaluated and came to be understood as
> climactic actions of the nervous system,
> symptomatic of hysterical epilepsy
> treated unto exhaustion
> in the work of Charcot
> and leaving traces
> in the case of Anna O.
> Oh Anna Oh

The philosophers are writing again of spirituality, a spirituality not so much opposed to the flesh, but a spirituality opposed to religion as faith is opposed to belief: "While belief sets down or assumes a sameness of the other with which it identifies itself and in which it takes solace (he is good, he will save me), faith lets itself be addressed by a disconcerting appeal through the other," thrown into a listening that we do not know ourselves.[5]

But should we not hear those who cannot speak
but who do make sounds
mixed with a violence unbearable:
the bombs and flames and crashing planes,
bodies, and buildings to the ground,
earth quaking, spitting blame, shame and pain?

What is this? Sounds of pain that the philosophers claim return us to a religion that is not spirituality, a belief that is not faith. The philosophers are hearing sound for which they do not yet have a musical taste. Their taste is for a secularism installed with the beats of an unmarked Western Christianity.

One, two *and* three, one, two *and* three.

My soul doth magnify the lord
My spirit rejoices in God my Savior
For He that is mighty hath done great things for me,
And holy is His Name.
Holy is his name. His name is wholly holy.

What was asked of sex now is asked of religion: "What might it mean today to be for or against religion, the way Christianity proposed to make its followers into adversaries for or against the body, the way it made them love some bodies and detest others, as if *free* from the body and later from religion?"[6] Western Christianity freed itself from religion as it produced a secular critique of religion that, at the same time, made a religious other in the "Orient": Islam as a religious fanaticism incapable of self-critique.

And Christianity forgot itself and it forgave itself.

I remember.
I remember.
I remember.
I do.

He didn't want to be an accountant he once told me. It was something else he wanted to be. What was it? Something more frivolous, he said.

Ah yes. A tugboat captain. But I wasn't sure he wasn't teasing me and I decided he meant he had wanted to write poetry. I never quite knew whether he was teasing me or ridiculing me.

And I still search for what poetry there might be in the counting. In the beating of minutes passing as I stood in the corner where I had been sent and would not be set free until I could read the time on the face of the clock near my parents bed.

This is how he punished me.

The clock was enclosed in a dome of glass,
a miniature cathedral, an airless space of time,
held still for me a horrid glimpse of eternity.

I had been left there.
My face awash in salty tears and fear
that I would never learn to read the clock's face.
Its hands moving from one Roman numeral to the next,
it said nothing to me. But there was a pendulum
hung with delicate wiring between the golden columns
that held up the clock
with its indecipherable face.
The pendulum's mechanical movement,
turning one way and then,
back again, made time flee.
I was amazed and terrified,
ecstatic, convulsive, possessed.
His meanness made some sort of penitent out of me,
one needing to be set free of the sins
that made a swarm of demons hurl me into the
corner of that place,
the bedroom.

I am the penitent
repeating the beating.

Like Mary Magdala, who "becomes the saint par excellence because she holds to this point," the point of abandonment, "where the touch of sense is identical to its retreat," where "she gives herself up to a presence that is only a departing, to a glory that is only a darkness, to a scent that is only a coldness." Beaten. It calms her for a while, until the panic and the unbearably wild sensation repeats.[7]

> Repeats the beating
> like the backbeat
> sounding at the birth of rock-and-roll
> and in the autobiographies of the early rock and rollers,
> who, had it hard coming from the country to the urban setting.
> Bo Diddly got beaten but finds a backbeat to beat back.
> And Chuck Berry too—his mother's whipping
> giving a rhythm in black and blue.
> And it is not merely that the stories are true
> but a fantasy too
> that makes of sound, music.[8]

And sexuality, and should we say Western Christianity too, breaks into the body, is beaten into skin made flesh. No matter whether there is actual beating, there is an accounting of the beats repeating, a counting that is sex, as the mother and the father, *the father, the father, the father,* become the stuff of fantasy through which all reality is made real.

Really? Really, reality does not absolutely come before, nor does fantasy necessarily come after, even though there is some sense in which there is indeed a delay between them. Reality, fantasy, reality, fantasy.

> There is an *afterwardness* that upsets
> the easy reading of the clock face of time,
> so that what seems to be a prior unnamable incident
> comes through the unconscious reserve as sexuality,
> perceived by the subject as a break in
> perceived as an inner foreign body
> which breaks out from within the subject.
> Breaking in, beaten in and through,
> backbeating to you.[9]

I remember. I remember. I remember.

And the breaking in that is the fantasy breaking out in reality is not so much derived from what was seen, but more from what was heard.

Snapping fingers and clapping hands, the organ music swelling, and the sounding of the piano accompanying me.

I remember the repeating beating of sexuality,
of Western Christianity. But not simply
Western Christianity. Knotted through the backbeat
is vodou and the call of the drumming to the dancers
to dance in ecstasy, in a frenzy as beings possessed.

The repeating backbeat of rock-and-roll resonates
a people's resistance to the shattering impact of slavery.
Dispossession realized in slavery,
countered by possession in vodou,
a spirituality that nonetheless
would be accused of primitiveness.[10]
An exorcism is called forth,
and the displacement of drumming
with the disciplining of the metronome.[11]

The metronome sat on the piano just beside the sheets of music in front of me. It beat out instruction to my fingers as I practiced.

Adagio, andante, allegro, vivace.
Sound and mood shifts.
Lento, grave, mysterioso.
I felt the piano feeling, feeling for me,
feelings that resisted the rigors of technicality.
So the metronome often seemed to be accusing me
of an infidelity. One, two *and* three.
One, two *and* three.

One
Two
Three.

The metronome, first patented in 1812, was meant to be used by musicians in order to maintain a constant tempo while practicing. Beats beating by the minute perfectly, exactly. But great musicians always have been wary about the mathematical regularity of the metronome. Not only has there been doubt that human beings actually can keep themselves exactly in time with the metronome's beating, but there has been the fast turning of this human insufficiency into a capacity for the sublime. The sublimity of music, in Kantian terms, is in the disjuncture of apprehension and comprehension, in the disjuncture of a purely mathematical and nonhuman number with no limit and an embodied aesthetic number whose limit is subjective apprehension itself.

> For the human,
> the sublime comes with the giving way to,
> the falling back into
> incomprehension.[12]

But we might open our ears to black metal sound or electronic noise. Their swarming pulse let to push the Kantian sublime a bit and the psychoanalytic too. Rethink the relationship of number and sound to swarming, that capacity of demons to be heard before being seen, if ever seen.

> An incorporality that is a materiality
> unbodied noise, which has neither origin nor end.
> Swaths of sound between and across notes,
> a metronomic monstrosity,
> hundreds of them beating in dead time.

> I heard and felt it that night
> the affect of demons
> that night, when he first took all comprehension away.
> That night he took and looked away.
> And left me trembling with a repeating beating,
> the rhythm of shame and pain.

> Turning into word impressions
> typing themselves onto the page.
> Here and now to be spoken.
> I am moving still, nearer to you,
> carrying the stain of evil,
> the power of evil to create
> anew.

Gendered Security / National Security

POLITICAL BRANDING AND POPULATION RACISM

Patricia Ticineto Clough and Craig Willse

On September 8, 2002, a series of photographs and text advertising fashions by Kenneth Cole appeared as an insert in the Sunday *New York Times Magazine*.[1] To the right of the insert's cover photograph, a sentence appears: *Some statements are more fashionable than others. Kenneth Cole Fall 2002*. The first photograph appearing on the inside of the insert shows a young, seemingly heterosexual white couple. She wears a white coat and tan boots; he is wearing gray, brown, and black. They sit in front of building on an extended stair in what feels to be Lower Manhattan. The sentence to the right of them reads: *Wearing protection is the new black.* On the next page there is a photograph of a black woman standing with a bike. The sentence to her right states: *Not voting is so last season.* The center photograph of the insert is of a white man dressed fully in black, bent on one knee over a briefcase in which he is putting a newspaper. Just below the fold of the newspaper, one's eye catches the word "hopes." There is no sentence accompanying the photograph, but there is one on the next page. It runs across the body of a white boy dressed as a soldier. The boy bends on one knee while aiming a gun at another boy, also white, dressed like a cowboy. The cowboy's arms are extended, held up under arrest. The two young women from earlier photographs are also in the picture; the black woman has passed the boys and the white woman is just doing so. All four are pictured on a city street, again seemingly Lower Manhattan. Across the soldier boy's body is the statement: *Gun safety . . . it's all the rage.* On the next page, the two women are on either side of a security guard in front of a building with a wall sign: *The United States*

Federal Courthouse. Across the body of the black woman, who is dressed in black, is written: *Security . . . The Accessory for Fall.* Two more sentences will appear on the next two photographs. The first of these shows a young man with a newspaper, the headline reads, "HOLY WAR," and above it the word "bombers" can be glimpsed. To the right of the man is a white woman dressed in white at a newspaper stand eyeing with some suspicion another man dressed in black who is dark haired and bearded. The sentence just below this man and woman reads: *Mideast Peace is the must-have for Fall.* Finally, there is a photograph of the two women showing the bottom of the leg of the black woman as she comes down the stairs of what appears to be a government building, with the white woman to her right sitting on the stairs. Across the white woman's body the sentence reads: *Choice . . . No woman should be without one.* And again: *Some statements are more fashionable than others. Kenneth Cole.*

Borrowing from the advertorial genre, the Kenneth Cole photographs and text make the theme of security a matter of fashion, just a year after the attacks on the World Trade Center and a few months before the invasion of Iraq in March 2003.[2] Through the gendered codes of fashion, the photos and text link national security to personal security, proposing that the former is essential to the latter and that the latter might be gendered in such a way as to concern women in particular. The photographs and text both point to and all but erase a distinction proposed with the concept of *human security,* given that human security policy was promoted by international organizations such as the United Nations post-1989, when the end of the Cold War was taken to signal an opportunity to shape policy that would ensure the security of persons as distinct from a national security based on militarism and war. With the surge of U.S. militarism and the intensification of war after 2001, human security discourse and human security policy would not disappear; they would, however, increasingly be suspected of being unable to ensure a distinction between personal security and national security. Human security discourse and human security policy even came under suspicion for its complicity with militarism and war, a complicity that would be elaborated in debates among cultural critics.[3]

For example, antiracist and anticolonial feminist critics would become critical of those efforts to make human security policy sensitive to the specific needs of women, rather than taking the opportunity to offer a more general critique of the concept of human security and human security policy. In outlining the specific human security needs of women, it was argued, a certain view of gender was promoted; a universal norm of behavior was offered that could be imposed on others as it was taken up by legislators, policy makers, advocates, and activists. This deployment of gender was concerned not only, nor primarily, with the differential treatment of men and women. It also pointed to a "political branding" of policy and programming in which brand does not so much signify, but rather arouses, or affectively activates.[4] Here, gender as a political branding arouses an interest in the protection and/or the liberation of women as modern, progressive, and civil, activating democratic action aimed at what, in the Kenneth Cole advertorial, is described as "ensuring choice"—the choice to be personally safe and nationally secure, to be invested in peace.

As such, gender is used not to distinguish human security from national security, militarism, and war. Rather, national security again is made necessary to human security, as war and counterterrorism are promoted as the means to liberate women in certain designated parts of the world. Indeed, a number of scholars who helped shape the debate over the use of gender in the promotion of war and counterterrorism addressed Islam and the historical figure of Muslim woman/women, pointing toward what the Kenneth Cole images and text evoked and affectively circulated with words like "holy war," along with their placement so close to the word "bombers" and at a distance from the word "choice." Lila Abu-Lughod urged that: "We should be wary of taking on the mantle of those nineteenth-century Christian missionary women who devoted their lives to saving their Muslim sisters. . . . One can hear uncanny echoes of their virtuous goals today, even though the language is secular, the appeals not to Jesus but to human rights or the liberal West."[5] Gender as political branding here rests on Orientalist and racialized histories at the same time that it folds memory into affective intensities, reductively absorbing the force of histories into preconscious bodily irritations or activations so to generate a *sense* of safety and fear without having to point explicitly to the source or location of those feelings.

In saying that gender "brands" war and counterterrorism, therefore, we mean to point to a shift in the understanding of brand from its being a sign of subject status to its making objects things that exude and transmit affect or potentiality, the way we might think of the things that commodities have become in what Christine Harold treats as "aesthetic capitalism."[6] As another tag for grasping the changes in capitalist economy, aesthetic capitalism points to a shift in branding, moving branding from the auratics of the circulating sign to a matter of things being designed to function affectively to stir bodily propensities or initiate activation in mood shifts. Here, branding seeks to produce a surplus value of "audience effect" or affect in a political economy that embeds what Luciana Parisi and Steven Goodman have called the "mnemonic control" of a preemptive logic.[7] For Parisi and Goodman, the operation of preemption through branding seeks to remodel long-term memory through an occupation of or the "parasiting" on the dynamics of short-term intuition where past, present, and future coexist as affect, a pre-individual, preconscious incipience or potentiality, an intensity that repeatedly instigates activation in the neurophysiological plasticity of the body-brain. Branding's occupation of short-term intuitions is something like "a distribution of memory implants" that provides you with the bodily or affective sense of an experience you have not had or a memory you have not had, giving a base for future activation or repetition.

In what follows, we will trace political branding through two other media presentations: the first a story about "cyber-farming" conducted by Chinese laborers, and the second a series of advertisements selling storage space. What brings these seemingly unrelated circulations together, we will argue, is the political branding operative in the Kenneth Cole advertorial. If those images and text gender human security toward reproducing a discourse of national security, these further cases point to the way political branding operates to make other characteristics, such as ethnoraciality and sexuality, less the effect of a gaze embedded in scenarios for disciplining the individual subject and more a matter of modulating life capacities at population levels above and below the individual—a matter of biopolitics in terms of what Tiziana Terranova, following Maurizio Lazzarato, describes as "the ontological powers of time memory."[8] In other words, what has been understood as characteristics of identity, a personal property, such as ethnoraciality, sexuality, or gender, now can also function in terms of "audience effect" through a political branding that is a source of value in which the economy is speculative, informational, or affective.[9] It is in this light that we want to explore political branding and the way it is linked to the power of biopolitics. This necessitates revisiting the relationship between subject identity and populations to which Michel Foucault pointed when conceptualizing biopolitics. At the same time, this requires going beyond Foucault's treatment of state racism to a "population racism" that, we will argue, political branding circulates affectively.

SECURITY . . . THE ACCESSORY FOR FALL

For Foucault, biopolitics is one trajectory of a form of power that he described as biopower, which, he argued, arose in eighteenth-century Europe when "the old power of death that symbolized sovereign power was now carefully supplanted by the administration of bodies and the calculated management of life."[10] The two trajectories of biopower—anatomopolitics (or discipline) and biopolitics—both bring life described as biological into political calculation. Anatomopolitics does so by fostering life and focusing on the disciplining of the subject within an ordered space, such as the school or the prison. Anatomopolitics takes on the life of the individual in terms of "infinitesimal surveillances, permanent controls, extremely meticulous orderings of space, indeterminate medical or psychological examinations, an entire micro-power concerned with the body."[11]

In contrast, biopolitics turns to the life capacities of populations or the regulation of the productive economic and biological capacities of human life at a mass scale. Biopolitical technologies are a matter of making-live, but at the level of populations. As Foucault put it: "So after a first seizure of power over the body in an individualizing mode, we have a second seizure of power that is not individualizing, but, if you like, massifying, that is directed not at man-as-body but at man-as-species."[12] While Foucault's remarks seem to suggest a linear progression from individual body to species, Foucault more often and more convincingly suggested that biopower always works as the governance of a constituted multiplicity that must also govern in depth, at the level of the fine points and details of the individual or the singular.[13]

Foucault's history of sexuality demonstrates the relationships between the disciplinary and biopolitical. He argues that the deployment of a technology of sex spreads out between the disciplining of the individual subject and the biopolitics of populations, and so it offered "a whole series of different tactics that combined in varying proportions the object of disciplining the body and that of regulating populations."[14] Similarly we are suggesting that there is a relationship between a biopolitics and a deployment of the political branding of what we will call a population racism.[15] While Foucault argued that the biopolitical power over the species or life-itself is a matter of fostering life, such that the sovereign right over death is put at a distance, he also argued that, "to improve life, to prolong its duration, to improve its chances, to avoid accidents and to compensate for failings," it might be legitimate to kill, at least to let die.[16] Foucault argues that it is a form of racism that allows for death in biopolitics, the death of some populations that are marked as inferior and harmful to the larger body of the nation. He refers to this racism as "state racism in its biologizing form." But we prefer to use the term "population racism," not only to emphasize the biopolitical register at which such racism operates more ordinarily but also to attend to the ways that distributions of life chances and death probabilities operate transnationally, at a global scale not confined to state bureaucracies. The war on terror demonstrates forcibly that the kinds of life that are taken in service of a state may be located far outside the boundaries of that state.

As histories of racism are elided into programs and policies of a population racism, these populations are opened to becoming the stuff of a political branding, such that the histories of racism are subsumed into a circulation of affect, as when gender branding circulates insecurity and fear, and thereby justifies an exceptional treatment of some populations as a matter of biopolitical manipulation. But as a political branding, gender further "frees" the histories and identities of populations such that they too can be used in the process of politically branding. Through political branding, extreme versions of a population racism, extermination, for example, can be allowed to resonate with the more ordinary biopolitics of branding policy and programming, or what might be referred to as the "technical solutions" of making live and letting die.

WEARING PROTECTION IS THE NEW BLACK

The more ordinary deployment of a population racism in neoliberalism functions in a field of many populations, all of which are differently targeted for manipulation through technical solutions. Technical solutions deploy a population racism not only as a matter of governance, but as a matter of economy as well. That is to say, population racism functions on behalf of a capital accumulation by enacting a fragmentation of the biological field, enabling differences to be cut into the biological, which, as life-itself, had been made abstract. The calculation of biological differences enables a process of value production in the differences of race, or in the differences of life capacities rendered as racial probabilities to be circulated as data. Not only do probability statistics activate a population, but the probabilities draw future possibilities of life and death into the present and, in so doing, generate and circulate value, or what might better be called the biovalue of risk or life and death chances.[17] As Aihwa Ong suggests, here all populations, even those marked for the extreme violences of political exclusion, are included economically, as the excluded are made targets of calculation,[18] or when there is, as Foucault describes it, "a sort of complete superimposition of market mechanisms, indexed to competition, and governmental policy."[19]

Technical solutions have been made ordinary practice in neoliberalism, where economy and governance together have had as their primary function the evaluation and management of risk through processes of technically supported calculation, digitization especially. As Randy Martin has noted, twenty years ago the financialization of the economy concerned the opportunities of the market, while risk concerned the societal provision of damage control, especially for technological threats. Today, in neoliberalism, economy and society have been brought into "a grand, nonlinear matrix," what Martin refers to as securitization.[20] Securitization, rather than reduce everything to economy, instead has enabled economy and governance to engage common techniques of management. Governance obtains its legitimacy from markets of information, including the financial market, such that indices give shape to feelings of and capacity for well-being or the lack thereof. Fear, for example, is modulated not simply as a matter of national security but also as a matter of producing and sustaining confidence in markets that, in turn, offer veridiction of government decision. Here, population racism also plays an important part in producing affect, as, for example, it circulates fear along with statistical profiles of populations, providing neoliberalism with a rhetoric of motive in the process of political branding.[21]

Populations, therefore, are not simply groupings of human beings or individual juridical subjects of right, but rather are statistically organized and manipulated as groupings of characteristics, features, or parts. As Foucault put it: "Population will henceforth be seen, not from the standpoint of the juridical-political notion of subject, but as a sort of technical political object of management and government . . . dependent on series of variables."[22] The manipulation of populations through a population racism, therefore, is a manipulation of life capacities, of vitality, and is operated as well to produce sensation, affects, and somatic effects that are felt not only at the individual level, but more importantly at the population level through political branding. These manipulations are not meant to produce behavior of individuals or groups so much as they are meant to produce affective states, states of attention or activation with indeterminate albeit already to-be-sensed future effects.

As such, population is not only a matter of biology, of the life of species. Population may also be grasped in terms of what Foucault referred to as "publics," or populations under the guise of opinion, a milieu in which political branding might be said to operate best.[23] Tiziana Terranova describes these publics as "addresses of communicated affective states."[24] To be sure, publics are not *the* public, imagined to be engaged in discourse about and argumentation over narrative knowledge with truth claims. Publics, rather, are engaged at the level of affect and sensation, being drawn into images and commentary that are full of passions and prejudices in order that affective states might take on a facticity without employing a logic of evidence. Constituted on the same ontological plane as populations, publics come and go in time and, as such, they "express a mobility of the socius that further deterritorializes the relation between individuals and collectivities."[25] Terranova argues that there is no relationship of belonging-ness that characterizes the individual elements that constitute the public of a population. Belonging-ness or relationality is itself an effect of the mediated modulation of affectivity.

And not surprisingly, Terranova concludes that digitized technologies are fundamental to the deterritorialization of the relationship between individual and collectivity, as well as to the constitution of the publics of populations. These technologies are not only able to bring all sorts of populations to calculation but also able to produce publics through the provisional capture and dissemination of affect.[26] As the digitization of biopolitics allows for the calculation and distribution of life and death capacities for a greater number of types of populations at increasingly greater speeds, value itself has been undergoing a transvaluation, such that populations and their publics can be brought together into the production of value in the circulation of affect. That is, populations and their publics labor together in the circulation of the political branding of technical solutions in an affect economy. Here, what has been called affective labor or immaterial labor encompasses the laboring of calculation for technical solutions and the production and consumption of politically branded opinion about population capacities for life and death. The latter even is put to work in producing a division of affective laborers or an affective division of laborers—a sensibility circulated about workers working around the world, as in our next case, where there is the "feminization" of laborers who are presented as male and who are working endlessly for little pay in those parts of the world that are characterized in public opinion to have dehumanizing labor practices.

SOME STATEMENTS ARE MORE FASHIONABLE THAN OTHERS

As much for the style of reportage as for the story reported, a 2007 article in the *New York Times Magazine* seemed, at the time, as shocking as expected.[27] Its writer, Julian Dibbell, author of the book *Play Money,* tells of Chinese who work twelve hours a night, seven nights a week, for a wage of thirty cents an hour—more or less.[28] It is more or less thirty cents because just how much a farmer makes depends on how many gold coins he harvests. Gold coins? Yes, the farming that workers do takes place in cyberspace, where they participate in multiplayer online role-playing

games, or M.M.O.s, such as *World of Warcraft*. Millions of players participate in this fantasy world of combat and adventure, playing for months,
or even years, as their avatar, a virtual stand-in for the computer user.
The farmers play to gather the "gold coins" that buy the magic swords,
enchanted breastplates, and the like needed to earn the points required for
advancing through levels of the game. Gold coins worth about thirty cents
to the laborer are sold online for about three U.S. dollars, and then to the
final customer, usually an American or European player, for about twenty
U.S. dollars. Dibbell suggests that gold farmers labor in ways imagined
to be "typically" Chinese. The gold farmer usually works with others in
one of the two rooms of a small commercial space. There are thousands
of such places all over China, neither owned nor operated by owners of
the games but part of a 1.8-billion-dollar worldwide trade in virtual items.

Because "the grind," or playing to get the virtual loot that is needed
to get to higher levels of the game, is both time and patience consum-
ing, some players choose instead to buy virtual loot with "real" money,
a practice that has gone on for some time through auctioning on eBay.
While eBay recently has ended its operation of players auctioning their
hard-won loot, there are now high-volume online specialty sites for selling virtual items like gold coins, where working players are replaced by
retailers. But gold farming goes on, and game owners, not surprisingly,
have responded to the underground market in gold coins. Yet, rather than
crack down on buyers (otherwise good-paying customers of games), they
crack down on gold farmers by banning their accounts. Meanwhile, there
is also legitimate auctioning within the game being developed by game
owners, an official virtual economy that parrots and delegitimizes the
underground economy Dibbell's workers labor in.

But there is also a response like that of Donghua Networks, where
players actually play for others who give over their account names and
passwords and pay a fee. Inventiveness also has been displayed around
the end game, where a customer is escorted by a team who plays for the
most valuable rewards that cannot be bought, only won in rounds of
playing near the very end of the game. Once the team has enabled the
customer to get a valued item, they stand back so he can bag it—for a fee,
of course. Developing a deep sense of cooperation, these teams forced

the development of guilds for training in the skills of end gaming. Dibbell writes that, when this market for end gaming proved less than lucrative, some team workers found it difficult to go back to farming on their own. It seemed boring to return to the repetitive rounds of playing for nothing but gold coins, even though gold farmers often play in their down time, not only as a matter of R&D, but also for pleasure.

Perhaps it may still seem shocking that some play as work and still want to play when not working, or that there are players who don't want to play even though they are in the game, or that there has been a stratifying of game playing, defining some of it as boring, a grind, while some of it remains exciting, worth playing—or more generally, that play has begun to do real work and that virtual loot makes real money. It seems a lot less surprising that the work of playing defined as boring is outsourced to groups of players-made-laborers, paid by the piece. And not surprising at all is that the gold farmers who make for a good story, at least in the *New York Times Magazine,* are those working in China.

The story of gold farmers points to conceptualizations of immaterial or affective labor, conceptualizations that, by the 1990s, were meant to register a change in work, production and consumption, ownership, and personal property. Laboring in "a realm of atomless digital products traded in frictionless digital environments for paperless digital cash," gold farmers, as Dibbell would have it, do produce product, gold coins.[29] However, the value of their labor is based on their immaterial and affective capacities as players—not only those capacities they already exhibit, but more on those that they are capable of developing in response to the sophistication of other players of the game and, therefore, their further development of the game itself through ongoing play. Gold farming is a continuous laboring that absorbs play and more, if not all of life.

As if another side—the under side—of playing and gaming in the *financial* market, gold farming is part of the laboring of an assemblage including scientific and technological advances, corporate resources, research and development of capitalist modes of producing desire, and complex sets of game-playing practices. And more, the gold farming story plays its part in this assemblage as it politically brands and, through branding, deploys population racism. It does so differently from the gender branding of the Kenneth Cole campaign, which draws from those senses of woman as vulnerable, in need of protection, and desiring choice in order to code national security in terms of individual safety and protection and, therefore, to invest affective energies in national security. With the gold farmers, political brand operates to evoke a Western capitalist fantasy that aligns feminization with a communist de-individualization of Chinese workers presented as male. The policing of farm work taking place among the Chinese gold farmers becomes, then, a way to realign proper divisions of work and play, or legitimate work and entitlements to play, with an American nationalist-capitalist masculinist imaginary. In asserting the illegality and illegitimacy of gold farming, here the protection of labor and play (rather than of woman) becomes a matter of racialized economic superiority felt to be a defense of proper capitalism. In the political branding of the gold farmers, there is an overlay of a population racism that functions to draw the productive assemblage of potential back to various population publics through reference to past media coverage of a "*'dehumanizing' labor typically Chinese*" and, thereby, also shaping the meaning of humanness in human-rights or human-security discourse.

That is to say, just as the story of gold farming recapitulates some things already well-known about labor, production, consumption, ownership, and personal property in contemporary capitalism, that this is a story set in China cannot be taken as incidental. After all, gold farming activities are not unique or confined to China. Thus, as Rey Chow would remind us, not just the gold coins but also the story of their farming has to be understood as circulating in an economy in which "Chinese ethnicity" itself has been made valuable—serving as a political branding.[30] Although the specifics of the working conditions endured by laboring gold farmers is not news, their labor is nonetheless made surprising or given a shock-value through its infusion with the contagious affectivity of population racism.

In 2007, when Dibbell's piece was published, "China" was, and continues to be, of great interest to a United States characterized by economic insecurity and an apprehensive sense that the only thing more dangerous than Chinese communism might be Chinese capitalism. This insecurity pointed to the way in which Cold War ideologies that demarcated an ethical nationality against an easily identified foreign threat had disintegrated, and as the open field of capitalism comes not just to include but also to affectively circulate "the other," the accompanying production of fear and insecurity is itself invested in and modulated. Thus, the case of Chinese gold farmers occasions not only the circulation of virtual currency in exchange for money (really, one system of credit interlocking with another), but the circulation of a branded population racism enjoined to the securitization of market confidence in the face of a "creeping Chinese" threat of capital takeover. None of this, however, merely stops or even is meant to stop the farming. Even when attacks on gold farmers' play are mobilized by nonfarming players, the players who object to the labor of the Chinese farmers and who spend *their* playtime working to contain the threats the Chinese gold farmers pose will only intensify the value of play. That is, given the circulation of the affect of a population racism, the play to contain the threat of the Chinese farmers can only invest the gaming with affective force, with impetus for ongoing and competitive play, and as such, the labor of farming is made more valuable.

As value undergoes a transvaluation, drawing the ethical to the economic and deploying the ethical to enable economic circulation, Chow reminds us too of the other but related interest in China and argues that the concern with China's "human rights abuses" is not contrary to or even separable from economic circulation. Arguing that an economic circuit has been put into play with human rights demands concerning political prisoners, Chow reports that Chinese authorities respond by releasing "political prisoners" (from whom, she also reports, body parts are taken for exchange in the global market). The prisoners are released a few at a time, even as others are imprisoned, nonetheless compelling Western nations to soften their rhetoric so that China can gain more trading privileges and opportunities. The circuit, being dependent on the ongoing evaluation of human rights abuse, leads Chow to conclude: " Human rights can no longer be understood purely on humanitarian grounds but rather must also be seen as an inherent part—entirely brutal yet also entirely logical—of transnational corporatism, under which anything, including human beings or parts of human beings, can become exchangeable for its negotiated equivalent value."[31] All this goes into a construction of "the

Chinese," into the use and further intensification of a population racism.

Far from a negotiation with a transcendental morality (for example, the rights of humans), ethical value in an affect economy is very much a material operation, an immanent force drawing attention or activation toward sites of investment for capital and neoliberal governance. It is this forceful attraction at play in neoliberal governance that has made possible the deployment of political branding in the field of human rights and human security simultaneous with and embedded in a deployment of a population racism. Chow, as we have done with human security, takes her discussion of human rights and Chinese political prisoners to the history of feminist efforts to enter "woman" into representation in human rights policy, but she also implicates the drive of all identity politics for representation in her criticism. Chow argues that the claim to representation made for women could be realized only as a supplement to man in that it required the undoing of the erasure of woman in the construction of the "essential identity" of man. But, by the time woman enters representation by unveiling the fictionality of man's essential identity, the coupling of man–woman is "already obsolete."

This is "not so much because its twosomeness is heterosexist as because such twosomeness itself will have to be recognized as part of something else, something whose configuration—as class or race, for instance—becomes graspable exactly the moment of the supplement's materialization."[32] This undoing of gender identity, and other identities as well, in the application of the logic of supplementation, or deconstruction, has behind it the ongoing transformation of the certain configuration of the separate social spheres of the state, the economy, and the public and the private domains that, in Western modernity at least, has provided the institutional arrangement for the regime of subject formation, the condition of possibility of the individual's rights, freedoms, and obligations in relationship to a national collectivity. The shift of emphasis in neoliberalism from discipline aimed at the subject to the biopolitical manipulation of populations that we have been tracing turns to the ethical, producing the transvaluation of value in the context of a reconfiguration of social spheres, the private and public domains, the economy and the state.

CHOICE . . . NO WOMAN SHOULD BE WITHOUT ONE

In the summer of 2007, around the same time that Dibbell's story was published, a far-from high-end photo ad appeared on billboards and in train and bus stops, one in a series of advertisements for Manhattan Mini Storage, a storage facility in New York City. The ad showed an iron hanger tilted slightly to the right. To the left of the hanger and crossing over the corner of the hanger, the copy reads: *YOUR CLOSET SPACE IS SHRINKING AS FAST AS HER RIGHT TO CHOOSE.* The ad, with a flurry of response on the blogosphere, also instigated a rethinking of affect, gender as brand, and population racism. Though in a more pedestrian fashion, the Manhattan Mini Storage ad, like the Kenneth Cole advertorial, suggests there is a particularly gendered insecurity that requires this defense. Like the Kenneth Cole advertisements, this ad for storage space also links a gendered personal security with consumer choice. But if Kenneth Cole gestures toward an external nonspecified threat that nonetheless recirculates the racialization and Orientalization of threat, these ads point to the internal threat of a spreading neoconservatism. In this case, Western society must be defended against itself.

If, during the consumption boom of the mid-twentieth century, U.S. corporations learned to tie a product to sexuality, producing advertisements that offered a layer of implicit and explicit suggestions that a particular commodity would improve a consumer's sex appeal or experiences of sexual pleasure, both of which would be normatively raced as well as gendered, affective advertising does not work in quite the same way. To connect with an affective register, advertisers must activate a circulation of moods, desires, impulses, pleasures, and attentions that pass through a brand but do not need to be directly tied to a product of that brand. Branding does not rely on the attachment of connotative associations to a commodity. The Kenneth Cole insert with which we began makes the selling of fashion the stuff of political commentary, but not by explicitly suggesting that there is national security or personal safety in wearing Kenneth Cole fashions. Rather, the commentary works along with the bright surface of the photographs—the sheen of bodies and buildings, the sense of movement captured yet still in motion—to elicit a mood that draws in a reader's attention, attention to be mixed with sentiments and affects that do not have to be sorted into cognitive thought or directly exchanged for a commodity. This is advertising and marketing that is easily the matter of political branding.

In separating advertising from a product, branding like that of the Kenneth Cole fashion photographs opens itself to more ready replication, as it moves in a pool of affect that cannot be contained by a product (if it were to solidify that way, it would not be working as affect). So it is not surprising that other corporations have followed Kenneth Cole's lead. Though perhaps less artful, the campaign of Manhattan Mini Storage is nonetheless quite effective/affective, and its lack of artiness may register as a populist lack of artifice, eliciting feelings of solidarity between the "common folk" reader and the corporation. The clothes-hanger ad is but one in a series. These ads—no high-end photography pictorial in the *New York Times Magazine,* indeed, more Comedy Central than NPR—are directed at city dwellers lacking space in small cramped quarters. They have taken equal aim at celebrity and political culture. One ad stated, *Your closet's so shallow it makes Paris Hilton look deep,* while another attacked the reader's inadequate storage space by admonishing, *Your closet is so narrow it makes Cheney look liberal.* During the 2008 U.S. presidential campaigns, a photograph of a woman dressed from the neck down in an unmistakably Sarah Palin-esque jacket, accompanied the question, *What's more limited? Your closet or her experience?* There is something to note here about how an affect economy encourages the erasure of distinctions between some kinds of fame and others (for example, that of a media figure versus a politician) as fame is set not to produce meaningful aura but to marshal the rapid movements of attention. This is politician as celebrity and celebrity as political branding.

In fact, not only what a politician might be but also what politics itself might be is the question raised. Although the *New York Sun* reported on this advertising campaign in terms of how its liberal politics might dissuade conservative customers, the politics of this campaign, not to mention its effect on consumption patterns, might not be so clear.[33] To be "against" neoconservatism is not to subvert the circulations of political branding and population racism. Thus, we might agree with a blogger who, writing in response to the ads, pointed out that they work simply to "get people emotionally moved."[34] For example, *Your Closet Space Is Shrinking as Fast as Her Right to Choose,* drew various responses. Commentators on one feminist blog were content to accept the ad as a pro-choice statement in defense of women's reproductive health and freedom; a photograph of the ad appeared on this blog in 2007 under the headline *Yet Another Reason Why I'm Proud To Be a New Yorker* and was captioned with the line *We love you, Manhattan Mini Storage.* The last bit is, of course, hyperlinked to the Manhattan Mini Storage website. Other bloggers remained skeptical— though of exactly what is not clear. Blogger Subway Fox also presented a photograph of the billboard under the questioning headline *Does This Ad Go a Little Too Far?* followed by responses that include the suggestion that "it has crossed a line." *What* line is not specified, and neither is the direction that this might have gone too far in. Responding bloggers commented that any defense of abortion goes too far, that a joke about abortion goes too far, that there is no too far in politics, or that it is images of aborted fetuses used by anti-abortion activists that have gone too far.[35]

The openness to interpretation of this question signals the openness to interpretation of the ad and gives further evidence, if any was needed, that traditional models of a political spectrum that moves from left to right lose bearing in a context of affect economies and population racism. The Manhattan Mini Storage ad campaigns operate, rather, by mobilizing and intensifying attention, carrying the brand in the gone-too-far-ness or excess of affect produced by the ad and its distributed internet-based reproductions and commentary. They also function to make a political ground for marketing, advertisement, or capitalist exchange such that the choice that the ad advocates, like the one advocated in human rights and human security policies, is a neoliberal choice, gender-branded to fuse consumer options with freedom, producing an indifference between access to closet space and access to abortion. This is no misread of what freedom truly is; it is rather a rearticulation of freedom exactly as it is mobilized by the occupying forces of democracy that open markets and liberate consumers, making available whole populations of occupied territories to affective investment: the life of the oppressed Other-woman offering a branding of legitimacy to military intervention.

If the invasions of Iraq and Afghanistan never really were about the "liberation" of women, this ad also was not really about women, especially not those women whose bodies have undergone the torments of the clothes-hanger abortion. Nor was the ad about the history of the joining of reproductive technologies, including contraception, sterilization, and abortion, to eugenics programs of race population control such that some women, poor women and especially women of color, have needed protection from those technologies at least as much as access to them. Even as this ad evokes woman—the "her" that is losing out (unlike the "you," who can at least buy more storage space)—it makes abortion not about women, which is to say it disaggregates an identity or subject bound up with rights and redistributes gender, in the figure of woman, as brand. Here, woman is a set of feelings and senses about freedom and capitalism; woman is a way to think and feel about choice. In the gender branding of certain social and political policies and programs, a certain sheen of fashionable modernity and civility is given them, while populations are held in fear and terror of other populations in the gender deployment of a population racism. We nonetheless can see, although barely, the differential effects on each of us as we differently take up the risk and try to live the various lives cut out for us through these programs and policies of governance and economy.

MIDEAST PEACE IS THE MUST-HAVE FOR FALL

If the historic election of Barack Obama was hoped by some to signal a break from some forms of racism, the backlash that has risen in the first years of his administration suggests instead another affective configuration and circulation of population racism. In this round, population racism is bolstered by a political branding that connects populist white racial resentment to a conservative hostility to "big government" and any forms of social welfare democracy. While some public outrage followed, for example, the circulation through email of an image depicting the Whitehouse lawn planted with watermelons, circulate it did, along with defenses of "free expression" that recalibrate democracy along familiar lines of racialized subordination, determining what kind of society (and what parts of it) must be defended.[36] In a context of Tea Party protests and an intensified terrorizing of (presumed) immigrant populations, the imagination of how government should respond to crises of the economy and healthcare is mired in the affective forces of a renewed and insecure racialized nationalism. Defenses of racial profiling in the name of national security, panics of supposed nuclear threat posed by North Korea, Pakistan, and Iran, and the further deployment of U.S. military troops to Afghanistan—all these and more suggest that the political branding of population racism will remain at play even as we have been invited to imagine that an economic neoliberalism is facing its demise and that racism has had an historic reversal in the election of an African American President. No doubt there is reason to wonder about the future, about the indeterminacy of the present affective background of hope and what it will yield. There is no doubt as well that this hope and what it yields will come in some form of governance of capitalism attached to projects of militarized securitization against internal and external threats.

As the economic crisis, unemployment, and foreclosure continue to expand, the marshalling of populist backlash by entrenched economic and political powers both demands "something be done" and calls for governmental nonintervention. Much hangs in the balance as to how governance will respond to this double-bind of demands for and against regulation, what the relationship will be or can be between financial markets and an economy seeking again to enhance infrastructure and produce the jobs to do so. These questions open into the future, but we want to underscore the force of the past, especially in terms of its affective background of fear. As conservative neoliberal governance has found support in the manipulation of affect and gender as brand in the deployment of a population racism, future governance will continue to engage methods of manipulating affective potential. It is these methods that we must become more able to critique. Our engagement with the event of media circulations sought to be a model for such criticism.

My Mother's Scream

She shook and shook
until my ear drum burst.
Her screams penetrated my body unheard
more like a vibrating afterward
leaving a broken ground for the sounding of my soul.
And there was no set rhythm.
Her expression of rage was uncomposed,
like a CD being burnt into me
only a blistering sensation left.
Where an arrangement of affects
was meant to be assembled with voice
only dense noise
traumatizing my senses.

I would
appear to be
deaf, dumb, and blind
lost in time
immersed in space
gone to a place
somewhere else.

It has been said that the child learns to speak "by imitating the sounds made by the mother, fashioning its voice after hers." The "child hears itself initially through that voice. It first recognizes itself in the vocal mirror, supplied by the mother."[1] Not the mirror staging of vision, the acoustic mirroring sets up a circuitry from outside sound to inner ear that makes it impossible to hear only oneself in one's voice. In the echoing of the other's voice, one feels the sonorous cave, the resonating drum that one becomes, that one is when sounding, speaking, singing.

In this mirroring, the self that the child becomes is not a presence to which one could be present but "the resonance of a return": a coming and a passing, an extending and a penetrating. It is "a present in waves on a swell not in a point on a line; it is a time . . . that becomes or is turned into a loop" that stretches out or contracts, envelops or separates, and so on. It is this delicate looping that is listening or being heard.² It is what a violent screaming disturbs.

> Without the resonating circuit of coming in
> and going out from,
> no lullaby is sung
> that does not become
> a scream,
> a violation from her to me
> the raging sound, left in me
> silently repeating
> the beats on a bursted ear drum.

A perforated eardrum is a condition in which there is a hole or tear in the tympanic membrane that separates the external ear from the inner ear. The perforation disturbs the transmission of sound from outside to inside. Some things that can rupture the eardrum include sticking objects into the ear canal too deeply. Also a direct strike to the ear or an intense shaking of the head can cause the tearing of the eardrum.

And I would learn to pray for someone to come and take the sound back out of me, to take the screaming away, once and for all, to come pray with me, silently. At the end of prayer I imagined myself answering the call not of a mother's voice but of some other voice, and then once again: breath, exhalation, inspiration.

> A pressure, an impulsion
> against the violent compulsion in
> the presence of someone to tell my story to
> as now once again I hope to do.

But are we not beyond the exhausting repetitions of autobiography? Is there not an expiration date on self-representation? Is there not a cessation of storying the self for therapeutic ends, for alleviating traumatic effects that were at the turn of the millennium configured with the repeated demand to give voice to what could not be said, a privacy that now has no end of publicity? Has not sound become a matter of noise, not voice, as the shattered matrix of being reconfigures with the near end of articulating subjectivity with memory and forgetting pressed into narrative's beginning, middle, and ending? Self-representation is thinned, dispersed, and the ethnographic other's representation too. The inner drum leaves the body, leaving the body to resonate with repeated beating at a technical remove: sensory residues across distributed networks of body machines.

Still, the child has not ceased her crying. I hear her sobs coming from afar, from the world all around. My crying but not only mine. The cries are of a sonic warfare, which back then, when I was a child, was inside and outside the three-room apartment where my family lived, midst mid-twentieth-century urban renewal and the informal refusal to desegregate the schools, a clamorous politics in black and white. This was my first invitation to find a common beat within me and in the environment, to translate statistical populations of racialized lives into vibrations, coming up from the street, affecting me bodily, resonating with the slow painful beating in my stomach and the fast irregular beating of my heart as I walked.

I walked to the church before it was fully light, still lost in the sounds of the night. I walked carefully full of fear, and even before there, I could hear the large dog's bark. It awaited me on the last length of street just before I could see the church's steeple

> looming over me and everywhere the people
> letting out "the basic growl of blackness,"
> the blackness of a "non-originary drive"
> that inheres in the force that brings governmental regulation
> into existence at the very same time
> that criminality, fugitivity, waste, and debt.
> come into being.[3]

It has been proposed that the physicality of loud sounds can be understood in a number of ways—as "an ill defined sonic force exerted en masse, or as the conveyance of the materiality of sound" complementing the experience of sound as "hearing only with the ears and the mind," or "as the experience of the intensity of vibrations on the whole body as

well as within it," or as the physiological response to sound "as a potentially dangerous action" such that loudness "ultimately is governed by
injury," and in this way "the body refuses to indiscriminately allow all
sound."[4]

> But the body cannot always refuse.
> Screams can enter unheard
> when they come all at once
> when they come from everywhere,
> as if disembodied
> or of a body too monstrous to imagine
> or to hold whole in the imagination—
> a shattering body of sound,
> shattering the child's body.

Sonic warfare has been defined as "the use of force, both seductive and
violent, via a range of acoustic machines . . . meant to modulate the affective dynamic of populations, of bodies, of crowds." Sonic warfare is more
about imperceptible sounding below or above human hearing, but which
nonetheless affects the human, pushing it to the edge of nonhuman-ness.[5]
It is "a war of vibration" and "the production of vibratory fields," bringing
forth from before the theory of information a sense of noise as weapon,
blasphemy, plagues, dirt, pollution, and destruction.[6] But it is now of a
sophistication too, of a technoscience that has taken up the transsensorial
or the affective sensorium in order to find ways to modulate perception
through the indiscriminate rhythms of vibration.

> I did not sleep easily at night
> and this is nearly all I remember
> of us all being there,
> in the dark of the bedroom,
> in the three room apartment,
> except for the pattern thrown up at night
> coming through the curtain on the window,
> the light of passing cars onto the ceiling
> sliding down the wall
> never quite still,
> the lines and angles spiraling and curving

propagating in a fluid frame.
But perhaps not from outside at all
rather something coming from within,
unhearable sounds, vibrating,
with what was jumping onto my skin
and pushing in.
Once I was made to swallow the pattern whole.
Choking I could not control
the screaming now inside me echoing silently.

"[The echo] cannot occur without a distance between surfaces for the sound to bounce back and forth. But the resonance is not on the walls. It is in the emptiness between them. The echo fills the emptiness with its complex patterning. . . . And although it is complex, it is not composed of parts. It is composed of the event that it is which is unitary. It is a complex dynamic unity . . . where the bouncing back and forth multiplies the sound's movement without cutting it." The movement "remains in continuity with itself across its multiplication." "With the body, the 'walls' are the sensory surfaces." "The emptiness or the in-betweeness filled by experience is the affective dimension of the body. . . ."[7] A relay between the affective dimension and experience is not yet a subject but may well be the condition of possibility of the emergence of one.

The pattern in me an echo chamber for an insipient subjectivity. The pattern a bloc of outside-in, a bloc of colors, postures and sounds, beastly figures of a spasmodic deformation, a transformation of human bodies into vectors of matter energy. My only zone of comfort became a zone of undecidability. And there, I would learn to speak in tongues and to articulate what a third ear could hear but could not be directly said. Formed to channel voices and frequencies, a third ear allowed communication between the living and the dead, between sanity and insanity and disparate locations in space and time.

All that is left of this now is the rhyme
and this compositional form to make you linger
in the cut between singularities,
that generative space that fills and erases itself:
a space for the development of a musical faculty.

Her screams as if an intensive camouflage for words,
transposed by me into rhythmicity.

This is not autobiography
But rather a turn in me
to perform a vibrational artistry,
to become an ontologist of vibrational force.

An ontology of vibrational force delves below a philosophy of sound and the physics of acoustics toward the basic processes of entities affecting other entities. Such an orientation therefore should be differentiated from a phenomenology of sonic effects centered on perception of a human subject, as a ready-made interiorized center of being and feeling. "If we subtract human perception, everything moves. . . . At the molecular or quantum level, everything is in motion, is vibrating." "All entities are potential media that can feel or whose vibrations can be felt by other entities," allowing for "contractions of forces of the world into specific resonating milieus." Or, ecologies of sensation. An ontology of vibrational force objects to a "linguistic imperialism that subordinates the sonic to the semiotic register, . . . forcing sonic media to merely communicate meaning, losing sight of the more fundamental expressions of media's material potential as vibrational oscillators." But neither should vibrational force be misconceived as "a naïve physicalism." What is to be prioritized instead is "the in-between of oscillation, the vibration of vibration, the virtuality of the tremble."[8]

Let sound come to the rescue of thought, rather than the other way around, forcing thought to vibrate, loosening up its organized or petrified body. And there might well be a shift in the thought of trauma too, from its being conceived as a blocked unconscious repetition to its being engaged as a bloc of matter energy through which a vibrational force forces a new path, allows for a swerve, a difference in rhythm.

This is not an inscription of the self so much as a presentation in the speeds, the quickness and slowness, with which one slips in among things, how one connects with something else. Not commencing, but slipping in, entering in the middle, "taking up or laying down rhythms." This deprivileging of a phenomenology that takes the human as center of being and feeling meets with a rethinking of the digital that no longer privileges the analog against which the digital often is thought "to be simultaneously exact and reductive." An ontology of vibrational force directs thought of the digital elsewhere, to the "numerical dimensions of the virtual," "the rhythmic oscillations of the microsonic and the molecular," so to come to appreciate "an affective calculus of quantum, and the potential for mutation immanent to the numerical code itself."[9]

Ah, a sensual mathematics that would add to the calculus of probabilities "vague or incomplete quantities at the limit of 0 and 1," transforming "the logic of binary states, yes and no, into the fuzzy states of *maybes* and *perhaps.*" This is not merely a matter of qualitative renderings of a digital binarism, but rather a matter of new processes of quantification and, with that, new rhythmicities. It is upon this development of new processes of quantification and the social formation of which they are a part that rests much of what will become capacities and incapacities to sustain communication, to arouse affective connection, or to isolate and surveil, to free or control with regulative governing force. It is what will inform the future direction of self-representation and representation of us all.[10]

In between the wild pulsation of her screams, I dream of stopping time and moving myself through space to another place where I am lured into existence by abstractions. I will come to find some ease in numbers, calculus, algebra, and geometry—their rhythmicities. These become for me the means of both dissociation and creativity in a propensity for identifying the computationally open within every count or measure, opening every method to the enabling rhythmicity of sound, a rhythmicity in me but also all around.

And now, when I go back to where I once lived, just outside the door of the apartment, I am overwhelmed by the sound of rap, the beat so loud, so strong, I cannot stay there very long without being thrown back to the screams that disturb my dreams. I feel again resonating in me a violence, not only personal or cultural, or the dialectic of the two. Violence must be thought anew. It must be thought in terms of a governance that comes so close to life, comes so close to vitality, so close to rhythmicity, bringing

war, a war that engages us all, especially those who also walk the streets
where I once lived.

> hearing again the screams,
> feeling again the violence
> that comes all at once,
> that comes from everywhere.

> I walk to the church to pray.

Feminist Theory

BODIES, SCIENCE, AND TECHNOLOGY

The social studies of the body owe a considerable debt to feminist theory. Yet, feminist theorists have not always taken science and technology as a central concern in their treatment of the body. When they have, it often is with a good deal of anxiety about science and technology. Pointing to what they take to be the increasingly tight joining of the aims of science and technology with the aims of capitalism, feminist theorists have focused their treatments of science and technology on a detrimental displacement and devaluation of the human body, especially the female body. While there is reason for concern, there also is good reason to examine in order to critically engage what is presently occurring in science and technology. In what follows, I will present the work of a few of the feminist theorists who have participated in recent turns in critical theory, the turn to affect and the ontological turn, both of which are engaged with current developments in science and technology. Each of these turns has followed the philosophical thread articulated in the last decades of the twentieth century, which has led beyond the deconstruction of the subject to posthumanism, profoundly troubling the feminist conceptualization of gender and sexuality as only a matter of human subjects and human bodies. The feminist theorists I will be presenting, Elizabeth Grosz, Karen Barad, Tiziana Terranova, and Luciana Parisi, have engaged in rethinking gender, sexuality, and bodies while taking up a number of thinkers who have informed—indeed, have been central to—the ontological turn and the turn to affect, thinkers such as Gilles Deleuze and Félix Guattari, Michel Foucault, Alfred North Whitehead, Charles Darwin, Niels Bohr, Baruch Spinoza, Henri Bergson, and more recent thinkers such as Brian Massumi, Keith Ansell Pearson, and Steven Shaviro.

Grosz, Barad, Terranova, and Parisi have contributed to moving feminist theory from epistemological concerns to addressing ontological ones, including the ontology of asubjective, nonconscious affect, and have thereby opened the study of bodies to bodies other than the human body. They have instituted within feminist theory a deconstruction of the opposition of organic and nonorganic life, the living and the inert, nature and culture, a deconstruction that already has become central to new media studies, science and technology studies, and most recently, philosophy. While it is hard not to think immediately of Donna Haraway's work, especially her work on the cyborg, the feminist theorists whose works I instead will be engaging present a certain trajectory of thought leading to the ontological turn and the turn to affect while showing the challenges to feminist theory posed by these recent turns in contemporary critical theory.[1]

Perhaps the most formidable of these challenges that these feminist theorists faced was moving beyond the limitation of the social construction of gender or the constructionist approach to the body generally. In meeting this challenge, these feminist theorists often have drawn on Judith Butler, whose work has been foundational in making the body an object of study in a way that would shift feminist theory from its founding assumptions about gender and sexuality. The 1993 publication of Butler's *Bodies That Matter: On the Discursive Limits of "Sex"* and her *Gender Trouble: Feminism and the Subversion of Identity* two years before that, together, produced a stunning critique of the social constructionist approach to gender.[2] In just a few years, Butler's works would not only contribute to the establishment of queer theory; they would raise a question about the nature of matter, inciting a turn to ontology and a rethinking of technology, bodies, and matter.

SOCIAL CONSTRUCTION, BODIES, AND TECHNOLOGY

With her publication of *Gender Trouble,* Butler made it clear that the feminist conceptualization of gender as the social construction of sex needed to be troubled. Butler not only argued that the social construction of masculine and feminine genders leaves heterosexuality uninterrogated, thereby taking for granted, if not enforcing, what she referred to as hetero-normativity, but also proposed that social construction forecloses critical examination of how the body becomes sexed in the first place: how the sexed body comes to matter. Yet, Butler's queering of the sexed body, drawing as it does on a mix of Lacan's treatment of the oedipal complex, Foucault's treatment of power, and Derrida's deconstructive approach to discourse, takes the sexed body to be culturally or "unnaturally" (per)formed. The body is never given; it is performed, a performance of a material cause that is inseparable from its historical formation and meanings.

As a specific mode of discursive power, one that shows how a certain biological difference had become a historically situated norm, Butler's performativity nonetheless leaves certain oppositions in play, such as human and nonhuman, nature and culture, form and matter. So, although, for Butler, neither form nor matter preexists the other, only form is productive. Her treatment of bodily matter, as Pheng Cheah described it, assumes "a hypertrophy of the productive power conventionally accorded form," elaborated, however, "as socio-historical forms of power, that is *of the human realm.*"[3] Cheah concluded that Butler had not answered the question her queering of bodies had raised: "What is the nature of matter, such that discourse can have a formative or even causal power over bodies that the ideational scenario of psychical (oedipal) identification implies?"[4]

With the publication of her *Volatile Bodies: Toward a Corporeal Feminism* in 1994 and *Space, Time and Perversion* in 1995, Elizabeth Grosz would offer a critique of Butler that would further shift feminist theory toward an ontology of bodies and matter as well.[5] Grosz's treatment of bodies as volatile, although drawing on psychoanalysis, does not privilege the human body the way Butler's performativity does. What Grosz does instead is point to a level of dynamism subtending nature and culture. For her, the natural and the cultural are interimplicated, and therefore, their relationship is "neither dialectic (in which case, there is the possibility of a supersession of the binary terms) nor involves a relationship of identity but is marked by the interval, by pure difference."[6]

In these terms, derived mostly from the works of Gilles Deleuze and Félix Guattari, Grosz argues that, while the body is in no sense "non- or pre-social," the body also is not "purely a social, cultural, and signifying effect lacking its own weighty materiality."[7] Grosz takes up Deleuze and Guattari's conceptualization of the body-without-organs, in terms of which she deconstructs the way body parts have been organized, for example, in terms of a disciplining of the organism into an oedipalized unified sexed body. Against the oedipalized body, the body becomes, for Grosz, a matter of "a discontinuous, nontotalizable series of processes, organs, flows, energies, corporeal substances and incorporeal events, speeds and durations. . . ."[8] The body is what it can do, not what it is.

As such, the body engages in desiring production, where repetition is not to be understood in the psychoanalytic terms as a regression to an earlier state, but rather as the condition of possibility of difference or invention: a swerve in inheritance. Instead of aligning desire with fantasy opposed to the Lacanian Real, and therefore seeing it as an always unsatisfied yearning, desire is understood instead as a series of practices, bringing things together or separating them, making machines, making other bodies. Thus, the desiring unconscious also is reconceived. As Deleuze had put it: "The unconscious no longer deals with persons and objects, but with trajectories and becomings; it is no longer an unconscious of commemoration but one of mobilization, an unconscious whose objects take flight rather than remaining buried in the ground."[9] This view of desire displaces the Lacanian Real with virtuality or potentiality. For Deleuze, following Bergson, the virtual is to be contrasted with the actual, rather than the real. The virtual is never realized; instead, it calls forth actualization, but the actualized has no resemblance to the virtual. The virtual–actual circuit, therefore, is different from the possible–real circuit. The possible anticipates the real or the real projects backward to its possibility as if always having been. Actualization is not a realization of possibilities. Actualization is not a specification of a prior generality. Actualization is an experiment in virtuality. It is a divergence to the new or the future.

For Grosz, to think virtuality along these Deleuzian lines is not only to rethink the body, but to rethink form, to rethink frames, grounds, figures, and social structures: the constructed, the architectural, and the built. Not surprisingly then, when Grosz rethinks bodies, she thinks them becoming cities or becoming architecture, while she rethinks architecture and cities as productions of desire. Bodies, cities, and architecture are thought in terms of speeds, allowing and disallowing the actualization of virtuality in the reconfigurations of social spaces. As such, form moves and is moved by or in sensation; it is moved and moving affectively, where affect is to be distinguished from emotion, referring instead to bodily capacities to affect and be affected: the capacity to act, to engage, to connect. While emotions are commensurate with a subject, affect, being bodily, traverses, even is beyond, a subject. Affect is nonconscious, asubjective potentiality open to entanglement with technologies that modulate affective intensities below cognition and consciousness. As such, form, for Grosz, refers to the trajectories of bodies prior to, and remaining alongside, relations of subject and object, before and alongside figure, ground, and narrative structure. Form calls forth an ontological perspective in which matter and form are interimplicated or deferrals of one another like nature and culture, like biology and technology.[10]

Grosz's works would not only invite feminist theorists to engage with the works of Deleuze and Guattari, especially their ontology of bodies; she would also ask feminists to reconsider feminist criticisms of science and technology, especially in relationship to biology and evolution. In *The Nick of Time* and *Time Travels,* Grosz would argue that what is at stake in rethinking evolution and biology is an understanding of time or, better, duration in matter.[11] This is because the thought of evolution frames not only what we think about the emergent, the new, the future, but also how we relate these to matter. The question is whether emergence, newness, or futurity arises from a dynamic immanent to matter or whether they derive from transcendental categories of time and space. Grosz addresses these old philosophical questions through readings of Deleuze, Bergson, and Merleau-Ponty and turns these readings into philosophical meditations on Darwin. Grosz finds in Darwin's theory of evolution a connection to the volatile body, the virtual, to an ontology linking matter, energy, creativity, and invention.

Beginning with natural selection, Grosz makes clear that Darwinian evolution should not be thought as a matter of preservation, of the "victorious species, the winner of evolutionary struggle at any particular moment." It should be thought as a matter of selection that is "most open and amenable to change."[12] Indeed, there must be ever-changing criteria applied by natural selection precisely because it is meant to provoke change in relationship to an environment that changes. Natural selection presents "incentives for the ever inventive function of species in their self-proliferation."[13] It is the potential of individual variation, its inventiveness in the face of time's surprise, that makes Darwinian evolution creative: undirected, highly unpredictable, and inexplicable in causal terms. Grosz also argues that Darwin's theory of evolution turns the thought of evolution to time as a force of life, or time in matter. This leads Grosz to an understanding of technology—what she describes under the heading of "the thing" and "the prosthesis"—as effects of the challenge that time in matter poses to life. For Grosz, living bodies, organic bodies, invited or challenged by matter, tend toward prosthesis; as far as the body goes, technology is to be thought as a "prosthetic incorporation."

But, for Grosz (and here is the payoff of no longer depending on a Lacanian psychoanalysis), the organic body makes things that function as if they were bodily organs not because the body is lacking. Rather, what it makes, it makes as a matter of a supplementary invention, an aesthetic and proliferating reorganization. Grosz underscores what she correctly finds to be an extraordinary passage from Bergson: "Life, not content with producing organisms, would fain give them as an appendage inorganic matter itself, converted into an immense organ by the industry of the living being." For Bergson, this is the function of the intellect, which "always behaves as if it were fascinated by the contemplation of inert matter," thereby adopting its ways in order to direct them.[14]

While Grosz rightly refuses to oppose technology to nature as if it pre-existed technology, it is not clear that thinking technology as prosthesis will not allow these oppositions to return, as "inert matter" returns in Grosz's reference to Bergson. In her works on Darwin, Grosz does not rethink technology as other theorists would who also take up Deleuze's thinking about the body. These theorists rethink technology and the body in order to rethink matter as self-organizing or informational. They return to the genealogy of information theory—from nineteenth-century thermodynamics and equilibrium-seeking systems to late-twentieth-century complexity theory and far-from-equilibrium systems at the intersection of informatics and quantum mechanics, contemporary molecular biology, and computer science. These theorists allow us to see matter as informational all the way down and, therefore, to rethink the organism as bodies of information. This is especially important in relationship to a biopolitical economy, where "information," as Eugene Thacker argues, is "seen as constitutive of the very development of our understanding of life at the molecular level," while it provides the conditions for biology to surpass itself and gear itself "toward extra organism ends." For Thacker, in a biopolitical economy, biology is "the process of production," and in replacing machines, biology "is the technology."[15]

Although by the turn of the twenty-first century, Foucault's work on biopolitics, sexuality, and the disciplining of the subject already exerted influence on feminist theory generally and feminist queering of bodies particularly, it was Luciana Parisi and Tiziana Terranova who, as feminist theorists, would take up the organism as a way to rethink gender, discipline, systems, and bodies in a biopolitical economy. In their 2000 essay "Heat-Death: Emergence and Control in Genetic Engineering and Artificial Life," published online in the journal *CTHEORY,* Parisi and Terranova would draw especially on Deleuze—not so much the Bergsonian Deleuze, but rather the Spinozian Deleuze—in order to argue that bodies are not always organisms and any organism is constituted of many bodies.[16] Like Grosz, they would describe the body as a composition of fluids, flows of forces, and affect that precede and exceed the phenomenological self. But, unlike Grosz, Parisi and Terranova extend this thinking about bodies as fluid compositions from philosophy to political economy and the governance of capitalism. Echoing Donna Haraway, who had declared that the "organism is not born . . . but made in world-changing technoscientific practices by particular collective actors in particular times and places," Parisi and Terranova would point to the way in which the organism, with the rise of Western industrial capitalism, became what the body could be and do.[17] They then go on to outline the conditions of the current political economy that are making the body-as-organism a less dominant definition of the body, drawing on current technosciences that are concerned with information and post-thermodynamic far-from-equilibrium systems.

THE MAKING AND UNMAKING OF THE BODY-AS-ORGANISM

For Parisi and Terranova, the body-as-organism is a definition of bodies resulting from investment by capital and technoscience in the context of Western industrial capitalism. Described in thermodynamic terms, the body-as-organism is understood to function by borrowing energy from outside that which already is organized for production—that is, from the yet ungoverned fluids, forces, and affect—and to discharge entropy or unproductive energy to the outside. Thus, the body-as-organism is defined as homeostatic and equilibrium-seeking, a closed system, befitting industrial labor and reproduction. As such, the body-as-organism becomes an object of governance, an object of what Foucault called disciplinary practices meant to monitor the psychic and physical aspects of the individual subject. These disciplinary practices find their place in the enclosures of civil society as the nuclear family, the factory, the prison, the labor union, and the clinic become closed spaces for the socialization of the individual subject through a disciplining of the body.

The body-as-organism is not merely a definition of bodies; it also "presents a bio-physical pattern" or a diagram for the arrangement of social institutions in Western industrial capitalism, primarily for governing labor and reproduction, in which the body is fitted to a thermodynamic cycle of accumulation and expenditure of energy. It is this biophysical pattern governing the body and social institutions that produces a certain gendered economy or circulation of energy, where the woman's body becomes the figure of both maintaining homeostasis and threatening it. That is to say, the woman's body is subordinated to filiative reproduction, and as such, it renews the energy of the individual and the population. But as a primary source of energy outside production, the woman's body also threatens disequilibrium with the intimation of ungoverned flows.

Of course, the industrial system of production has its limits, and one surely is the difficulty of securing energy and using it without heat death or without energy being lost to other than production. Given that the loss of energy is understood primarily to be a matter of technology, as for example in closed mechanical systems like the steam engine, not surprisingly then, the response to heat death can be traced through a history of technoscience, from thermodynamics to a redefinition of matter/energy in terms of information, where creativity and invention finally are observed to arise when systems are far-from-equilibrium. This redefinition of matter/ energy as information, connected first with post–World War II cybernetics, affects the body-as-organism as the diagram of the governance of capitalism. As the body-as-organism gives way as the diagram of governance, a new diagram is invested. To critically engage this diagram, Parisi and Terranova turn to Deleuze's definition of control societies, which he developed in part as a reading of Foucault's discussion of the waning of disciplinarity.[18] Parisi and Terranova suggest that this shift of emphasis in governance from discipline to control coincides with three waves of cybernetic theory, initiating a redefinition of the body.

If post–World War II cybernetics first sought mechanisms of control that were equilibrium-seeking, treating the body as homeostatic, by the 1970s, the so-called second wave of cybernetics would theorize systems taking into account an observer or a point of view from which the functioning of the system could be understood—that is, the presence of a governing, reflexive feedback loop. Control would be theorized in terms of autopoietic informational systems, befitting the body-as-organism even while opening up the body to redefinition. Characterizing the organism as autopoietic or as closed to information but open to energy, Humberto Maturana and Francisco Varela defined the body-as-organism not only as a self-organizing system but also as a self-producing one.[19] The autopoietic organism has as its primary aim the continuation of its life in the preservation of its organization, its informational economy of functioning parts. With that as its aim, the body-as-organism selects as its environment only what supports its survival and its capacity for ongoing self-production. By this definition, the organism becomes reflexive, self-observing, internally doubling the point of view of an outside observer, thus giving the organism the inner capacity of an outside observer apparent in the organism's maintaining its boundary or its closure with each interaction with the environment.

As all living systems come to be defined as autopoietic, the body-as-organism becomes the figure of life-itself. But, as Parisi and Terranova argue, characterizing life as autopoietic "does not account enough for transformation and complexification" of life.[20] The circularity of auto-poiesis, preserved in every situation of the organism, is contradictory to evolution, where species evolve through continuity, but also through change and genetic diversity.[21] Parisi's mentor, Keith Ansell Pearson, would argue that autopoiesis "blocks off access to an appreciation of the dynamical and processual character of machinic evolution," which "con-nects and convolutes the disparate in terms of potential fields and virtual elements and crosses techno-ontological thresholds without fidelity to relations of genus or species."[22] As Pearson sees it, the organism must be rethought such that it is open to "the wider field of forces, intensities and duration that give rise to it and which do not cease to involve a play between nonorganic and stratified (or organic) life."[23] This would introduce into autopoiesis the complexity of nonlinear, far-from-equilibrium conditions.

Here the definition of the body is closer to Grosz's volatile bodies: a composition of fluids, flows of energy and affect. But it is also closer to what Parisi and Terranova argue befits the ongoing developments of genetic engineering, on one hand, and new media or digital design, on the other. It is a definition of the body as open to technicity. Or better, it is an understanding of technicity as the nonorganic always integral to life, if however under-theorized as such or disavowed in privileging the maintenance of the organism's boundaries as characteristic of life-itself. But if technicity or the nonorganic is integral to life, then the body must be conceived as a nonunified assemblage in which neither organic nor nonorganic can be privileged, in which the organism is many bodies, some nonorganic, and in which a point of view is not the internal doubling of an outside observer, but the very mark of the assembling or composing of the disparate. Here the nonorganic is a point of view, as there are many points of view, not only human ones. In these terms, the body-as-organism is replaced by the body as machinic assemblage, where machinic is neither mechanistic nor organismic, but rather a matter of affectivity, fluids, and energy flows, luring the disparate to each other, as well as sustaining the continuous.

As a definition of the body, machinic assemblage derives as much from science and technology as it does from capital investment. As Pa-risi and Terranova argue, the closure required for self-organizing and self-producing systems becomes a hindrance for the expansions of what they call "bio-cybernetic capital," in which "preservation of 'vivified matter in the face of adversity and a universal tendency toward disorder' is too conservative a goal."[24] By the late twentieth century, what is needed for capitalist expansion, Parisi and Terranova argue, is offered by technology and science in the capacity to draw profitability from life in turbulence, at the edge of chaos. Capital seeks to put the noisy to use in opting for invention or creativity beyond any human plan or program or where the plan or program is flexible, choosing variation as one of the components. There is something of a return here to Claude Shannon, who, before autopoiesis would become central to second wave cybernetics, had defined entropy not as heat-death, but as the condition of possibility of information, the noise and disorder against which information can be put to work.

This definition of information is extended through technologies of genetic engineering and its practices, where, as Parisi and Terranova point out: "It is not an individuated DNA which determines development but a relation between different bodies within and outside the cell. Selective pressures are immanent to the symbiotic process of combinations of molecular entities hinging on a multiplicity of relations and affects." This takes evolution even further than Darwinian and neo-Darwinian evolution; as Parisi and Terranova argue, "mutations are not random occurrences which are then selected by an external force but are already guided by an immanent and creative selective pressure." Here, "both beneath and across the strata of the organism, fluid dynamics and molecular life display a different mode of existence of a body, one that exceeds the thermodynamic cycles of finitude trapping the organism."[25] For Parisi and Terranova, however, invention and creativity, which are let loose with a "third wave" of cybernetics, are not merely a matter of freedom, specifically freedom from discipline. They are, rather, a letting loose of control of the unpredictable or the improbable in order to take the unpredictable as a resource for capitalist expansion and an object for governmental management.

In describing societies of control, Parisi and Terranova would follow Deleuze's take on Foucault, who distinguished a governmentality aimed at disciplining the individual subject from what he called biopolitical governmentality.[26] In biopolitical governance, the focus is less on the individual subject and more on species-life, expressed as the differential capacity or potential for life across populations. Here population is not, as Terranova later would argue, "a collection of subjects of right—constituted by the partial alienation of their natural rights to the sovereign—but a dynamic quasi-subject constituted by a great number of variables" pertaining to the "the environmental milieu that constitute and affect it."[27] The life of a population is unpredictable or improbable at the pre-individual level but reveals "probabilistic regularities once considered at the mass level."[28]

Along with regularity, probability brings the possibility of improbability, the unpredictable, especially at the pre-individual level. There always is an excess of information keeping a population metastable, or in "a continuous state of drift—caught up in deterritorializing movements of migration, mutation, recombination and creolization."[29] It is this excess, this improbability, that is sought as both an economic and political resource in biopolitical governing as the improbable becomes central to the market circulation of risk and where "populations" refer not only to human populations but also to populations of genes, stem cell lines, or blood banks; all can be calculated along with terror-risks, risks of mass deaths from HIV/AIDS, risks of imprisonment.[30]

While Parisi and Terranova express no nostalgia for disciplinary societies, they also caution that, in control societies, power is not gone, but only working differently on bodies and the body politic through ever more refined measures. As for the woman's body, often linked with fluidity, Parisi and Terranova also warn that control societies are not necessarily feminine or feminist. Control societies are less concerned with the coupling of bodies with subject identities or with identities generally because the shift to the governance of populations is about indeterminacy garnered from measure and made productive in an economy of risk. In control societies, a question is raised as to how to measure functions? Massumi points to what he describes as "beyond biopolitics," where risk leads to preemption as measure is opened up to the gamble of forecasting.[31] How does measure become a probe for the improbable or the unpredictable beyond statistics and probability?

Parisi and Terranova also refer to preemption when discussing cloning, where the cell seemingly is brought back to a virtual stage of growth also defined as a zero degree of development. Of course this zero degree only seems to be a reverse of development; it actually is a measure of the future from where a distinction of the cloned and the clone can be made only retroactively. The question of measure, of course, is raised here, as it often has been in relationship to the body as a matter of technology, performativity, and experimentation. That is, the question of measure is a question about boundary making: the cloned and the clone, the present and the future. But while Parisi and Terranova see bodies as a function of measure, they also take the flows of forces and affect to be in excess of any measure, the machinic assemblage to be in excess of any body, a conceptualization that Parisi later takes up in her work on queerness and abstract sex.[32]

QUANTUM ONTOLOGY, MEASURE, AND EXPERIMENTATION

If Parisi and Terranova would explore the space opened up by Grosz in her swerve away from Butler's take on the body, there would be an opening for rethinking the body suggested by another critique of Butler that would take up the ontology of the body not from the point of view of biology but from that of quantum physics. Two years earlier than "Heat-Death" appeared, Karen Barad's "Getting Real: Technoscientific Practices and the Materialization of Reality" would appear in the feminist journal *differences*.[33] As if to make her point from the very start of her essay, Barad would follow an opening epigram drawn from Foucault's description of the disciplined body by shifting the focus to another body: the piezoelectric crystal. Rather than take the human body as her subject matter, Barad takes up "a material instrument, the 'soul' of an observing apparatus, through which not simply signals but discourse (in the Foucauldian sense) operate" (89). Following Haraway's conception of agency in terms of what she has called "material-semiotic objects," Barad develops her conception of "agential realism," which would allow her to pay attention to matter in a way Butler did not do.

As Barad sees it, Butler had theorized how the human body came to matter as a sexed body, but she did so by showing how discourse mattered in materializing the body. What she did not do, Barad proposes, was show how matter came to matter. Here, again, Butler's account of the body is criticized for treating matter as passive, inert, receptive to and dependent on discourse for material transformations. Barad suggests that a return to the question of agency in relationship to matter is necessary, also requiring rethinking performativity and realism. Barad begins a revision of Butler by turning to technology, to what Barad calls "technologies of embodiment." Drawing momentum from works of feminists studying technologies, reproductive technologies especially, Barad goes on to offer an ontology of bodies by showing the way matter comes to matter through an entanglement of discourse and a measuring or observing apparatus in an experimental or performative context.

Barad takes as her primary example the work of Niels Bohr and his search for "a coherent interpretation of quantum physics" (94). Barad proposes that Bohr's search should be a guide, showing us that the question of bodies and technologies necessarily is a question of scientific method and objective measure. Moved by critiques of representationalism that feminists already had developed, Barad will further revise method and measure toward a realism commensurate with Bohr's perspective, which holds that there is an inseparability of the object of observation and the agencies of observation. There is an emergent and co-constitution of object and agencies, an interdependence of material and conceptual constraints and exclusions, demanding a reformulation of causality and the material conditions for objective knowledge. Thus Barad offers as a starting point, the proposition that "theoretical concepts are defined by the circumstances required for their measurement" (ibid.). Thus, the discursive is always part of an intra-actional performativity, part of the particular technological arrangements that define concepts. Barad's performativity therefore differs from Butler's in that it is not a mediation of signifiers but rather a formation relative to an observing or measuring apparatus.

Of course, the question of measure looms large in quantum mechanics, given the impossibility of simultaneously measuring the position and momentum of an electron so that the materialization of particle or wave is dependent on the particular measuring device in a particular experimental setting. Drawing on this characteristic of quantum measure,

Barad makes clear that the performativity of different measures is not about the uncertainty of the observer but about the indeterminate nature of matter—wave or particle: an ontological position rather than an epistemological one. Matter is indeterminate because that is how it acts under conditions of measure in the context of a specific experiment. To emphasize the inseparability of measured and measuring in the context of experimentation, Barad introduces the idea of "intra-action" displacing interaction, in which a dichotomy always is reinscribed. Intra-action is the production of a performative measure, an assemblaging of the measured and the measuring that constitutes a determinate body to which the measure retroactively has reference, as does conceptualization.

So, it is not a preexistent physical object that is measured; it is measure that performatively produces a determinant body or a "phenomenon-without-consciousness" out of the indeterminacy of matter, what we might take to be a production of a surplus of being or, better, a surplus of ordering. While, for Barad, performativity is a way to account for the different phenomena that are produced with measuring, measuring is irreducible to human agency, or human agency alone. In intra-action, all relevant features of the experimental arrangement count and, as such, are inseparable from the measured. What the measure does is exclude possibilities such that wave is produced rather than particle or particle is produced rather than wave. Following Bohr, Barad concludes that the classical idea of causality no longer fits. Causality is not a matter of an observation-independent object, but a matter of a phenomenon that excludes others. These are the conditions of objective knowledge.

Barad's agential realism has profound implications for an ontology of bodies that she draws out by elaborating the meaning of apparatus, moving beyond Bohr's theorizing of it back to Foucault's theorization of body practices in political and social terms. Turning to Foucault's treatment of "disciplinary apparatuses," or what he also called "apparatuses of observation," or "apparatuses of production," Barad focuses on the way Foucault points to the panopticon as a technology that served as an observing instrument for making disciplined bodies. For Foucault, while the bodies produced by these technological practices do not preexist them, he does not emphasize, as Barad would want him to do, the intra-action of bodily matter. She therefore returns to the piezoelectric transducer to further elaborate her idea of agential realism and intra-actional bodies. She makes the case that, in ultrasonography, "the transducer does not allow us to peer innocently at the fetus, nor does it simply offer constraints on what we can see; rather, it helps produce and is part of the body it images" (101).

For Barad, then, the sonogram refers not to a physical object we might call the fetus but is itself part of the phenomenon referenced by the observation or measure. Of course, the apparatus is also coproduced, as the apparatus does not preexist the measuring; ultrasonography is part of a range of practices involving many other material configuration and discursive formations. And here, the body cannot be separated from the apparatus except in its exclusions of other bodies; in the time of the measure, boundaries are produced. Beyond each measure, what we take to be the same body in fact is another body, a body produced differently. Agential reality "is continually reconstituted through our material-discursive intra-actions" (104). Intra-actionality is constraining rather than determining; intra-actional reality remains uncertain, open to being reconfigured.

In elaborating agential reality, Barad is bringing technology and science studies to bear on feminist theorizing of the body. For Barad, bodies arise intra-actionally as phenomenon, and therefore, intra-actional bodies are not just a matter of shaping the surface of a body or a body's morphology, as Butler proposed. Barad is taking up the very atoms or the very volume of bodies as nonconscious phenomena, not as a citational iteration but as an intra-actional iteration (106). For Barad, intra-actionality is how bodies materialize, how boundaries and volumes are produced. It is only through intra-action of observed and observing or measuring apparatus that there is an agential cut able to reconfigure matter, reconfiguring boundaries and separations, or where indeterminacy is resolved for specific experimentations. As such, Barad recasts agency. For her, agency is not something possessed, preordaining the distinction between human and nonhuman, subject and object; rather, agency is making changes to particular human and nonhuman practices. Like causality, agency is in the intra-actional production of nonconscious phenomena, or what Barad also calls "things-in-phenomena." Rather than things being entities behind phenomena or being things in themselves, phenomena are prior to any given or preexisting relata.

While Barad treats bodies as intra-actional phenomena that are both human and nonhuman, it is nonetheless not clear how one phenomenon or body becomes another. In her critique of Barad, Luciana Parisi would ask if "Barad's elevation of quantum mechanics . . . to metaphysics does not risk reiterating the discursive approach to science, which she refuses, insofar as by rejecting what is given in materiality, that is abstract bodies (the given or pre-existing relata), she also rejects what is implied in quantum mechanics: the event of experiencing quantum, imperceptible bodies before these acquire the qualitative properties of phenomena."[34] In putting abstract bodies against Barad's intra-actional bodies, Parisi wants to theorize the in-between of bodies; against Barad's rejection of the experience of the imperceptible, Parisi elaborates "a materialism of continuity."

MACHINIC ASSEMBLAGES, AFFECT, AND EXPERIENCE

By treating bodies in terms of "a materialism of continuity" that allows for the experience of imperceptibles and takes reality "not as agential realist intra-activities, but as the occurrence of *singular events*, . . . as *throbs of experiences* in duration," Parisi also draws on quantum physics.[35] Whereas Barad, like Bohr, allows quantum imperceptibles to be real only in being in intra-action with measure, Parisi takes them to be virtual and a matter of experience. For her take on quantum, Parisi turns to Alfred North Whitehead's reading of it, adding to it Deleuze's treatment of virtuality, discrete entities or occasions (object), and the experience of time.[36]

Beginning with Whitehead's definition of event as the dawning and perishing of an actual occasion (object), an experience of the passing from one state to another, from one present into another past, Parisi proposes that "what is becoming is not the actual experience but the continuity between one occurrence (or occasion or object) and another" (84). There is what Whitehead describes as the concrescence of elements into a novel assemblage by means of prehensions. For Whitehead, conscrescence is actual becoming through a novel production of togetherness or the coming together of multiple prehensions, where prehension is the preconscious, pre-individual act by which one actual occasion takes up and responds to another. Prehension is a kind of knowing, an affective knowing, prior to individuation and consciousness; as Parisi puts it: "Prehension may be better described as enactment . . . an affection that coincides not with here and now but with a vector connecting here with there, immediately before and after" (84–85). Everything, not just humans, prehends, in that each thing orients toward withdrawing from or advancing toward the world. That is to say, prehension is a "decision," to use Whitehead's term, eliminating potential occasions and delimiting a specific occasion, which, after perishing, becomes the past or "datum" for another occasion or for a grouping of occasions that endures as a "society," to use Whitehead's term. For Whitehead, "eternal objects" (or potentiality) also play a part, uniquely contributing or adding indetermination to each actual occasion, which allows the occasion to become a past or datum to another occasion. That is to say, as the potentiality of indetermination, eternal objects "ingress" actual occasions when they are selected by actual occasions. This is an immanence of concrescence and prehension that allows for both continuity and discreteness. Whitehead refers to this as extension: "the most general scheme of real potentiality."

Parisi puts Whitehead's thought to use in taking up what Deleuze and Guattari conceive of as an "abstract machine" or "machinic assemblage," which she describes as:

> . . . the gelling together of pre-individualities, a felt continuum that embeds discrete bodies within a field growing by its edges, adding and subtracting components: an ontogenetic process in which all elements play a part and yet no element can form a whole. The abstract machine entails an engineering patchwork of partialities passing from one state to another, fusing and breaking into each other, and yet belonging-together at points of transitions, which are less irreducible dots than inflections, critical thresholds, curvatures of imperceptible continuities. (82)

Differing with Barad, Parisi argues that the abstract machine permits a connection between things without the necessity that they be phenomena; rather there are "the insides of and spaces between atoms, the atomic and subatomic particles," an "incomputable materiality," which is nonetheless held-together in virtuality (ibid.).

In contrast to agential intra-action, there is an experiencing of virtuality, what Parisi describes as a real experience of "time as a continuous relation of enveloping" and "space as a relation of linkage," where experience, however, is affective and not only human (90). There is a kind of freedom here that seems absent from intra-action in that there are occasions that begin and end without end, or not without ending and falling back into potential—all independent of the observer's choice of reference. The event of an occasion is unique; it is a decision, a prehension, a freedom not only because the occasion is free from determination by an observer but because there is no situating in experimentation, but rather a displacing or relocating by means of experimentation. About this freedom, Steven Shaviro quotes Whitehead, who proposed that: "The vast causal independence of contemporary occasions is the preservative of the elbow-room within the Universe. It provides each actuality with a welcome environment for irresponsibility."[37]

Yet, for Parisi, this freedom must be understood as in her earlier work with Terranova, as a matter of value and, therefore, both to influence and to be influenced by the interests of governance and economy in control societies. If this also is a matter of measure, as it is for Barad, Parisi's view of measuring nonetheless differs from Barad's. The difference follows on Parisi's assumption, like Deleuze and Whitehead, of the ontological givenness of the virtual or potential that is nonetheless really experienced. And as such, the measure that Parisi takes account of is linked to the advances in the mathematics of digital design or digital architecture, software programming: simulation. What is of particular interest to Parisi is experimentation attempting to afford architectural software programming the ability to operate on the information or numbers between 0 and 1, to allow digital architecture to capture and manipulate the curvilinearity and variability of what Parisi refers to as the experience of a materialism of continuity. This, for Parisi, is not a matter of intra-action, because it assumes a different ontological understanding of quantum than the one Barad inherits from Bohr. Thus, the mathematics or digital architecture Parisi engages does measure, but only by intensifying or modulating that which measures itself, that is, the throbs of experiences in duration all the way down to matter, to life itself.[38]

Drawing on Whitehead and Deleuze, Parisi returns to sexuality and queerness, proposing that queerness is not an identity and surely does not belong merely to the human body or human sexuality. Queerness rather takes the body back from or beyond the constrictions of the organism, placing it into life where life is organic and nonorganic. For Parisi, queering raises the question not of who, but "how when where queer?" Queering makes for wondering how many sexes are implicated in the abstract machines of desire in the concrescence of multiple prehensions, in the givenness of the virtual. If once Grosz, paraphrasing Deleuze, would argue that there are "a thousand tiny sexes" traversing the human body, Parisi would take this thought to the machinic assemblage and, thus, not only the human body, but to matter, to life-itself.

CONCLUSION

The feminist theorists I have considered raise important and challenging questions for a feminist theory focused primarily on the sex and gender of human bodies, as well as for a feminist theory focused on science and technology that does not take into account more recent developments in science and technology. The feminist theorists I have engaged are focused on bodies other than human bodies. In shifting the focus, they retheorize the relation between human bodies and technologies, especially those technologies that are presently bringing into human experience what only technology can enable, the experience below human conscious and cognition, outside the current understanding of life-itself. They also are concerned to alert feminist theorists to the changing definition of the body that is arising to fit what the body can now do, but also what economic and governing interests, including science and technology, have and might yet invest, seek to control, or modulate in relationship to life and existence generally.

A Dream of Falling

PHILOSOPHY AND FAMILY VIOLENCE

The violence of her touch,
the crudeness of her gestures,
the distain of her address
transformed her beauty—
like the iridescence of a horrid bug's wing
caught in the flicker of sunlight—beautiful.
Then, light gone
and in shadow's fall,
even uglier,
if it can be believed.

Do you? Do you believe?
That the hurt repeats,
repeats its passage into eternity,
in iridescent blue, purple, and red
of her hand print on my face
and the banging in my head,
I cannot cry out.
The words can barely form in my mouth.
"What are you doing to me,
Mommy?"

Falling back into an ecstasy of fear,
young, and at the edge of despair,
abstraction will become in me
a call to philosophy.
Bold thoughts to suspend her hand in mid-air
so that it can not bear
down on me.
And then,

> oh lovely philosophy,
> the possibility
> of comforting thoughts,
> quieting thoughts
> for a cessation in the realm of sensation.
> To sleep, perchance to dream,
> to dream in place of waking
> amidst the night's violent scenes.

We are told that we do not fall asleep, but that sleep falls upon us. Or, it is not an "I" that falls into sleep, not an "I" that can distinguish itself from anything else, "from anything more than its own indistinctness." "I fall asleep—that is to say, 'I' fall. . . ." "In my own eyes, which no longer look at anything, which are turned toward themselves and toward the black spot inside them, . . ." I am "isolated from all manifestation, from all phenomenality, the sleeping thing . . . not measured, not measurable."[1]

But there is measure and measuring for those who cannot fall into sleep. So many of them now: women, abused by those whom they know or who know them. And, like women, children, too, are badly mistreated by mothers, fathers, sisters, brothers, uncles, cousins, doctors, teachers, therapists, ministers, priests.

> Three in ten girls. Three in twenty boys.

> A silent epidemic, they say,
> and with that,
> and the making of a statistical population,
> I fear no one will hear
> each woman or child crying,
> sleeplessly not dreaming,
> those who cannot let sleep fall,
> who cannot let consciousness fall into that unconscious
> that never simply was theirs: the world's unconsciousness,
> the unthought, that obsesses in ghostly figures walking
> the endless day of sleepless night. The dark night of the soul.

Is it that philosophy now is failing us? What bold thoughts for this overwhelming abuse? What comforting thoughts in the shameful shade of family violence? In our biopolitical state of governance, has a necropolitics brought philosophy to an end? Or must it come undone and begin again? From "the dust of this planet," a start?[2]

> Start again, the philosophers are saying, with objects withdrawn from all relations.
> Start again with no presumed correlations between human and world, reason and life.
> Start again on a groundless ground, in a negation of negation.

And I?

> I try to hide. I go inside myself
> where some few objects are put away:
> A rubber doll with washed out eyes,
> a stuffed yellow dog nearly life-sized,
> so dirty from being dragged along the street,
> outside the window
> where no one sits.
> And the clock and the metronome—
> time machines, mysterious to me,
> and the books of fairy tales and poetry

> All beloved
> the objects more to me
> than the humans can be
> The objects still
> awaiting me
> there always
> therefore, me.
> Attending objects
> truly being,
> only being,
> glistening in the shine
> of the bright lights of dissociation.

We who have been forced to insight might perhaps have the foresight to see objects otherwise before we see with only human eyes, seeking an ontograph and discompose of hurt in the objects of a childhood faith.

But what of childhood faith? Can it withstand the profound perversion of what the psychoanalysts have told us: that "the infant's first subjective experience of the object" is "less as a significant and an identifiable object than as a process of accumulating internal and external transformations" and that the first transformational object is the mother, "as a recurrent experience of being, as the rhythms of processes that inform the nature of the object-relation rather than the qualities of the object as object."[3]

And alongside the perversities, there is the history of the relationship of politics and philosophy that inserts itself between process and object, between object and the name of mother. Most recently, the history has found itself again in yet another unsettling turn. From a generative ontology, or "an ontology of generosity," of given-ness and giving, of being and becoming, there has been a turn to the speculative realism of an object-oriented ontology.[4] Will this philosophical turn call forth a more speculative psychology for our biopolitical state of governance?

After all, the genealogists tell us that there has been a shift from the family as model of governance, from the sovereign as a good father, who will provide, to the family as instrument in the biopolitical governing of populations. As the family becomes the privileged instrument for obtaining data pertaining to the life and death capacities of populations, the population becomes *the* medium of interests and aspirations. Family violence, if not violence in general, is made a normal matter, a matter of statistical populations. It is in terms of this socio-normalization through populations that governance resets the limits of perversion, such that, along with the hyper-familialism of our times, family is abandoned to sadness, pain and fear.[5]

> All subjects, objects, and environs are here
> to stand not before lack but before estimation and valuation.
> No longer in relationship to desire,
> our bodily wounds go to number and accounting.
>
> Freed in a way,
> although by some other hand than we might have imagined.
> Freed of family ties
> long after the reader of dreams revealed
> a mix of desire in the story of abuse,
> incest put in the shadowy grip of fantasy
> and turned from the real: the becoming of the impossibly real.

But alas, philosophy begins again; it returns as a speculative realism to validate the realness of experience and the experience of the real, including that which is beyond human knowing. Speculative realism refuses the presumption of a primordial rapport between human and world. Its object-oriented ontology claims that objects are real in that they are forever withdrawn from us and from each other. They can come to us and to each other only through sensuality or each object's sensual profile: color, texture, tone, taste, height, weight. It is by proxy of the sensual that a real object touches a real object in the interior of some other entity or surround that has been called "an intentional whole." But by no means is this only about human intentionality. The relations between objects are a matter of a vicarious causality, a causality where the sensual lures objects to each other. Causality is alluring: "a lure to feeling," to an experiencing beyond human consciousness, perception, and cognition.[6]

A new metaphysics is called forth as philosophy returns to the real while freeing thought from being bound to human consciousness, even human unconsciousness. And, along with this freeing, the family shifts from model to instrument to us being bits and pieces of populations, numbered, with only some small part left for poetry. And incest slips from fantasy's hold to the rhythm of the counter's bidding, a lullaby of probabilities, a rocking back and forth of a statistical cradling.

Are you dreaming yet? Are we dreaming together?

And there is no human hand on the cradle.
The mother's hand nowhere near,
I dream of falling.
I feel my body shake
and pivot down to a groundless ground.
Falling, falling,
into ecstasy wide awake

As everything is drawn to the count of endless measuring, counting, like causality, becomes alluring, and it is no surprise that measure becomes a matter of aesthetic judgment. Against a surfeit of measures, each measure is designed to be singular or subjective, able to change its metric or perspective with each measuring so that, with each measure, there also is a probe for the incalculable excess of calculation. This is not a matter of the sublime, however, but of the beautiful, not about truth or falsehood but about attraction and repulsion: measure becomes a speculative grasp of futurity or potentiality. An intense passion, repeatedly repeating.

> I crawl to a spot on the floor,
> damp with pee and tears.
> Small bits of grey condense
> into a hazy halo around my vision
> as through a child's dirty glasses
> no one cared to polish clean.
> I cannot see.

> But there was a moment, I remember,
> when we sat, my father and me, on the floor.
> There was a tunnel of light
> that blocked my peripheral sight
> of her standing there.
> My vision instead was directed straight ahead
> to the shelf of books he read to me.
> Leather bound with golden letters,
> poetry and fairy tales inside
> and fancy illustrations
> in iridescent colors of purple, blue, and red.
> But the moment does not hold.
> His fingers on my leg,
> bent at the knee,
> my thighs go clammy
> and there is a much too intense sense
> of a volcanic trembling in my stomach's pit
> Blinded by the light,
> ruined in her sight,
> no one now will sit
> with me.

Neither about truth nor falseness, measure is made to reach for the beautiful in assemblaging objects that otherwise are indifferent and disinterested. If one object lures indifferently or without caring which object it lures, the object that has been indifferently lured nonetheless finds the alluring object beautiful. For the lured object, the alluring object is beyond interest, use, or need; it rather is an object of a disinterested but intense passion. It is this reach for the beautiful that makes measure alluring and gives it the capacity to probe for potentiality or the incalculable excess of calculation. But when need is not met or when there only is the drive of sheer interest or utility, the allure of measure may offer no potential but instead incite an avaricious repetition; the beautiful freezes the lured object in a repetitive reductive response to the alluring object's superfluous self-exhibition.[7]

And ought we not allow the psychoanalysts another word about the infant who they claim takes in not only the contents of the mother's communications but also their form. "The mother's aesthetic," as they call it, is a facilitative environs that ought to make thinking irrelevant to the infant's survival. Sensual survival and the survival of the sensual: even the dream has its dramaturgical form thanks to this. That is, the mother's touching hold gives form to the way the ego will hold instinctual needs. The dream holds as the ego does as the mother did.[8]

Beautiful Mother, alluring Mother
there, ice cold in the mirror,
combing your lead black hair.
Lips painted red
your blue, purple dress thrown on the bed.
Repulsive Mother,
mouth twisted
in a bottomless howl,
a hissing growl.
Hands raised like claws
too near
ready to tear.
Destructive Mother,
imploding the space of dreams
my bodily intensities unable to cohere.

A critical aesthetic is, perhaps, our only hope. At least this is what the philosophers tell us; it is a way, they say, to bring on the shock of love and, with that, activate potential once again.[9]

The Datalogical Turn

Patricia Ticineto Clough, Karen Gregory, Benjamin Haber, and R. Joshua Scannell

In 2013, the Chief Technology Officer (CTO) of the United States Central Intelligence Agency, Ira "Gus" Hunt, addressed a crowd of software developers, coders, and programmers at the "Structure: Data" conference in New York City.[1] In a fast-paced and nearly winded PowerPoint presentation, Hunt tried to articulate both the challenges and possibilities that "big data" present to the agency.[2] Suggesting that the world has already become a "big data world," the CTO charted a simultaneously frightening and captivating vision in which social media, mobile technologies, and cloud computing have been married to the "unbounded, promiscuous, and indiscriminate" capacities of nanotechnology, biotechnology, and sensor technology. Given this queer bundling of capacities or this capacity to bundle, as we would put it, Hunt proclaimed that "it is nearly within our grasp to compute all human generated information" and that human beings are now "walking sensor platforms" generating endless seas of data. How to find "a signal" amidst all this "noise," suggested Hunt, is only one of the challenges posed by such a world.

While the scale of data is often simply referred to as "big," it is not necessarily the scale that troubles and excites. Rather, it is the speed with which data can now be collected and the adaptive algorithmic architectures that organize these data in ways beyond simple instructions leading to optimized solutions. Algorithmic architectures are no longer exclusively aiming to predict or calculate probabilities, but rather operate so that "any set of instructions is conditioned by what cannot be calculated," the incomputable quantities of data that are "included in sequential calculation . . . so as to add novelty in the actual architecture of things."[3] Adaptive algorithmic architectures point to what Luciana Parisi describes as "the residual power of algorithms, the processing of rules and the indeterminacies of programming, which are able to unleash novelty in biological, physical and mathematical forms."[4] As adaptive algorithmic architectures come to play a greater role in the parsing of big data, technology is felt to move faster than and differently from institutions and humans. Algorithmic architectures are not only offering epistemological resources, but ontological sources as well, allowing, as Hunt suggested, for the "inanimate to become sentient."[5]

In this essay, we explore how the coupling of large-scale databases and adaptive algorithms are calling forth a new ontologic of sociality or the social itself. We propose that this ontologic, or what we refer to as the "datalogical," is especially challenging to the discipline of sociology, which, as the study of social systems of human behavior, has provided a modern frame for configuring bodies, subjects, contexts, or environments in relationship to the political and the economic. Focusing especially on the entanglement of what George Steinmetz has called sociology's "epistemological unconscious" with the systems theory of cybernetics in the post–World War II years, we rethink sociality as moving from an operational logic of closed systems and its statistically predictable populations to algorithmic architectures that override the possibilities of a closed system and predictable populations, opening sociality to the post-probabilistic.[6] Characteristic of what we are calling the datalogical turn, the postprobabilistic is transforming the epistemological foundations of sociology and challenging the positivism, empiricism, and scientism that form the unconscious drive of sociological methodology and its ontology.

We further argue that the datalogical turn is resonant with the move from representation to nonrepresentation, often thought to herald the end of the modern or the becoming of the postmodern.[7] Instead, we argue that the move to nonrepresentation unconsciously has driven sociological methodology all along. Here, then, we take nonrepresentation to differ from representation. In representation, there is a present absence of what is represented. But for us, the present absence in representation is displaced in nonrepresentation; rather, nonrepresentation points to the real presence of incomputable data operative in algorithmic architectures parsing big data. As we will discuss below, these architectures have automated the selection of incomputable data, allowing for indeterminacies in the capacities of programs to reprogram their parameters in real time. We are proposing that what has been hailed as big data and the algorithmic architectures that sort it serve less as a fundamental break with the unconscious of sociology than as an intensification of sociological methods of measuring populations where individual persons primarily serve as human figures of these populations.[8] Taking this claim further, we see the algorithms currently being built to parse big data in the sciences, finance, marketing, education, and urban development, as well as in military and policing policy and training, as a more fully developed realization of the unconscious drive of sociological methodology that is, nonetheless, outflanking sociology's capacity to measure. That is to say, adaptive algorithmic data processing is forcing fundamental questions of the social, challenging our understanding of the relationship of measure to number taken as mere representation authorized by an observer/self-observer of social systems of human behavior. Big data is not simply a matter of the generalized deployment of new technologies of measure, but the performative "coming out" of an unconscious drive that has long haunted sociology and is now animating an emergent conception of sociality for which bodies, selves, contexts, or environments are being reconfigured in relationship to politics and economy.

In the first part of this chapter, we trace the entanglement of cybernetics and sociology to show how sociology's unconscious drive has always been datalogical. While sociology has been driven to go beyond the human and to become a science that could run only on statistical data, it has been hindered by the very speeds of its technologies of collection and analysis and has had to fall back on the supplementary figure of the observing/self-observing human subject. But once again, sociology's unconscious drive is being stirred, drawn out to meet new technologies that have given rise to nonrepresentational forms that run at the speed of contemporary capital. In the second part, we chart the arrival of big data, which we identify as the performative celebration of capital's queer captures and modulations. New technologies such as parametric adaptive algorithmic architectures have given rise to a mathematics reaching beyond number to the incalculable and are no longer slowed by the process or practice of translating back to human consciousness. The concern is not so much that these technologies are being deployed in the academy, but rather that there is a usurpation of social science by instruments of capital markets, beyond the state, leading to what Mike Savage and Roger Burrows have termed the "crisis of empirical sociology."[9] While some in sociology have responded to this crisis by trying to move faster (by learning to data mine, for example), the turn to datalogics is fundamentally a more profound challenge to the underlying epistemology and ontology of sociological thought that has yet to be seriously grappled with in the discipline, even as its foundational dualisms like structure–individual, system–agent, human–world, and even lively–inert increasingly are untenable.

Finally, in the third part, we look to the social logic of the derivative to chart the global disintegration of the human form under nonhuman spatiotemporalities. At a time when the spread of datalogics creates new profits through novel derivative modulations of liquidity, we suggest that sociology has doubled down on the human phenomenological project—on slowness, the bounded body, and the human figure. This representational retrenchment misses or ignores the new sociality being created and revealed by the performativity of the datalogical. We end then by proposing that nonrepresentational theory and other philosophical moves toward becoming and movement provide new space for critical inquiry on the social.

CYBERNETICS AND THE SOCIOLOGICAL UNCONSCIOUS

This emergence that we are calling the datalogical is contingent on contemporary availability of processor speeds capable of rapidly accumulating and sifting petabytes of data, but the datalogical has always haunted the sociological project.[10] The redistribution of the human body and the figure of the human subject into datafied terrains has underlined the discipline from its inception and points to some of the interesting resonances and entanglements between orders of cybernetic study and sociological methodology.[11] Cybernetics, of course, has been focused on the disintegration of the biophysical into the informational and, in turn, has articulated a complex informatics of sociality. Since its post–World War II reconstitution as the premier science of the state's reckoning with the social, sociology unsurprisingly has held a deep fascination with cybernetics.

While there is not strictly a causal relationship between cybernetics and sociology, we aim to sketch the entanglement of the disciplines with one another through the production of a data-driven human subject, a subject imbricated with data. In the case of sociology, the process of slowing down the information intake in order to make sense of relationships (statistical correlations, etc.) always was a methodological requirement of translating data into meaning befitting social systems of human behavior. Sociology has tied this slowing down of data to the figure of an observing/self-observing human subject. Our investigation of the entanglement of sociology and cybernetics shows that liquefying this congealed human figure always has been the unconscious drive of a discipline that, nonetheless, in the current moment, is defensively blocking the becoming conscious of that drive.

The epistemological unconscious of sociology arises in the post–World War II years with the presumption that the social world can be objectively studied. As positivism, empiricism, and scientism became its center of gravity, sociology aimed to be a usable, predictive state science. According to the basic premises of sociological methodology, data collected was only as good as the researcher's ability to assemble it and present it back to an invested public. At the most basic level, this meant that the methodologies of sociology were designed to modulate the speed and scale of the accumulation and circulation of data in order to fulfill the representational requirements of social systems of human behavior. It meant a marriage of phenomenology or the epistemology of the conscious/self-conscious human knower with the technical demands of the state, enabling institutions to agglutinate population data to systems of human behavior, on the one hand, and to rationalize the figure of the human subject for state instrumentality, on the other. A mode of inquiry of statistical models and replicable experiments "made it increasingly plausible that social practices really were repeatable . . . a wide range of human practices could be construed as constant conjunctions of events while ignoring the historical conditions of possibility of this patterning."[12] If the historical, in all its contingency and uncertainty, was not the reference for statistical models and replicable experiments, it was because the historical was displaced by the more powerful concept of "system."

By the 1950s, the notion of a generalized system had come to refer to interdependent components or parts and the principles by which interactions and interconnections of parts are to function in reproducing the system as a whole while maintaining its functionality. In terms of sociality, to maintain a system and its functionality is to reference the capacity for social reproduction in terms of a boundary—that which marks the "outside" of a system. This boundary, combined with a regularity in the interactions or interconnections that constitute the system, allows it to be modeled so that its behavior becomes predictable, usually at statistical-population levels. Aspects of sociality outside the system are "made static," turned into control variables, in order to see the patterned movements of the experimental variables. This movement, if repeatable, could be translated into durable predictions about behavioral dynamics that are technically expressed as the statistical probabilities of populations.

Statistical modeling can generate useful correlations only if a relatively closed system can be presumed such that the introduction of dynamic forces can have an impact that will be observable. In the social sciences, systems theory led to the development of evolutionary models of human behavior (most prominently in the work of Talcott Parsons) that viewed sociality as a hierarchically organized series of subsystems, each of which is, by necessity, discrete and relatively closed to outside information. Thus, for Parsons, both the biophysical or the organic and the sociocultural are self-contained systems driven to evolutionary reproduction. It is the breaking up of sociality into discrete systems that can be held static in relationship to an outside that allows for populations capturable by statistical models.

For this model of inquiry to proceed, it had to depend on an epistemological stance similar to first-order cybernetics. As in sociological research, first-order cybernetics is predicated on a homeostatic, equilibrium-seeking model that presumes a certain durability of reactions to observed stimuli that allow for a probabilistic prediction of future patterns.[13] In first-order cybernetics, the researcher stands to some degree *outside* the system that is being observed and applies technical apparatuses to convert incoming data from shifts in a stabilized system into repeatable and decipherable patterns. First-order cybernetics maintains a duality between the systems to be observed and the apparatuses of observation (in the case of sociology, the apparatuses are the method of the research project). The apparatuses extend through, but are not of, the systems that produce an implied dis-identification of researcher and researched. In this, first-order cybernetics and post–World War II sociology mirror each other as essentially positivistic, empirical imaginaries that presume a distinction between the observer and the observed. Ontologically, there remains a separation between a stable researcher, on the one hand, and a systematized research environment of human behavior, on the other.

If both first-order cybernetics and a positivistic, empirical, scientistic sociological unconscious presume a distinction between the observer and the observed, in second order cybernetics and the critical social theories and methodologies that would arise in the 1970s and 1980s, reflexive interventions would be imagined that were meant to "correct" the dis-identification of the observer with data resulting in the human subject being figured not only as observing but also as self-observing. Of particular concern to second-order cyberneticists and social scientists who sought to apply second-order cybernetics to research is the notion of "autopoiesis." Coined by Humberto Maturana and Francisco Varela, an "autopoietic system" is

> a machine organized . . . as a network of processes of production (transformation and destruction) of components which: (i) through their interaction and transformations continuously regenerate and realize the network of processes (relations) that produced them; and (ii) constitute it (the machine) as a concrete unity in space in which they (the components) exist by specifying the topological realization of such a network.[14]

In other words, autopoiesis suggests that the internal construction and networking of a machine, organism, or system reproduces itself in novel iterations as a response to—and through interaction with—the outside environment. Most famously translated into sociology through Niklas Luhmann's systems theories, the concept was more broadly used as a theoretical and methodological guide among so-called postmodern or critical theorists and researchers of the 1970s and 1980s.[15] For them, an autopoietic framework made the dis-identification of the researcher with the researched an untenable ontological position. Methodologies such as autoethnography and textual analysis would demonstrate that, in an autopoietic system, the researcher cannot stand outside the system and observe its feedback loops (as in first order). Instead, the researcher is a part of the system's feedback loop. No observer can be outside the system observed because, under autopoietic conditions, the system self-organizes around and within inputs, including the observer as input. The autopoietic system nonetheless maintains the boundedness of the system, as the observer serves as a double for the boundary. That is to say, the boundary between system and environment is taken as an effect of the observer observing, including observing him- or herself observing, as second-order cyberneticists would have it.

Such a stance has commonly come under fire for sliding into solipsism. If the system is constantly reorganizing against an "outside," then the system is totally enclosed and detached from any external "reality." A common discourse in debates over theory and methodology in the social sciences comes down to a conflict between those who would argue for a more positivist, empiricist, and scientistic social science and those who argue for a more reflexive one that includes taking account of the observer or insisting on his or her embodied self-consciousness being made visible. These debates have been tiresome for some time, given the archaeologically deep links between the two positions. They both rely on the figures of the human subject and the insular, thermodynamic system. In both cases, the role of the observer is one of calculated disturbance and translation. In sociology, the lessons of the second order have been taken up primarily as a simultaneous acknowledgment of one's presence in the field of observation via "reflexivity" and then the dismissal of this presence's importance to the overall project of drawing and articulating human relations. In the wake of critique, the championing of reflexivity often has taken the form of a defensive insistence on the capacity and obligation of the researcher to "speak for" the researched.

The sociological adoption of second-order cybernetics has, then, if anything, retrenched the discipline firmly in an insistence that it is articulating a human, phenomenological project and denying its unconscious datalogical drive. Poised between first-order and second-order cybernetic logics, but without acknowledging in either case the underlying datalogical drive of the discipline, sociological reasoning has stagnated. The constant resuscitation of the false dichotomy of observed and observing, along with that between quantitative and qualitative, micro and macro levels, has hamstrung much of sociology from rethinking its assumptions at a pace with the development of new modes of computation closely associated with postcybernetic computational technologies. We now turn to these new modes of computation, or what is being called "big data," in order to illustrate how their very logics, speeds, and capacities are troubling these long standing dichotomies.

THE DATALOGICAL TURN

According to IBM, every day, we create 2.5 quintillion bytes of data—so much that ninety percent of the data in the world today has been created in the last two years alone. This data comes from everywhere: sensors used to gather climate information, posts to social media sites, digital pictures and videos, purchase transaction records, and cell phone GPS signals to name a few. This data is big data.[16] Descriptions like this one have rapidly proliferated across increasingly widely distributed media. The big data scientist has been billed as the "sexiest job of the twenty-first century"—and sociology is only one of the many disciplines trying to "get in on the action."[17] But sociology always has been part of this action, unconsciously driven by the datalogical, with its capacity to escape the capture of apparatuses of arrest such as regulation, the law, and indeed, the biopolitics of the human figure—putting the datalogical beyond the representational without necessarily being inherently attached to the resistant or the liberatory.

However, the coming out of the datalogical means a redistribution of the technologies of collection and analysis of "social" data away from the academy, challenging empirical sociology, if not putting it into crisis. Sociology no longer has a monopoly on "social" data collection and analysis; rather, human lives continually pass through datafied terrains. Even though data collection processes are unevenly distributed throughout the world, many quotidian behaviors such as making a call from a cell phone, using a mobile device to access the internet, clicking through web links, swiping a credit card to make a purchase, or even visiting a hospital or accruing a speeding ticket have now become dynamic sites of data collection.

The movement within these sites, however, is not unidirectional. Data fields pass in and out of bodies, feeding on novel and emergent connections within and between bodies. Indeed, the ability of data to smoothly travel away from its original site of collection is highly valued within ecologies of big data. The translation between behavior and data point is often less than clear and subjected to numerous third- and fourth-party interventions that multiply the networks through which data will travel. For example, salary and paystub data that is collected by employers will become part of the data that is bought and sold by credit-reporting companies and data brokers that work to compile these reports, along with other "public" information, in order to buy and sell data profiles. Another example is gamified marketing strategies that require an individual to go through a series of clicks in order to make a simple purchase or that require a bit of "free labor" before a transaction can be completed—producing data that is only tangentially related to the express purpose of the individual's behavior.[18]

In other words, data—or what comes to populate a database—is no mere representation of the social activities that produce it, as sociology and first- and second-order cybernetics have suggested. The "point" of the datalogical is not to describe a stabilized system or to follow a representational trail, but instead to collect information that would typically be discarded as noise. Indeed, it is that data that is most typically bracketed out as noise in sociological methods—such as affect, or the dynamism of nonconscious or even nonhuman capacity—that is central to the datalogical turn. The adaptable algorithmic architectures that parse such data are not merely representational; rather, they are nonrepresentational in that they seek to prehend incomputable data and, thereby, modulate the emergent forms of sociality in their emergence.[19] Put otherwise, the datalogical turn moves away from representation and its reliance on sociological correlation and correlative datasets and moves toward the incomputable conditioning of parametric practices in algorithmic production. In contrast to these practices, the rules of operation for serial algorithms state that one sequence after another must complete itself to arrive at relationships (such as in the case of crosstabs and linear regressions— that is, stochastic approaches) in which datasets are to be pitted against one another in order to uncover durable relationships between sets of numbers. The postcybernetic analysis of big data is oriented away from this sort of seriality and toward an analytic not of numbers, per se, but of parameters, leaning toward the nonrepresentational.

What is crucial in postcybernetic logic is not the reliable relationship between input and output, but rather the capacity to generate new and interesting sets of relationships given certain inputs and rules.[20] In order to achieve this productive novelty, the analysis of big data relies on adaptive algorithmic architectures that add patternless quantities of data that allow parameters to change in real time.[21] Instead of establishing an order of rules that must be followed to result in a relational number, adaptable algorithmic architectures allow rules and parameters to adapt to one another without necessarily operating in keeping with a progressive or teleological sequence. These adaptations do not lead "to the evolution of one algorithm or the other but to a new algorithmic behavior."[22] For example, the U.S. Air Force is creating an autogenerating virus that builds itself out of snippets of code snapped up from various "gadgets" (short texts of pedestrian code) distributed across a number of programs in a computing network. The virus builds itself based on certain parameters that define the rules of the algorithm and adjusts those parameters as needed in order to develop more interesting, complex, and dynamic networks of relations.[23]

The operative mathematics underlying big data analytics is functionally a mathematics reaching beyond numbers, a mathematics reaching to the incomputable, calling into question the opposition of quantitative and qualitative methods of measure. The unfathomably huge and diverse clouds of data that are generated from the ubiquity of digital surveillance effectively render them beyond number, and it is only in the context of adaptive algorithms that the noise of the data cloud can be rendered.[24] In the case of personal data, it is not the details of that data or a single digital trail that are important. It is, rather, the relationship of the emergent attributes of digital trails en masse that allow for both the broadly sweeping and the particularized modes of affective measure and control. Big data doesn't care about who you are so much as about the bits of seemingly random information that bodies generate or that they leave as a data trail; the aim is to affect or prehend novelty.

This is precisely how big data calls into question relationships of individual and structure, actor and system, particular and general, and quantitative and qualitative. For Bruno Latour and his followers, the trails and trajectories of ubiquitous digital data collection allow for a more fully realized actor-network theory in which, instead of the two "levels" of micro and macro, big data gives us visualized tracings of "individual entities taken severally," where entities can be a person or a city, attributes of a person or characteristics of a city, etc.[25] With the datalogical turn, therefore, not only is there a decentering of the human subject, but the definition of the bodily also broadens beyond the human body or the body as autopoietic organism, and as such, bodily practices themselves instantiate as data, which in turn produces a surplus of bodily practices. So too, the difference of the inside and the outside the system is undone and a question is raised as to what environment is.

All this is to suggest that it is especially important that we not filter our understanding of the social through representational frames that are understood to supplement reductive quantitative measures when, instead, through complex processes of calculation, computing technologies cannot be thought merely to be reductive: they neither quantify biophysical and cultural capacities nor are calculation or information understood simply to be grounded in such capacities.[26] In other words, digital computing has its own capacity to be adaptable and "creative" in ways that challenge the assumption that the "artificial" nature of computational intelligence is inherently limiting; rather, big data is revealing digital computation's immanent potential for indetermination in incomputable probabilities.[27]

Computational shifts in the algorithm-driven analysis of big data have allowed a form of qualitative computing that has been considered exclusive to human cognition and the self-conscious observer. Digital computation is flattening the opposition of quantitative and qualitative methods of measure. In doing so, digital computation or architectural algorithms are problematizing the observing/self-observing human subject of social systems in which the environment can be represented or registered only in the limiting terms of the ongoing functioning or autopoiesis of the system.

Whereas the self-conscious observer of critical theory and second-order cybernetics implies an autopoietic feedback that reproduced the whole or system, albeit while increasing its complexity with the ever returning epistemological excess of a blind spot, the architectural algorithms of big data make use of the unknowable or the incomputable in a nonconscious manner that points to the further decentering of human cognition, consciousness, and preconsciousness. Here, parts are not reducible to the whole or the system, since parts can be large, quantitatively incompressible, and as such, bigger than the whole. Algorithmic architectures work with parts that are divorced from a whole. Indeed, the incomputable or the incompressible information that would necessarily be excluded or bracketed in cybernetic logics is folded into algorithmic architectures such that, at any time, the incomputable may deracinate the whole. This moves representation beyond systems and the observing/self-observing subject in the enactment of a nonrepresentational theoretical orientation.

FROM SOCIAL SYSTEM TO DERIVATIVE SOCIALITY

Although it has been claimed that big data represents the "end of theory," we are suggesting that the datalogical turn is, rather, the end of the illusion of a human and systems-oriented sociology.[28] Sociology's statistical production of populations in relation to systems of human behavior is being disassembled and distributed in derivative and recombinable forms operating in the multiple time-spaces of capital. This is to say, the sociological production of populations for governance, while being the central mechanism through which securitized power's taxonomies have coagulated, has found itself in the odd position of being outflanked by measuring technologies beyond the discipline that are running at the hyper speed of capital.

Sociology's insistence on durable, delimited, repeatably observable populations as a prima facie for measurement has situated it as a quasi-positivist, empiricist discipline between first-order and second-order cybernetics. Its assumptions about the nature of information and noise, such that the sociological mission is to cleanse the former of the latter, fundamentally miss the point that, under contemporary regimes of big data and its algorithmic architectures, noise and information are ontologically inseparable. The noise of the incomputable is always already valuable information since it allows for resetting parameters. Big data technologies seek not only to parse, translate, and value noise but also to enhance its production by taking volatility as their horizon of opportunity. Such volatility can be felt tingling, agitating, or, to use a rather commonplace market term, "disrupting" knowledge formations across numerous disciplines, but is particularly challenging stable sociological articulations of the demos. Given the datalogical's challenge to sociological methods of measure, the very project of tracing or tracking populations presumed to be held static through statistical analysis is put under pressure, if not undone entirely.

Traditionally, statistical and demographic data accumulations are performed at complementary but cross-purposes. Demographics tend to accumulate the raw material from which statistical analyses (plotted, generally, on an x–y axis) can be conducted. That is to say, demographics produce the populations that can be held still or made visible in order to measure relations in a statistical (that is, predictive) manner. Demographics, in sociological modeling, function as the condition of possibility for statistical relationships. Of course, the relation is recursive (or topological) in that statistical models fold back into future accumulation of demographic information and project backward in time to complicate historical demographic calculations. And yet, the relationship between statistical and demographic data is still logically distinguishable.

However, the distinction effectively disintegrates when the datalogical turn allows instant geospatial realization of histories of environmental, consumer, criminal, domestic, and municipal datasets to be reconciled in real time. Here, coded bodily practices—walking, sitting, waiting, smoking, cell phone use, for example—get read through ubiquitous distributed methods of digital surveillance and fed back through big data sorting that is designed to collate seemingly unrelated sets with the intention of producing novel relations. The temporal and spatial differentiations upheld by the distinction of statistical analysis and demographic data breakdown. We are suggesting that the datalogical leads less toward an articulable demographic than towards an ecology of Whiteheadian "occasions."[29] Occasions, while temporally and spatially discrete, are in actuality a movement that itself traces multitudes of becomings in which the social itself continually formulates or reformulates, as do the boundaries of any population. This blending of demography and statistics is part and parcel of the process of smoothing that big data accomplishes.

Here, the ongoing formulation of the social replaces what historically have been considered social formations. The latter are smoothed out or flattened into derivative circulations in a digitally mapped/mapping universe that means to stretch to folded information or the incomputable. The deployment of folded information or the incomputable is the deployment of indeterminacy, and it remains unclear how this indeterminacy will affect ongoing calculation and its ongoing performativity of measuring the social. What is enabled, however, is that flattened structural categories like social formations or racial, sexual, ethnic, or class identity can be mobilized statistically in instantaneous, computationally driven assemblages with indeterminacy at work. It is our contention that this is a measuring that is always adaptive and, indeed, a self-measuring dynamic immanent to ongoing formulations of the social. Under datalogical conditions, measurement is always a singularity—a productive, affective materialization of dynamics and relations of recombinable forces, bundling parts or attributes. Rather than a reductive process, calculation remains computationally open and the digital is no longer easily contrasted with a putatively thicker, qualitative computation. As such, big data allows for a new, prehensive mode of thought that collapses emergence into the changing parameters of computational arrangements.

It would seem, then, that the datalogical turn is drawing together a form of Whiteheadian process theory of occasions and a social logic, that of the derivative, both of which share an interest in the deployment of excess—an excess that is necessarily bracketed out by sociology and the two orders of cybernetics in their quest for replication and repeatability.[30] In a system that seeks to cleanse noise from information, what cannot be rigorously and falsifiably repeated or what seems qualitatively beyond the scope of probabilistic calculation (affect, or the dynamism of nonconscious or even nonhuman capacity) is necessarily bracketed out. But what is beyond the scope of probabilistic measure is relevant not only to the algorithmic architectures of big data; it is also relevant to the queering of economy, what Randy Martin has called the "after economy" in his elaboration of the derivative.[31] Calculation beyond the probabilistic is especially central to the pricing of derivatives, which, as Elie Ayache argues, is the very process of "market-making."[32] The market is made with every trade in that "trading (this process supposed to record a value, as of today and day after day, for the derivative that was once written and sentenced to have no value until a future date . . .) will never be the reiteration and the replication of the values that were initially planned for the derivative by the theoretical stochastic process and its prescribed dynamics."[33] To put it another way, pricing through trading is an occasion, a radically contingent one where pricing makes no reference to any preceding trends, tendencies, or causes. These are better grasped as retro-productive aspects of market making.

The pricing of the derivative through trade "extends beyond probability." The derivative "trades after probability is done with and (the context) saturated" (41). When the context is saturated with all its possibilities, it opens up to what Ayache calls "capacity" that allows for the context to be changed (42). Pricing through trading "is a revision of the whole range of possibilities, not just of the probability distribution overlying them": not changing possibilities, but changing context, the whole range of possibilities of a context (44). For Ayache, this means "putting in play of the parameter (or parameters) whose fixity was the guarantee of fixity of the context and of the corresponding dynamic replication" (42). There is an excess, an incomputable affective capacity that takes flight in the vectors of the derivative. As Martin puts it: "Here is an excess that is released but never fully absorbed, noise that need not be stilled, a debt registered yet impossible to repay."[34] Excess, debt and noise all point to that drive for liquidity upon which the derivative sits, "at once producer and parasite."[35] In this way, derivatives, as Gregory Seigworth and Matthew Tiessen argue, "work to construct a plane of global relative equivalence through processes of continual recalculation on sloping vectors of differentiation."[36] Pricing derivatives through trade is a process of "forever calculating and instantaneously recalculating value based on monetary value's latest valuation."[37]

Extrapolating from its common perception as a mere financial instrument that bundles investments against potential risks, Martin points to changes in sociality informed by the derivative that also are indicated by the algorithmic architectures of big data: undermining the conceit of the system or the taken-for-granted reduction of parts to the whole. For Martin, "as opposed to the fixed relation between part and whole that informs the system metaphysic, the derivative acts as movement between these polarities that are rendered unstable through its very contestation of accurate price and fundamental value. . . ."[38] Indeed, derivatives "turn the *contestability* of fundamental value into a tradable commodity . . . a market benchmark for unknowable value": an incomputable value that is nonetheless deployed in measure.[39] The way the derivative bundles suggests a "lateral orientation," as Martin puts it, that displaces the relatively recent descriptors of a postmodern sociality:

> A transmission of some value from a source to something else, an attribute of that original expression that can be combined with like characteristics, a variable factor that can move in harmony or dissonance with others . . . derivative logic speaks to what is otherwise balefully named as fragmentation, dispersion, isolation by allowing us to recognize ways in which the concrete particularities, the specific engagements, commitments, interventions we tender and expend might be interconnected without first or ultimately needing to appear as a single whole or unity of practice or perspective.[40]

The very act of cutting the commodity into aspects of a derivative not only freed the commodity from its ontological status as "a thing," but freed the vectors of time and space contained within the commodity. A house is no longer a home, but rather a forecast of possible futures, understood as risks to be hedged or profited from. Big data follows this forecasting logic as it seeks not only to gather infinite data points but also to put these points into motion as datasets aim to generate unique patterns. In this way, big data is moving data. It cannot be captured or held static, or it would lose its very value both socially and monetarily. As such, big data serves the derivative logic that is running on perpetual debt- or credit-based liquidity.

Here again are ties to a Whiteheadian theory of process in which discrete occasions of experience both come into being and dissipate back into a continuum of generative excess. While working with the notion of occasion requires a conceptual attunement to a world pulsing with change, we argue that such an attunement is essential if we are truly to grasp the breadth of social shift currently afoot in computational world. This basic move allows not only that things—both human and nonhuman—are in continual process of becoming, but that they do not necessarily require a human, cognitive subject to act as their interpreter. In fact, we might ask if the computational itself is beginning to reach toward the notion of the continuum, possibly coming to stand in for what we will perceive is a life-generating flux of information capable of again and again forming the social just as the market is made again and again in the information-driven pricing of the derivative where liquidity is the flux.

If we can concede that the datalogical is drawing thought beyond stable and static objects of statistical analysis, we might then conclude that the datalogical is delivering to us a version of nonrepresentational theory and a "radical empiricism" that Nigel Thrift aligns with a lineage running from William James to Alfred North Whitehead.[41] Radical empiricism moves past a sense- or observation-based empiricism to look to the processes and practices by which discrete events or occasions come into being. In other words, this empiricism recognizes the reality of that which is pre-individual, other or below human perception, cognition or consciousness, which, as we have seen, are key to datalogical production. Nonrepresentational theory therefore also proposes that methods of study be rethought in terms of performativity, or what Thrift refers to as "play" or "experimentation."[42] For Thrift, performativity brings into play all kinds of bodies, human and nonhuman, along with their varying temporalities, thereby forcing sociological thought, method, and research to break away from the oppositions of nature and technology, body and machine, the living and the inert. However, this drawing together of computational flux and radical empiricism is not necessarily a project of celebrating of discovering excess. Rather, as we have suggested earlier, we do not wish to carry resistant or liberatory hues into the datalogical turn. Indeed, the comfortable fit between the datalogical turn, new computational logics, and nonrepresentational theory may need to be pressured in order to ask new and difficult questions, and not only about the status or effects of actors beyond the human now traveling or circulating their affective capacities, giving rise to what Thrift has called an "expressive infrastructure" and materializing a sociality in which thought itself must open to the mathematical.[43]

CONCLUSION

We have followed Michel Foucault in claiming that sociology has functioned to produce statistical populations for governance.[44] Furthermore, we concur with his sense that these statistical populations have never been ontologically reducible to humans; populations instead are articulated by sociology such that they are epistemologically grafted onto a human figure and locked into place representationally by a reflexive sociological practice. To move Foucault's critique into the realm of contemporary practices of big data and algorithm architectures requires a politically uncomfortable but disciplinarily inevitable move from critique of governance and economy based on a humanist sociology toward a critical sociology of a mathematically open sociality that can recognize the after-economy of the derivative where the political, usually excluded from economy in liberalism, instead has been fully included as the political effectiveness of governance is subjected to market measures, here treated in terms of big data and algorithmic architectures.

A critical sociology recognizes a postcybernetic logic of computation that desystematizes the methods of collating and analyzing statistical and demographic data while decentering the human subject; the observing/ self-observing human subject collapses as the basis for a data-driven project of understanding sociality. The oppositions of individual and structure and micro and macro levels, as well as embodiment and information, nature and culture, the living and the inert, are called into question. We follow Latour et al., who refuse the presumption of these oppositions and argue that the consequence of their presumption "is that almost all the questions raised by sociological theory have been framed as the search for the right pathway" between these opposed terms—how to explain the relationship between them.[45] For Latour and his collaborators, these oppositions are the result of the very technology that has been employed in the sociological method of data collection and data analysis. As they write, "'Specific' and 'general', 'individual' and 'collective', 'actor' and 'system' are not essential realities but provisional terms . . . a consequence of the type of technology used for navigating inside datasets."[46] However, as data becomes big and analyzed through algorithmic architectures, the oppositions by which sociological correlations have been made have become "flattened."

Although we agree with Latour that the methods of measure that sociology has deployed are inadequate, we insist that the critique of sociology must be taken further. What faces sociology is not a question of how better to use a dataset. The growing focus on data mining in relationship to slow sociological methods of measure is less a matter of catching up with algorithmic architectures of measure in order to reclaim a dominant position as the science of society. Rather, it is necessary to face the technical realization of sociology's unconscious drive to articulate and disassemble populations in real time and how the nature of sociality has radically changed. There also is the question of the subjectivity of this sociality in which the subject is no longer an ideologically interpellated subject of a system.

What is at issue, however, is not an ideological failure in constituting the subject. Seigworth and Tiessen suggest instead that the appetite for liquidity—by no means simply a human appetite, but substantially a technical one—precedes ideology.[47] They argue that ideological discourses of privatization, neoliberalization, corporatization, and securitization are "*effects* of, or *responses* to, credit money's appetite for liquidity."[48] Drawing on Latour's conceptualization of "plasma" and Thrift's of "a moving frame that is not a frame at all but a fabric," Seigworth and Tiessen argue that liquidity might well be what Latour describes as the "in between the meshes . . . of a flat networky topography."[49] As such, the methods of measuring big data and derivative pricing and trading—meant to sustain liquidity and deploy the incomputable—are central to today's sociality.[50] They also may be central for rethinking the subject of this sociality, the subject without reference to a system.

Given that the algorithmic production of big data has no reference to human consciousness, or even the human behavior from which data arises, the subject cannot be the conscious subject of modern thought. Recently, Mark Hansen has argued that the subject must now be of a consciousness that is after the fact of the presentation of data, since there is no possible subjectification of big data; instead, big data is "fed forward into con-sciousness *not* as the material basis for an emergent mental state but, quite literally, *as an intrusion from the outside.*"[51] As such, "consciousness comes to learn that it lags behind its own efficacy."[52] This is not to argue that there has been a reduction of the conscious subject to technical processes that are themselves reductive; after all, in pointing to incomputable prob-abilities, we are arguing that algorithmic architectures are not reductive in this way. Rather, we want to suggest that the subject Hansen describes might be thought as one that is tracking tendencies, maintaining liquidity of capacity. This is not, therefore, a subject who is reducible to "a mere calculus of interests."[53] Instead, Michel Feher has described this subject as invested in the self not merely for monetary return, but to manage the appreciation of the self lest there be depreciation.[54] The self-appreciating subject is given over to practices at a distance from knowing the self or self-reflection in relation to a system; it is a nonrepresentational subject.[55] Feher refers to the "speculative subject" who, we would suggest, is engaged in practices to sustain a liquidity of capacity, and thereby, a subject who finds politics in debates over what practices of self-appreciation might be wanted and what kinds of alliances and collectives might be necessary.

The Object's Affects

THE ROSARY

Viscosity, the heat,
the oil drips
down my cheek. I sit,
my feet barely touch the floor.
The exorcism begins,
me, in a chair placed
up against the kitchen sink.
Frightened and fascinated too
I look up into her face over me
into the small black centers
of her eyes.
My mother calls out the evil spirit
that has been put into me
by some other little girl
due to jealousy,
she told me
that first time.

If only I could I would place my big sister there —
to sit beside me, hold my hand,
and insist we both resist.
My mother.
Unworthy of the office,
of doing what only the ordained were meant to do,
she proclaims evil living in me
before she casts it out and sets me free.

I did not move.

So it would seem that even *before I was I, God was displeased with me,*[1]
having been found guilty of some sort of receptivity, or complicity.

> Her illegitimate wielding of power fixed what would never come to be:
> Clarity, definition, not even an uneasy settlement between the real and
>   the unreal,
> the good and the bad, would there ever be.

I lived in my childhood not so much in my own skin, but in a shroud of undecidability and a loneliness in my sister's inability to attend to me—her means of psychic survival a denial of a mutual infection of wounds. Left to a private communion, falling back into an ecstasy of fear, my gaze would fix on his hands and feet, ripped through. Blood poured down from the gash in his side, and the ignominious crown of thorns driven into his brow. I did not fail to kneel, early in the morning and later in the night, each day translating something done to me, correcting an idolatry, resisting a false worshipping yet ever inviting an attachment to my mother and this sacrilegious confrontation with evil, this will to do violence with the violence of the sacred, a misappropriation of a divine violence.

> My fingers move from bead to bead, ten and then one alone, and then ten
>   again: feeling without seeing, tactile before being visible, like a blind
>   person's object or thing, counting and praying Hail Marys.

Although thought to be mostly a matter of the Reformation, iconoclasm existed in the late Middle Ages as a drive to rid spirituality of images or objects mistaken for the real, confusing the miraculous with the magical. In the late Middle Ages, iconoclasm was enacted in religious art as a movement from scenes of the crucifixion with the upright figure of the suffering Christ to those scenes of his body being brought down from the cross, on the way to the grave, dead and becoming invisible. Together, these scenes can be taken as an allegory of an iconoclasm of the image: the image making God visible in the body of the crucified Christ and then the body brought down to be buried, the image becomes mere image again, pointing only to an invisible God. But, by the late sixteenth century, the host of the transubstantiated flesh, Christ under the guise of the everyday, is held up for the adoring gaze of those who pray in a golden monstrance edged with a corona of light and administering angels all around, shifting weight from the commandment to turn away from false gods, mere objects or images,

> to believe and cherish instead
> the divine touching the human,
> two substances aligned:
> salvation by complex perception of the real,
> there to be felt more than seen or known,
> there in affect, advancing to what is without language
> more magical than magic.[2]

Iconoclasm may well be a violent start of a genealogy of philosophies of the object and relations, implicating the nature of reality. And again today, another turn in philosophy in an effort to touch vitality, in an effort to recover objects and their energetic powers, their virtuality: to recover objects from the assimilating act of human consciousness. The correlation between being and knowing is broken and the question of the image and the real is replaced by the question of substance and manifestations, objects and relations, the vibrations, rhythmicities, or oscillations of each and every thing.[3]

But is it idolatrous to say that objects are themselves lively, that they have capacities to affect and be affected? Is it idolatrous to say that objects withdraw from human consciousness and from each other, falling back into the networks of meaningful reference of which they are a part but from which they stand apart. And yet, do objects take measure of each other, feel and be felt by one another and, by feeling, become however slightly or massively changed, indicating the object's internal energy, its differing from itself, its nonidentity with itself from which the object radiates a lure to feeling, an aesthetic of forces of repulsion and attraction. Can we say that there is an aesthetic causality that once philosophers thought to be a force of evil, a demonic force beyond understanding and will?[4]

> Nothing left but this: aesthetic practices, ritual practices to think at the limit of thought beyond thought, beyond understanding and will.

> My fingers move from bead to bead, ten and then one alone and then ten again: the rosary, like a holy abacus for counting mysteries, as I laid in bed and prayed.

Perhaps an important marker of our similarity and difference was the position of our beds, iron cots pulled out each night, my sister's placed right next to my parents' bed, the three of them, head to head to head, while mine was placed at the foot of the bed near enough to touch their feet, moving, moving under the sheet. And just beyond and over their heads, the crucifix hung that my sister could not see from where she lay. It was there, I thought, only for me: to condemn or protect me, I could not be sure, from the evil spirits that I thought I saw all around. She with my parents, and me left to pray the rosary, counting Hail Marys against the return of some little girl's jealousy.

The rosary is a string of beads used to keep count of prayers as they are recited. First given to Saint Dominic by the Blessed Virgin Mary in the thirteenth century, the rosary would be popularly practiced with spiritual intensity. There also were rosary books, among the earliest vernacular devotional manuals to be printed, thus defining the role of print as a way of shaping and reflecting religious awareness. But the rosary was popular as much among those who could read as those who could not, as indulgences were offered granting a surplus value of grace in exchange simply for the number of prayers that were recited. And with this, a concern arose that the value given to sheer repetition would mix up quantity and quality, spirituality and superstition, depth and superficiality, faith and calculation. Against this mere repetition in the use of the rosary, a set of meditations were prescribed: scenes from Christ's and his mother Mary's lives. Mysteries, they would be called, joyful, sorrowful, and finally glorious, to be kept in mind as one prayed.[5]

> My fingers move from bead to bead, ten and then one alone, and then ten again. The beads vibrate with certain energies, having been touched for centuries. Hail Mary full of grace. Hail Mary full of grace. Hail Mary full of grace.

And so it would be that no one cared that my sister was not kind to me. As I struggled to comprehend another already born, in my place and yet different than me, I was turned to abstract thought and a philosophical wonderment that offers the very young child a sense of the mind like a womb, giving birth to ideas, numbers and numbers of them, in one series and then another adhering one series to the other, trying to bring together body and soul, quality and quantity, substance and sensuality, my sister and me.

By the sixteenth century, the host had become an object of adoration especially for women. Linked first to the Eucharistic feast, the host was believed to be the body of Christ in the consecrated bread. It was meant to encourage in the one who beheld it an imitation of Christ's life—for the woman mystic to be in her body as he was in his suffering and dying. This union gave her the experience of horrible pain, whether inflicted by God or by herself was not clear. But this was not an effort to destroy the body, not primarily an effort to shear away a source of lust, but rather an effort to plumb the depths of Christ's humanity at the moment of his most insistent and terrifying humanness, the moment of his dying. This embrace of physicality at the point where it intersects with the divine was thought to be a refusal of dualism: body and soul, matter and spirit put in ecstatic union. For the woman, this is a becoming Christ as a matter of fact, not imagination or memory. Of a tradition in which male is to female as soul is to matter, these women found in themselves a blessed physicality that endowed them with authority to point out uncomfortable truths about the male priesthood. Yet this, a women's power, often was seen as resulting from possession by demons rather than being of a godly inspiration.[6]

And what now of this history and a mother misplaced by centuries such that what was once of spiritual significance comes to have a psychic resonance, infecting my thinking, oscillating it between godly inspiration and demon possession and turning me most recently to those translations of theologies into philosophy, heeding a call to rethink a dark mysticism[7] and to find a prayer adequate to a world near destruction or violent extinction.

> To refind poetry
> to allude to what cannot be told directly
> of a mixture of hate and love unresolved,
> of tendencies to reproduce an evil of failed recognition and lack of care
> yet seeking a way to a new ethics and a political repair.

The reproduction of evil today is understood psychoanalytically and thought to be related to malignant trauma and the experience of intense loneliness. This loneliness is not "something wordless that can be ultimately rendered in speech."[8] It is "unformulatable." As described, it is a paradox: "The experience of traumatic annihilation produces the need to be known that continually meets the impossibility of being known." Experience in this mode exists only in the ephemeral somatic present and never becomes linguistically encoded, while it shapes bodies affectively with its full force.

So that, in bodies, there still can be a memory that points to trauma and beyond to a divine violence brought with the wild intervention of the dark angel of history, who, seeing the pile of debris of nameless, faceless suffering, a wreckage of injustices, and the misappropriation of the divine, she strikes back to enact revenge for the destructive lack of care, love having all but failed. Let us go meet this angel. Let us meet her without fear.

Rethinking Race, Calculation, Quantification, and Measure

> "It is hard work to hold race and computation together *in a systemic manner,* but it is work that we must continue to undertake."
>
> —Tara McPherson, "U.S. Operating Systems at Mid-Century: The Intertwining of Race and UNIX," in *Race after the Internet*

In response to the call to address dominant epistemological and ontological assumptions about numerical signifiers, I want to begin by turning to Roderick Ferguson's *The Reorder of Things,* where he takes up what he calls the interdisciplines established in the late 1960s and 1970s.[1] Focusing on ethnic studies, Black studies, Puerto Rican studies, women's studies, queer studies, and postcolonial studies, Ferguson offers a genealogy of the interdisciplines' subversion of that classical figure—the Man of Michel Foucault's *The Order of Things.*[2] He argues that this subversion only deepened the relationship of race to calculation, quantification, and measure.

Ferguson's reordering of Foucault's ordering provides a point of comparison for considering what today might be said about the relationship of race to calculation, quantification, and measure. As these now refer us to what I and my coauthors have called the "datalogical turn," or what Mark Hansen calls "the data-fication of twenty-first century media," I want to argue that new interdisciplines are arising that are different from those Ferguson engages.[3] These new interdisciplines bring the humanities, the arts, and the social sciences into a more intimate relationship with mathematical sciences, computer sciences, digital studies, and an array of natural sciences, again raising the question of the relationship of race to quantification, calculation, and measure.

FERGUSON'S REORDERING OF FOUCAULT:
FROM STATE RACISM TO POPULATION RACISM

What makes Ferguson's account of the interdisciplines of the late 1960s and 1970s a matter of calculation, quantification, and measure is its focus on the institutional arrangements and the material practices of bureaucracy that characterized the academic context in which the interdisciplines developed or the way in which the academy met what Ferguson calls the interdisciplines' "will to institutionality." In their ambitions to be recognized by the academy, the interdisciplines, Ferguson suggests, both informed and were informed by the ongoing deconstruction of the sovereign subject of Western modern thought, thereby contributing to critical theory as it was finding a home in the humanities and the arts. In their insistence on the recognition of subjects other than the sovereign subject of Western modern thought, the interdisciplines would participate, if not altogether consciously or willingly, in the administrative work of the social sciences; they would contribute to managing social difference in what was becoming more explicitly a neoliberal and biopolitical governance both inside and outside the academy.

For Ferguson, then, the interdisciplines became a force of biopower, turning minorities into subjects of biopolitics as biopolitics "would take as its representative the subject constituted through difference, the one who had to learn what it meant to have a particularized history, the one who would have to access how the probabilities for life have everything to do with these particularities."[4] More specifically, subjects would have to learn to think of themselves in terms of historic social differences, accounting for the present conditions of their lives in these terms. The academy played a central role in this "learning," as it ingratiated minorities by making ability or capacity—both physical and mental—a standard of incorporation and also a mode of surveillance and measurement. This "new interdisciplinary biopower placed social differences in the realm of calculation and recalibrated power/knowledge as an agent of social life."[5] Or to put it otherwise, the academy was central in aligning economy and governance with knowledge/power by turning knowledge/power into biopower and fostering the calculative manipulation of affective or life capacities as a reformulation of difference. Difference was to be incorporated into hegemony, not disruptive of it, and a "calculative ambience of sociality" was both supportive and supported.[6]

The academy's management of difference was part of, if not in part constitutive of, a change in the relationship between economy and governance. In this sense, it is hard not to think of Foucault, not the Foucault of *The Order of Things*, but the Foucault of the lectures of the late 1970s on liberalism, neoliberalism, and the change in the relationship of economy and governance.[7] In these lectures, Foucault argued that the liberal market functions as a limit to sovereignty in that the so-called natural circulation necessary to the market cannot withstand governance's direct interference. What distinguishes neoliberalism from liberalism, especially American neoliberalism, is that the government no longer functions as a principle of market limitation. Rather, the market has become a principle turned against governance. The market has become something like an economic tribunal that governance continuously faces, in which governance is no longer determined to be legitimate or illegitimate, but efficient or inefficient. This is an economy that is *after economy,* as Randy Martin describes it, in that the political, usually excluded from economy, instead has been fully included as the political effectiveness of governance is subjected to market measures, or what Martin calls "the social logic of the derivative."[8]

As such, the market functions as a principle of intelligibility and a principle of decipherment of social relationships and behaviors, not in terms of a measure of exchangeability, but in terms of a formal structure of competition, the underside of the liberal promise of equality. Foucault himself argues that this is a society where discipline is no longer central: "Nor is it a society in which a mechanism of general normalization and the exclusion of those who cannot be normalized is needed."[9] Instead we see "the image, idea or theme-program of a society in which there is an optimization of systems of difference in which the field is left open to fluctuating processes, in which minority individuals and practices are tolerated, in which action is brought to bear on the rules of the game rather than on the players, and finally in which there is an environmental type of intervention instead of the internal subjugation of the individual."[10]

As Ferguson puts it: "Without question, there was a new policing of minority difference by federal, state and local governments but alongside that repression was a veritable explosion in the affirmation of minority difference in both grassroots and official venues."[11] Ferguson continues: "Sometimes minority difference would be hegemonic, at other times it would be oppositional; many times it would be both. Each profile would be available for articulation and neither one would be 'false.'"[12] This of course follows on the efforts especially of those in the academy to correct the misrepresentations of women, African Americans, queers, and others. But, in a neoliberal environment where the matter of false consciousness matters less, difference not only becomes a matter of tolerance; difference fast becomes a resource for "political branding."[13] That is, difference is put to use to politically brand issues, regardless of where these issues actually fall on the political spectrum, as modern, progressive, and civil. Difference now functions as a technology deeply embedded in the discourses of humanitarianism and human rights, activating democratic action aimed at "ensuring choice." If, then, the subject of discipline is no longer central to biopolitics, the subject nevertheless becomes an individualizing figure of populations, a humanizing figure of political branding. Think for example of the figures of the starving African child, the Israeli queer, the trafficked prepubescent girl, and others that can be used as rhetorical figures in what I referred to above as political branding and population racism. These figures serve to individualize a collective phenomenon or integrate individual phenomena within a collective field, but in the form of quantification.

While the figure of the human subject may function to humanize populations, nonetheless, in biopolitical terms, the population is a technical object, a political object of management and government—not necessarily a collection of individual subjects. Population is, rather, a set of elements in which we can note constants and regularities. Populations have their own specific aggregate effects, irreducible to a smaller frame. Population is an effect of statistical analysis, a matter of probabilities, a measure of risk that constitutes an actuarialism, a racist actuarialism, which is productive rather than merely representational. It is the calculability of risk that underwrites the comparison of populations and their life capacities or lack thereof, thereby value-coding an expectation about populations, as populations are thrown into a market competition for life-itself.

After all, the matter of population is life-itself, and it is this competition for life among populations that Foucault treated as a racism particular to biopolitics, a state racism. I prefer to make use of the term *population racism* to point to a racist actuarialism that is before and goes beyond state racism, or what Foucault described as the maintenance of health of national populations, in marking some populations for debility and death.[14] With population racism, the calculations and measures of population in a variety of contexts—territory, class, ethnicity, gender, race—all are put in terms of an analysis of biological activity. Of course, this is a biology (and now neuroscience) that is infused with technicity or technicality—the technicity of measuring, for starters. In turning all contexts of populations into a biotechnicity of calculation, quantification, and measure, population racism makes way for the health or lack thereof of populations to be part of a global market, beyond national boundedness, beyond the boundaries of the body as organism.

Ferguson, drawing on Stephanie Smallwood, adds to this discussion, reminding us that these biopolitical practices of quantification have roots in slavery, where "Africans were placed at the center of calculation in order to see how far a life could be stretched and tried for the necessities of capitalist economic formations."[15] As a result, Ferguson proposes that "life would become a factor in capital's equations," releasing a "profound epistemic revolution in which slavery's computations would be the prototype to Marx's free laborer."[16] While slavery was subject to calculation as a measure of exchangeability in capitalist formations, the institutionalization of the interdisciplines in the late 1960s and 1970s, however, made difference a matter of competition in social life, part of, but not reducible to, production or economic exchange. It is this competition among populations for affective or life capacities that was operated successfully in the academy by factoring in minority difference in a regime of calculation that betrayed the kinship this regime had "to prior and emerging regimes of calculation and alienation."[17] In this, the specific historicities of the subject of difference are also made to function biopolitically, becoming a matter of calculative or quantitative reformulation.

THE NEW INTERDISCIPLINES

Today, in the wake of the institutionalization of the interdisciplines and their ongoing decline, both the humanities and the social sciences are facing a new regime of calculation, quantification, and measure. My coauthors and I have called this the "datalogical turn" in order to refer to the data mining of social media, tracking devices, and biometric and environmental passive microsensors—the full analytic capacities of twenty-first-century media—now deployed in but also outside the academy in business, culture, government, economy, and individuals' lives. Social sciences, sociology in particular, are facing what, nearly ten years ago, Mike Savage and Roger Burrows called the "coming crisis of empirical sociology."[18] Data, as they put it then, "is so routinely gathered and disseminated, and in such myriad ways that the role of sociologists in generating data is now unclear."[19] Thus, "the claims to jurisdiction" that "sociologists can make around their methodology repertoires" is challenged.[20]

Not only have sociologists become brokers of data rather than producers of it; the massive production of data outside the academy makes way for the aestheticization of data to make data more affective and to command greater market attention. To my mind, it is this aestheticization of data that has informed the critical studies of calculation, quantification, and measure, which today are forming the new interdisciplines, drawing the humanities, the arts, and the social sciences into a close relationship with mathematical sciences, computer sciences, digital studies, and an array of natural sciences. In the humanities and the arts, the critical studies of calculation, quantification, and measure are part of what has developed as "the nonhuman turn" to recognize other-than-human agencies.[21] In the social sciences, they are part of studying the impact of data-fication and its effects on the epistemological and ontological assumptions underlying methods for studying the social.[22]

But the data-fication of twenty-first-century media not only raises a question about methods for studying the social but also raises a question about the interrelationship of concepts and technologies for navigating inside datasets. As Bruno Latour and his collaborators have put it, "'specific' and 'general', 'individual' and 'collective', 'actor' and 'system' are not essential realities but provisional terms . . . a consequence of the type of technology used for navigating inside datasets."[23] For Latour and his colleagues, digitized networks specifically undo the assumption of the whole constituted by interacting elements—or a system-metaphysic. They argue, instead, that there is more complexity in the elements than in the aggregates; or to state it a bit more provocatively, they claim that: "The whole is always smaller than its parts." This characteristic of a network is termed "the one level standpoint" (1-LS) in contrast to the "two level standpoint" (2-LS) of micro and macro levels of social structure.

This provocative proposal about the displacement of the two-level standpoint by the one-level standpoint, or the network, I would propose, points to the effects of the current regime of calculation or the data-fication of twenty-first-century media that is calling into question assumptions about human experience, consciousness, and bodily perception, as well as agency, historicity, system, and structure. As Hansen sees it, twenty-first-century media no longer store human experience as such; rather, they store the bits of data that "register molecular increments of behavior" that are never an expression of lived human experience.[24] As such, twenty-first-century media have shifted from "addressing humans first and foremost" to registering "the environmentality of the world itself," providing a "worldly sensibility" that is prior to human consciousness and bodily-based perception and reembeds "consciousness in a far richer context of the causally efficacious lineages that have produced it."[25] The data-fication of twenty-first-century media shows that consciousness and bodily-based perception are accomplishments that involve "the coexistence of multiple experiential presents—multiple, partially overlapping presents from different time frames and scales."[26] In other words, bodily-based perception and consciousness are displaced as central to experience. The technical not only supplements consciousness and bodily-based perception, but is actually the condition of their arising.

For Alexander Galloway, what Hansen refers to as twenty-first-century media brings about the decline of forms of mediation such as hermeneutics, historicization, and immanent or aesthetic appreciation.[27] As Galloway puts it: "We can expect a tendential fall in the efficiency of both images and texts, in both poems and problems, and a marked increase in the efficiency of an entirely different mode of mediation, the system, the machine, the network."[28] For Galloway, the network, or a "microphysics of links and vectors," has become systemic.[29] However, it should be noted that, if network be system, it is one in which the structure of the micro and macro, or the two-level standpoint, has been displaced. In this, the system-metaphysic, the taken-for-granted relationship of parts constituting the whole, no longer holds. Martin has even argued that the undoing of the system-metaphysic is one of the effects of network that is better understood in terms of the social logic of the derivative. As he puts it: "As opposed to the fixed relation between part and whole that informs the system metaphysic, the derivative acts as the movement between these polarities that are rendered unstable through its very contestation of accurate price and fundamental value."[30]

For Martin, the derivative assembles the disassembled aspects of almost anything that can be given a risk file, and almost anything, it would seem, can be. As these risks can be hedged, and these hedges themselves traded, derivatives bring neither market equilibrium nor stable prices; it is as if no transaction is ever finished and there will always be potential for a better performance with every trade. Measure is a matter of volatility, the self-generating volatility of pricing the derivative through trade. As such, measure is "a point of reference after the fact that is treated as an intent, a target to be hit based upon something that has already occurred, hence a momentary conversion of an unknown into a measure that cannot hold."[31]

Eli Ayache describes this process of measuring or pricing through trading as "beyond probability." As he puts it: "This process supposed to record a value, as of today and day after day, for the derivative that was once written and sentenced to have no value until a future date . . . extends beyond probability."[32] The derivative "trades after probability is done with and (the context) saturated."[33] When the context is saturated with all its possibilities, it opens up to what Ayache calls "capacity," which allows for the context to be changed. Pricing through trading "is a revision of the whole range of possibilities, not just of the probability distribution overlying them." This puts "into play the parameter (or parameters) whose fixity was (supposed to be) the guarantee of fixity of the context and of the corresponding dynamic replication within a context."[34]

Hansen too rethinks probability in terms of the data-fication of twenty-first-century media. Providing "a wide swathe of environmental data," data-fication, Hansen argues, can only offer the opportunity to produce patterns or information that are not inherently there in the data, what he calls "probabilities in the wild."[35] As datasets cannot be totalized, probability ceases to function either as an "a priori calculus of probability" or as "empirical probabilistic systems"—that is to say, when probability is in relationship to the number of possible outcomes that can be considered equiprobable. Jordan Crandall argues that the latter is no longer the case. With data-fication, he proposes, a "probable construct exists that stands in relation to reality as its *tendency* . . . a silhouette that models future positions, a ghostly forebear into which reality flows."[36] Drawing on Crandall, Hansen concludes that data-fication "seems to yield an ontological transformation of probability itself: probability ceases to function on the basis of mere possibilities and instead comes to operate as the index of 'real propensities.'"[37]

In his take on propensities or tendencies, Hansen turns to Alfred North Whitehead, who proposes that "probabilities are expressions of real forces, of actual propensities rather than empty statistical likelihoods."[38] For Hansen, Whitehead's take on probability shows a shift from conceiving potentiality as residing in an affective excess or in the virtuality of conscrescence that is ontologically prior to actualization. Instead, Hansen argues that the potentiality of conscrescence "*bleeds* or *seeps* into the contribution the actual entity makes to the settled world."[39] Potential, then, is in "the contrast among already existing actualities . . . the real potentiality of the settled world at each moment of its becoming"—becoming different with each new actuality or data.[40] This is data's power to give rise to more data. For Hansen, following Whitehead, this power is the "causal force of the present"; that is to say, "every actuality includes in its present feeling, *its* potential to impact future actualities *but also* . . . that it feels the potentiality for the future in its present and indeed as part of what constitutes the causal force of the present."[41] As Hansen sees it, data-fication refashions the relationship of the present and the future, causality and probability. Data-fication makes causality a matter of tendencies rather than "acts of discrete agents," drawing on the continual becoming of the worldly sensibility that data-fication provides. As such, there is always a "surplus of sensibility," no matter the precision of the "predictive analytics" of twenty-first-century media, or the measures of data-fication.[42]

CRITICAL PRACTICE: RACE AND TWENTY-FIRST-CENTURY MEDIA

In turning to questions of criticism and the new interdisciplines, it is this surplus of sensibility that makes or can make a difference. Martin too points to a surplus in relationship to the derivative as a matter of the social relationships that can occur around transactions that are never done with, or, as Ayache would put it, when probability is done with and the parameters have the capacity to change.[43] As derivatives "articulate what is made in motion, how production is inside circulation," Martin goes on to argue that derivatives turn criticism to mobilization, "to see how we move together but not as one," to see what we are in the midst of, or what is in our midst, to take up what is remaindered, the excess of noise that comes back from the amplifying of risk."[44] He continues: "To suggest therefore that a derivative logic is present across cultural and financial practices is not to assign particular places in an architectural order (which was what the idea of structure was based upon), but to identify principles of movement that associate an array of activities, and flows of people, without forcing them to conform to a singular idea."[45]

Echoing Martin's concern to shift criticism to mobilization, and following on Galloway's treatment of network's deflation of hermeneutics, historicizing, and aesthetic or immanent appreciation, McKenzie Wark argues that criticism must yield to being a critical practice "of constructing situations for communicating otherwise," or alongside "the control of the portals which appear to govern the relation between what is possible and that which lays claim to command them."[46] In this moment of the undoing of the system-metaphysic and the becoming ubiquitous of the post-probabilistic measure of the current regime of calculation, it might be best for the new interdisciplines forming around calculation, quantification, and measure to be wary of their own will to institutionality and the ways it does or does not support a critical practice. It also may be a good time to rethink race, measure, calculation, and quantification, however, without seeking their systemic relationship, as Tara McPherson suggests is needed in the epigraph to this essay. The systemic is not our problem.

Recently, Wendy Hui Kyong Chun has proposed that, rather than considering race *and* technology, we consider "race *as* technology."[47] For Chun, this means that race be understood not for what it is but for what it does, and, like technology, what race does is function "to facilitate comparisons between entities classed as similar or dissimilar." For example, race has been "crucial in negotiating and establishing historically variable definitions of biology and culture." Like technology, race "is always already a mix of science, art and culture." It is central, as is technology, to the "changing relationships between human and machine, human and animal, media and environment, mediation and embodiment, nature and culture, visibility and invisibility, privacy and publicity."[48] Race *as* technology may be another indication of how race, in the post-1960s and -1970s, became a matter of minority difference and useful as such to the academy and to neoliberalism and biopolitics generally. But it seems to me that thinking race *as* technology fails to provide ways to think of race or technology in terms of twenty-first-century media *if* we do not ask if and how the simile, race *as* technology, still might or might not hold.

After all, when Chun links racism to race as technology, she turns to Martin Heidegger's post–World War II treatment of technology in terms of standing reserve. In this, Chun follows Heidegger in thinking that the essence of technology is not technological and so there is no need to specify which technology is being referenced. Yet, there is a growing awareness that it matters which technology is being addressed or what different technologies do.[49] This is especially important in relationship to the data-fication of twenty-first-century media, as they operate beyond the boundary between human and machine, human and animal, media and environment, mediation and embodiment, nature and culture, visibility and invisibility, privacy and publicity, the very boundary that race supposedly mediates, as Chun would have it. Indeed, it is beyond the boundary between human and machine, human and animal, media and environment, mediation and embodiment, nature and culture, visibility and invisibility, privacy and publicity, that calculation, quantification, and measure operate. As such, the new interdisciplines are pointing to the inefficiency of hermeneutics, historicizing, and immanent appreciation and calling for new methods of critique of media, race, and racism that take the specificity of data-fication into account.

Chun suggests that there is still possibility for criticism in pitting racism against the technicity of standing reserve, thereby hoping to make race *do* poiesis, become a mode of revealing. But twenty-first-century media take us beyond the opposition of techne and poiesis, and as Hansen reminds us, the compensation that twenty-first-century media offer for doing so, or for demoting consciousness and bodily-based perception, is not to give back to them their centrality in constituting or reflecting on experience. Rather, it is to offer human beings the experience of a worldly sensibility and, thereby, to make available to consciousness "aspects of its own causal background that it literally has no capacity to grasp directly."[50] I am not saying that twenty-first-century media gives us a post-racism; surely there is already a body of criticism of data-fication in the production of racist practices of risk, surveillance, and control, a matter of biopolitics and neoliberalism. I am instead asking the question Chun might have asked: what is race doing *as* twenty-first-century media beyond biopolitics and neoliberalism or in relationship to the social logic of the derivative and data-fication? Perhaps Chun does indicate what might be an apt answer when, in her reading of Greg Pak's film *Robot Stories,* she sees race as a matter of ethics, as an ethical question: what relationships does race set up? In light of twenty-first-century media, I would reformulate this question to ask: what mobilizations can race make possible? In this sense, what race does or can do is lead away from hermeneutic, interpretive criticism to critical practices of mobilization, from a humanism to a nonhumanism that is not inherently racist.

Wondering about the future condition of the interdisciplines that he has addressed, Ferguson ends *The Reorder of Things* not with a revolutionary plan, but with a moderate one. Addressing those who have been and still may be connected to these interdisciplines, Ferguson calls for small acts: "A syllabus, a job ad, a recruitment strategy, a memo, a book, an artwork, a report, an organizational plan, a protest. . . ." These small acts, as Ferguson sees it, can be deployed "in order to imagine critical forms of community."[51] Martin argues similarly: he proposes that the derivative social logic allows us to recognize ways in which "the concrete particularities, the specific engagements, commitments, interventions we tender and expend might be interconnected, without first or ultimately needing to appear as a single whole or unity of practice or perspective."[52] This shift to small acts might make a difference, Ferguson claims, but only if they serve a will to institutionality that "recognizes the world is not enough." However, such acts have already been all but caught up in the network of twenty-first-century media, or what Matthew Fuller and Andrew Goffey have called "gray media," like "databases, group-work software, project-planning methods, media forms, protocol, algorithms." These are "tangible, biddable things" that pose "problems of meaning [only] as a preliminary to a more efficacious problem of use or 'getting things done.'"[53] To make a difference with the little acts that Ferguson and Martin point to, it will be necessary to seriously and critically engage with twenty-first-century media––its affordances and its debilitations. I view this critical engagement as one example of the sort of mobilization that race may make possible as a nonhumanism.

We might also consider what Stefano Harney and Fred Moten have said of the university and those who refuse to be accounted for:

> What might appear as the professionalization of the American university, our starting point, now might better be understood as a certain intensification of method in *the Universitas,* a tightening of the circle. Professionalization cannot take over the American university—it is the critical approach of the university, its *Universitas.*[54]

> Perhaps then it needs to be said that the crack dealer, terrorist, and political prisoner share a commitment to war, and society responds in kind with wars on crime, terror, drugs, communism. But "this war on the commitment to war" crusades as a war against the asocial, that is, those who live "without a concern for sociality." Yet it cannot be such a thing. After all, it is professionalization itself that is devoted to the asocial, the university itself that reproduces the knowledge of how to neglect sociality in its very concern for what it calls asociality.[55]

And They Were Dancing

For Randy Martin

And they were dancing:
she in a salmon colored silk gown
and he in black patent leather shoes.
They were dancing to the big band music of those times, their times.
In waves of motion, they move oh so gracefully,
practiced at the intricate footwork of the Peabody.
And they were dancing in those times, in time, seemingly carefree,
until a bit off beat, a tangle of feet, she slips and falls.
He goes down with her, landing on his knee.
Slow motion to dead time.
Then, suddenly
she spits words of disdain directed at him
sending a spasm of violence
through the stylish choreography of the Peabody.

My eyes shut tight.
My ears refuse to function. But something passes through:
the musical tones and the dance steps.
Sensibilities ingressing into actuality, ghosting the present potentiality
Her afterlife and his: lingering lingering

If recently dance has captured the attention of critical theory, it is not only because its kinesthetic abundance instigates conceptual movement beyond the fixity of received categories. It also is because dance directly addresses what the body can do, and not only the human body but other bodies too—the choreographic body or object that tweaks the time of everyday movement, inviting movement to tend toward the time of the event and the experience of potential in the feel of the future in the present, when an object no longer seems to be quite what you thought it was and the experience of time no longer feels as linear. And time slips, and the choreographic objects dance:

> Her silk gown thrown on the bed
> and the white gardenias he gave her browning at the edge
> in my head playing like a black and white movie from 1934,
> before the fall, when they met in the glove factory.
> He always would say that he fell in love with her immediately
> hearing her sing over the din of the sewing machines.
> Did he whisper: *I adore you*
> in her ear, as they danced the Peabody
> seemingly carefree,
> in waves of motion oh so gracefully?

"Events are only events because they perish." "Perishing is inevitable." Events come and perish, but not into nothingness. Perished events are like memories ready for reactivation that, nonetheless, invent new movement.[1] And the violence too is reactivated inventively, even more cruelly for that: the spasm of violence from them to me through the stylish choreography of the Peabody.

The spasm begins "in stillness and crescendos to extreme intensity and then dissipates."[2] But it reiterates its presence again and again unexpectedly; sometimes, its effects disappear immediately, and other times they linger indefinitely, corrosive and tenacious, impregnating everything that I am resolved to grasp, bringing to ruin whatever beauty there might be.

> And she spits words of disdain and he to his knee again and again
> The spasm of violence from them to me
> I do not see.
> I do not hear.
> I do not know that I am there

The spasm happens from within as the body attempts to escape from itself. "It is not I who attempts to escape from my body; it is the body that attempts to escape from itself by means of . . . a spasm." In dance, the spasm performs the body at the edges of representation at the limits of sense as it moves into sensation.[3]

Sensations moving in both directions simultaneously
disorienting exterior and interior,
a motion that touches those who see
that touches me,
making unclear what of this spasming flesh will come to be
my body.

It was five years before she would agree to marry him, pitying him, she said, for having waited each and every day for her to reply. And it is as if I were there to see from the start, even before the fall, a tear in the movie from 1934. What was he waiting for? The block against love already was there, tearing apart body from psyche, tenderness from sexuality, leaving only isolated moments of release, there on the ballroom floor, leaving an excess of energy entering me bodily.

Their dancing, like a primal scene,
an event of violent agitation,
a spasm agitating the flesh of their bodies enmeshed
before I am me, if ever it is to be,
if ever there is to be a body for me
other than their bodies, laying there.
I should not see. I should not hear. I should not know what happens there.
So near to their bed I lay,
the fingers of my left hand tracing
a sensing without touching,
a dwelling in the shaping of the flowers
made of brownish-red mahogany on the foot board of their bed.

It is said that it was to cure a spider's bite that her female ancestors from Sicily first danced the tarantella and produced a trance-like frenzy that also struck fear especially in men who should care but didn't: fathers, brothers, husbands, doctors, priests. Later, they would dance the tarantella when Sicily resisted the North's imposition of the unification of Italy, and throughout the massive migration at the turn of the twentieth century, the dance continued among women who were left behind or who were on their way to factories here, there, and everywhere. Just as the dancing led to southern Italian women being characterized in Northern Italy as savage, superstitious, or crazy, a generation later, when the women arrived in factories, they often still were seen as primitive, insane, promiscuous, and racially inferior.[4]

> Was it the spider bite of history
> that made her spit poisonous disdain
> that made her female ancestors seem to others
> what she finally became:
> savage superstitious insane ?

> Spider (or Tarantula): It is the spirit of revenge or resentment. Its power of contagion is its venom. Its will to punish and to judge. Its weapon is the thread, the thread of morality. It preaches equality (that everyone become like it).[5]

The Peabody was danced from the early decades of the twentieth century to the years following a depression and a world war as consumerism was expanding and movies were giving ballroom dancing a wide-screened envisioning. But the dance would not be transmitted to the dancers' children. They would move to the beat of rock-and-roll in the years just before the onrush of postmodernity and after, when dance would take itself outside off the dance-room floor to the streets in hip-hop, break dancing, and skate boarding. The unity of technique and choreography broken, dance was opened to another sociality.

If recently dance has captured critical attention, it may be for its excess energy, the in- excess of choreography. Dance, no more than any other cultural practice, is not simply produced by following rules. The dancing body, in "its kinesthetic specificity formulates an appeal . . . to be apprehended and felt," encouraging participation and a return to the scene of dancing again and again. This is "its own version of unabsorbable excess" that comes back to the body and "overwhelms the senses" as a "dreaded figure of contagion," like a devil dancing jealously, spitefully, hatefully, in and around the pieces of bedroom furniture of a brownish red mahogany.[6]

> She dreamed that he would purchase them for her.
> Mirrors, chairs, dressers, and the bed,
> where they lay just beyond mine,

a cot with an iron frame
cold to the touch
of my fingers counting out the beats
fingers like dancing feet.
And I begin to wonder about the numbers in my head
that could be orderly
ordering the excess of energy
made into a choreography

Only in name primal, the scene always was meant to be blinding, deafening, stupifying so that its time seems to be forever after some past pleasure, etching in flesh the very definition of pleasure as endless guilty longing for what actually never has been.

The child left there only to see,
hungrily, awaiting what cannot be.
Yearning turning into the bitter haunting
of an abstract power,
the power of the past randomly
to drain the potentiality of the present
again and again, differently.
Yet always starting with a choice,
not made by me alone
but also by some force
of an arrangement of feet, of sheets,
of the metal frame of my bed
of my fingers tracing brownish red
feeling again for potentiality in the mahogany
feeling for the wild probabilities in a body
of artistic experimentation
for the proliferation of sensibilities
in-excess of choreography
now, more commonly realized digitally
in a program for calculating reality
but other species of actuality too
other genres of humanity.

"The program is bound up in the materialization of . . . a normative field." It is "a scrim of expectation overlaid upon the real" that all the actants uphold in "a web of influence, and motivation," defending against the violation of an expressive outburst or physical act. But "the event is a violent exception or amplification, an object of fascination or concern that destabilizes a stabilized field."[7] As such, the event also is the bearer of potentiality in excess of the program, in excess of choreography.

This is dance as it assembles the gestures of actual bodies with those of virtual bodies, with virtual movements. In this sense, to dance is to experiment. "Dance operates as a kind of pure experimentation" with the body's capacity to be whatever it assembles.[8]

I catch the gestures mid-flight immobilizing them in the night by means of "an ontological measuring" that nonetheless is receptive to the pressure of potentiality: "a living relationship that intermingles intensities with two extensive quantities," a mother and a father right there near my bed where I lay.[9]

I am looking back at them. Still looking back for them in the analysis of psychic memory and in a research in philosophy, studying that impossibility of fleeing in those moments when an extreme tension, a pain, a sensation of uneasiness, surges toward an outside that does not exist, something that is so constituted as to make fleeing impossible while also making it necessary. It is necessary to flee this impossibility of a no outside, no elsewhere. Like the drive of sexuality, this specific excitation cannot find its discharge outside psychic memory but may never cease in its efforts to do so. To dance.

And they were dancing. In my head like in a movie from 1934, they crisscross the ballroom floor. Their bodies facing each other, each slightly to the side of the other, they dance with some speed the intricate steps of the Peabody, indicating which steps next to take through eyes looking furtively and fingers pressing with certainty in the curve of the back or in the fold of the arm.

> Like Ginger Rogers and Fred Astaire
> they were dancing gracefully
> until a bit off beat, a tangle of feet
> They fall
> They fall
> They fall together forever.

The experience of falling, falling forever, is thought to have no language and, rather, be a wordless bodily memory of a body being without any relation or orientation and, instead, being in an ongoing, near complete dissociation as profound anxiety dances free in bodily memories.[10]

Yet, in its backward looking glance, the history of dance turns the error of the fall to insight about what has come to ruins and what can arise out of ruins: bodies dancing against destruction, with hope against despair, cutting through the verticality, falling into horizontality, a laterality of movement. If modern dance still is vertical while opening to the contraction, the spiral and the rapid fall to the ground, in postmodernism, there is a clearer break from the vertical, as the hinge between inside and outside is at least partially undone: dancing feet up the side of building walls and bodies flying down from high above. There is a release from being taut and vigilant. From responding in an upright position to the body's being on the floor and more, the body moves through elegant yet disjointed, unexpected articulations that call forth a reorientation of bodily spaces in relation to the forces of gravity. Traumatic drops to the knee and falling down to the ground become ordinary for bodies used to dangerous situations where risking may be the only relief. But there is more, as the body, still moving, may seize the moment where minor differences can make all the difference, where wild probabilities still prevail as forces of real potentiality.[11]

Ecstatic Corona

FROM ETHNOGRAPHY TO PERFORMANCE

I got to Hester Street later than the others. We were meeting in an old industrial building on the Lower East Side of Manhattan, a site of ongoing gentrification. We were meeting to practice "The Children of the Mercy Files," scheduled for performance in just three weeks' time at the 2014 Remix Festival at La Mama, NYC. Waiting for me were Elijah Wong, Omar Montana, Elizabeth Garcia, Mac Morris, and Yeong Ran Kim, to whom I usually refer as the Corona group. In three weeks' time, barely ready, we did perform. The festival director's introduction pleased us. He remembered our performance from the year before and informed the audience that they were in for a special experience. In 2013, we performed as a group for the first time, a performance piece that we called "Ecstatic Corona." As we have described it for promotional material: "['Ecstatic Corona' is] a visual and sound multimedia performance using a remix of field recordings and electronic sounds, spoken words, song and dance to bring Corona to you. We have found Corona; we still are looking for Corona. We ask you to join us in seeking your Corona too."

Corona is the town in Queens, New York, where I grew up in the years just after *Brown v. Board of Education,* years in which the informal segregation of Corona schools was coming undone. I lived in what was called "Black Corona," even though most white and Italian families like my own lived in South Corona. During those years of white flight, my family stayed in Corona longer than other families did. Other families had moved to houses on Long Island. But we stayed. My mother was afraid, afraid of moving. She was afraid of change. She was afraid, just afraid, and so we stayed. We stayed in Corona in the three-room apartment with one bedroom where we all slept until I was eleven, my sister fourteen.

So close but ever at an emotional distance, we stayed. We stayed without much love, yet somehow given over to longing rather than mourning all that had passed and had not fulfilled, leaving behind deprivation, sadness, and rage—all part of the longing. We stayed.

The metal door still looks the same but for the many more layers of paint. The halls are dirty, but the old black and white tile floors bring me back. I played there just outside the door in the hallways—indoor playground for apartment building kids. My hand can't quite touch. I hold back. I can't believe I am here. I don't dare knock. Blocked access to the tiny dark, three-room apartment.

I went back in 2007. I went back to Corona, sore with psychic pain, feeling lost without understanding. I went back to walk the streets of Corona, to take measure of the inside and the outside and how they touch, if not collide. Out on the streets, in Corona, late at night, I could hear from the outside the collision of the inside and the outside that Elijah once described as "the soundtrack of surveillance, police sirens, and NYPD helicopters, every technology deployed to take down, shake down, and then calm down the people in the aftermath of a sonic warfare." When I was growing up, I first heard the collision from the inside. Inside my head, my mother is screaming. She is afraid, but she also is enraged; it is more than any small body can take. It is the experience of an outside going in, taking over the inside and locking it in—more than a small body can take. In 2007, I went into psychoanalysis to recover that body, to recover from Corona. Corona was the name I gave my psychoanalytic search as I first explained it to my analyst: *I want to go back to Corona. I want to find out what happened to me there.* In 2007, I went back to Corona. I went back falling, falling into a collision.

I say collision when I know I should say that the inside and the outside interact or, even better, that they dialectically feed back one onto the other. But I think social theory must be more sensitive to lives where the inside and the outside collide into each other, collapse the time-space between one and the other, psychotic transferences leaving a body undone and a self without grounding—what has been thought to be the destructive effects of trauma. And are we not in posttraumatic times? Although not every one of us is traumatized, or not in ways that would make a notable difference to others, there are many directly experiencing war, dispossession, violence, abusive unkindness, oppression, and exploitation; many of us live with militarized borders and identity checkpoints, biometric surveillance and increased ill health, or a generalized demodernization of cities in destruction of urban infrastructure. Does not the collision of the inside and the outside speak to the posttraumatic times of these lives, and more generally, to the crisis of epistemology and ontology about what life is? And which lives are to be counted as livable versus unlivable, and by what calculations? There is a crisis of social theory and, more specifically, a crisis of sociological methods of measure in the collision of the inside and the outside in post-traumatic times, or what might be described as the "calculative ambience" of the biopolitical conditions of living.

Some of us have known each other since 2009. Elizabeth and I had met then. An undergraduate student in my Sociological Theory class, she wanted to do research on a church group in Corona that she had been attending since she was young. I wanted to be in Corona. So I went to the church group meetings with her. Soon after, Omar joined Elizabeth and me. Also an undergraduate who had been in my theory class, Omar didn't mind going to church meetings, but he was more interested in conversation about social research, theory, and ethnography. Yeong Ran joined next. She wanted a site, a community to do some photographing, some video, something with sound. The partner of a former graduate student of mine and just nine months in the United States, she wasn't sure what Corona was except that it was the place where I grew up. She came to church group meetings with Elizabeth, Omar, and me. But she also walked with me, photographing me and my memories. Yeong Ran was getting an MA in media studies, so as we walked, we also talked about sound studies, postcolonial studies, and media studies. There in the streets of Corona, on hot summer nights with loud music coming from still opened barber shops and out of cars touring the streets, I found myself talking critical theory.

Yeong Ran and I did do some interviews. But I had no plan. I just wanted to be in Corona, there to remember. But eventually Yeong Ran wanted to do something with the images and sound she had recorded. She wanted to do an electronic remix of Corona. We had interviewed Elijah, who, like Elizabeth, was born in Corona and now was living there after attending college. In a park near the church, we shared a cigarette or two, as Elijah spoke about his life. In poetic cadence, he sang, I remember, about his father and the family abuse, the violence, the rage, the sorrow, but the hope too that, as he told us, was common to so many Corona kids. These sounds of rage, sorrow, and hope, Yeong Ran felt, needed to be part of remix Corona. We were beginning to inspire each other as three, then four, then five of us now walked in Corona together.

The door opened and I suddenly found myself inside the apartment once again, long after I had been there as a little girl. Quickly finding myself in the bedroom, I looked to see the corner where, as a child, I had been sent as punishment. When I was left there then, I would hardly move, except to look around the room. It was as if I was memorizing the bed, the mirror, the crucifix, the engraving on the dresser drawers, the bottles of perfume and her hairbrush and comb, the window and, beyond it, the fire escape. And the sights and sounds became thought circling around in my head. Around and around.

They got into my head, into my private space, as we walked Corona streets. They were the last of the young adults I had met during my time in Corona, and I am not sure what first drew us to each other, what kept us together, except that we liked being together, learning, talking, walking. We walked sometimes for hours, me and them, young adults: Chinese, Colombian, Dominican, Korean, African American—queer and straight, feeling ethnic, feeling immigrant, feeling smart and talented but feeling wounded, all. We shared that.

Mac was last to join us, back home from college, living in Brooklyn. He came as a friend of Elijah's. After we got accepted to the first remix festival, he offered to help with the dance. Elizabeth had taken some few classes in dance and I knew that dance was a medium for her of hope, of prayer. When Mac offered to dance with her, I felt that something was happening. By then, I had composed a number of the performance scores. I shared these with the Corona group. Inspired by the conversations that followed, I became more confident that we were going to produce a joint performance. And we did perform at the first Remix Festival, 2013, that year held in Brooklyn. We performed what we titled "Ecstatic Corona."

Both psychoanalysis and sociology tell stories about people and the worlds in which we live—we might say, one tells the story from the inside and the other from the outside. But telling your own story deconstructs the boundaries between the disciplines; at least this was how I would describe it in *The End(s) of Ethnography,* where I made use of deconstruction as a critique of writing and authorship generally, ethnographic writing in particular.[1] While deconstruction was energizing, allowing for the intuition of new forms, it also carried the force of the traumatic collision of the inside and the outside that requires, beyond deconstruction, an expanded sense of safety in which to elaborate the intuition of new forms. Without this expansion of a sense of safety, there can be a rigidifying of form, even forms of criticism.

Returning to Corona, I was given the unexpected opportunity to work creatively with ethnography without obviating the criticisms that had been made about traditional ethnography in the late 1980s and early 1990s, including my own criticisms of ethnography. Then, my criticism was aimed at ethnography's disavowal of the autobiography of the ethnographic writer, including his or her race, sexuality, gender, ethnicity, and nationality, in producing the ethnographer's authority. And yet, ironically I wanted little to do with autoethnography as it then was being elaborated. It seemed to me that the author of autoethnography usually was a subject seeking to be heard in terms of an experience and an identity embodied and known but felt to be socially or culturally illegible. Without aspirations to be the author of an autoethnography, I was drawn, however, to a yet-to-be-subject who did not have a full body or a full-bodied voice, who was waiting to speak or to be made legible. I wanted to give this longing for voice—the unconscious struggle it implies—a presence in the writing. This is a struggle of the subject divided from itself or split into contradictory or dissociated parts, often dedicated to some other, or imprisoned by another's desire. At the time, these psychoanalytically inflected terms were a part of poststructuralist thought—feminist, post-colonial, queer—that posed a challenge to the ontological and epistemological assumptions of the social sciences but were not taken up there with much seriousness.

At the time of its publication in 1992, the reception of *The End(s) of Ethnography* suggested to me that the book was untimely or ill-timed or both. It was ill-timed for sociology, a discipline that had never been open to the play of the unconscious in methods of research. It was untimely too, even for critical theories. Whereas critical theories were focused on the unconscious and language in the production of meaning, I took up the unconscious in terms of technicity and media technologies. I addressed the ways different media affected the relationship between subjectivity, meaning, and narrative, turning finally to digital technology, which I proposed delinked narrative from meaning and subjectivity. Instead, digital media raised questions about methods of parsing and disseminating data, a question about the relationship between quantitative and qualitative methods—a matter that I proposed needed to be a critical concern in and beyond the social sciences.

Once we found the thick chain fence surprisingly unlocked, and we went down the broken cement stairs littered with garbage. The stairs led to the basement. I remember that, when I was a child, it was a dark and frightening place. I once stopped there, right there outside the basement door. It was winter and I was four and little more. I stopped to pick up a large chunk of glass, like a crystal laying there catching white light. When I trip, it rips open a finger on my right hand. The pain is winter cold, my blood splatters red in the icy white light.

Returning to Corona in the early twenty-first century, I occasionally thought that, in addition to recovering childhood memories, I might return to thinking about ethnography, even doing an ethnographic study of Corona. At least it seemed as if I were rehearsing for one. The elements were there: the history of a place to be captured, the populations to be studied in migration, assimilation, and/or transformation, and the array of social problems to be displayed, contrasted with the hope in the rhythms of everyday life. There was also the Corona group, itself. Walking in Corona, we did share our experiences. Elizabeth led us to the various places important to her when growing up in Corona. Omar talked about how his family first came to the United States and its ongoing effects on their lives. Elijah showed us where friends had been stopped and frisked. We stopped in playgrounds, at schools and churches. We drank beer and ate food along the way. We talked about Corona, about how to think of family, race, ethnicity, immigration, schools, and the police. Each of us might have been a representative of Corona, or of its ethnic, racial, class, sexual, age, and gender differences, as well as differences of ability, both physical and mental. And there I was, a white, older female, an accomplished sociologist, well-trained to be an ethnographer in Corona. We might have become an ethnographic cliché.

None of us became the subject of ethnographic research, and yet all of us were. None of us was the sole creator of "Ecstatic Corona," and yet each of us was. "Ecstatic Corona" is not a study of Corona, of race in Corona, of religiosity, of family, of police brutality, of class, ethnicity, gender, or sexuality. Yet, it is precisely all these; for each of us, "Ecstatic Corona" is an objective pull on our subjective experiences. Each of us pulling the others back to learn more, to think more, and hopefully to undo the rigidity of our forms of thinking, of living. Together, we turned the ethnographic, as well as the autobiographical, into a form of conviviality, a form of our being together that became study, including a deepening of our sensitivity to the genealogies of ethnographic capture, along with the ongoing intensification of the calculation of population comparisons, a racialization that naturalizes biopolitical production of life in Corona and elsewhere. As being together became study, study became performance.

The video projected on a large screen—the backdrop of our performance of "Ecstatic Corona," along with the photographs, projected just to the side of the large screen—all are of our time in Corona. They are images produced as we walked in Corona long before we knew there was to be a performance. For the video, the camera was trained on the crowded streets in front of it, producing the experience of the endless movement of bodies, feet in rhythm with arms swinging, teenagers throwing a ball back and forth, bikes and skateboards jutting in and out of the crowd passing by, signs in every color covering the store windows, competing for attention with the graffiti on every wall. And along with this anonymous but intimate movement, there is the cacophony of sounds arising from the street, the ambient sounds of Corona.

The sounds intensify the feeling of endless movement while the photographs alongside the video serve to slow down the movement; some are of inside spaces, the dirty hallways of my apartment building, the bedroom window, empty churches, hot playgrounds, a child alone on a swing crying, gardens and the statues there of the Virgin Mary, the elevated train and the train stations from which so many come and to which so many go, day and night. And there are the photographs of us walking and talking. Yet, even though the words, songs, dance, and images carry aspects of each of our lives and our life-experiences of the biopolitics of posttraumatic times, "Ecstatic Corona" nonetheless is something other than autobiography or ethnography without being a mere refusal of these.

Perhaps, then, "Ecstatic Corona" is better understood in terms of what Boris Groys describes as "documentation in biopolitical times."[2] As Groys sees it, in biopolitical times, the boundary between life and technology or technicality is increasingly more porous, if not effaced. As such, the dominant medium of biopolitics is "bureaucratic and technical documentation which includes planning, decrees, fact-finding reports, statistical inquiries and project plans" (56). But there is also what Groys describes as the documentation of art, as art becomes a matter of performance, installation, event—an art that aspires to be life itself. For Groys, art documentation "is neither the making present of a past art event nor the promise of a coming artwork, but rather is the only possible form of reference to an artistic activity that cannot be represented in any other way" (57). As art becomes a passing event with a "unique unrepeatable life-span," art documentation, as Groys sees it, aims to give the art "life as such independently of whether this object was 'originally' living or artificial" (ibid.).

Yet, it seems to me that, even for Groys, the distinction of the arts and art documentation from technical and bureaucratic documentation is increasingly hard to maintain in the age of digitalized circulation of anyone's art, every variety of self-documentation, as well as the circulation of beautiful expressions of research data, or when the inventiveness in the practices of producing, presenting, and disseminating data have become ordinary as well as the motor of economy and governance. Furthermore, with this aestheticization of data, ethnography's traditional claim to being a supplement to the technical documentation of a positivistic and scientistic social science has also become less meaningful. Or to put this otherwise, ethnography has had to adjust to the weakening of the distinction of art and art documentation from technical and bureaucratic documentation. The early experimentation in ethnography in the wake of the criticism of the 1980s and 1990s might now be thought to have been an intimation of and response to this—to the ongoing aesthetization of data.

Being neither autobiography nor ethnography, and faced with the weakening of the distinction of the arts and art documentation from the technical and bureaucratic, "Ecstatic Corona" instead is a performance documenting the Corona group's spending time together without a plan, an unending rehearsal, or a rehearsal of a rehearsal. Without a plan, we nonetheless created an opening for relationality, which compelled us. Over and over again, something starts off a relationality in being together with time. It is unproductive time, or what Groys describes as a "project of contemporaneity": being "comrades of time," helping time when unproductive time, if not time generally, has become problematic.[3] Of course, the value of this unproductive time is relative to the ever-intensifying demand for productiveness in the domain of life, in living itself, linked to the ubiquity of digital technologies.

For some in Corona, if not many, unproductive time is a way of living poorly, without resources. For the members of the Corona group, perhaps some of us more than others, it is the time of our being together, slowing down in the midst of ever faster and faster tempos. It is a withdrawal at least momentarily. It is for each of us a gift of time in the feel for the future in the present, even without knowing whether or what that future will be. It is the potential of the present that can be prolonged, delayed to make ground for an experience of affective resonance with each other and with the human and the more-than-human environment of Corona. "Ecstatic Corona" is an engagement with the residue of unconscious memory in the flows of affect, the networks of voices, messages, images, and virtual effects crisscrossing bodies as bodies come in touch with the infinitesimal dust of what Mark Hansen calls a "worldly sensibility" now amplified by the data mining of twenty-first-century digital technologies.[4]

Referring to and repurposing these technologies, "Ecstatic Corona" exceeds our bodies as the center of experience, adding "a new inflection to an understanding of the feelings, sensuous and nonsensuous, concrete and abstract, of all actualities."[5] As such, the performance is a commentary on current debates in philosophy and critical theory in which attention is shifting from intentionality as embodied in the individual to a postphenomenological interimplication of human and nonhuman animacies as the human body finds its "technosomatic correlate" that violates ontological assumptions at the limit of the body of the individual, suggesting at once the un- or non- or supernatural.

The punishment would end when I could read the time on the face of the clock near my parents' bed. The clock was enclosed in a dome of glass; it was a miniature cathedral, an airless space of time that held still for me a horrid glimpse of eternity. My face awash in salty tears, I feared that I would never learn to read the clock's face. Its hands moving from one Roman numeral to the next, it said nothing to me. But there was a pendulum hung with delicate wiring between the golden columns that held up the clock with its indecipherable face. The pendulum's mechanical movement, turning one way and then, back again, made time easier on me.

It was during a practice of "Ecstatic Corona" that I first heard Elijah singing. He is singing the Hail Mary: pray for us now, pray for us now and at the hour of our death. Mac and Elizabeth are dancing. Slowing their bodies to the movement of Elijah's voice, calming their bodies after a frenzy of dance expressions of domestic and street violence, they then fall to their knees in prayer: pray for us now, pray for us now and at the hour of our death. Pulling himself back up, Mac lifts Elizabeth's body above his chest and as she raises her hands to the heavens; I tremble with the sensation of something that had passed among us. How well each of us had been attending to the meanness, generosity, disappointment, and hope of the stories we told each other on our walks through Corona. In performance, we find ourselves again in an ecstasy of joy and despair, at least momentarily, just as when we are walking.

Our performances are ecstatic, mystical in the way that we find ourselves outside ourselves together, supporting each other in the risky but familiar movement of leaving ourselves, our bodies, for the ecstatic fall into beautiful pain that Luce Irigaray describes as "expectant expectancy, absence of project and projections. Unbearable sweetness and bitterness, aridity, dizzy horror. . . . Everything is relentlessly immediate. . . ."[6] Psychoanalyst Michael Eigen describes the ecstatic as being thrown in an unaccountable shift from "bursting with heavenly sensation and feeling" to being "alone forlorn in agony," but also "terrified and enraged at the other's indifference, cruelty, incapacity."[7] One feels grieved until one again is radiant with spiritually nourishing affect.

While ecstasy is a matter of prayer, mysticism, theology, the ecstatic state may also be easier to arrive at for those of us who, as children, turned inward to care for ourselves when no one else was there to do so or no one who was there was able to do so. In psychoanalytic terms, this can result in "a precocious self-sufficiency." That may sound less troubling than it turns out to be, since precocious self-sufficiency means an inability to recognize or express infantile need. It means intensified mental activity and projecting this mental activity outward to fill the void between one's own body and the other's lack of care. The child experiences a sense of disembodiment that comes from an identification with the absence of care, an identification with the other's needs, often those of an aggressor. The child takes in an imitative replica of the other's needs and finds a sense of self only in meeting these needs. Thus, the experience of disembodiment is associated with the very feeling of existence. At the same time, a tough or dismissive way of being can be produced with outbursts of anger and rage tearing through the surface of denial over wells of fear, loneliness, and an ontological insecurity.[8]

Precocious self-sufficiency may be one way of understanding the collision of the inside and the outside, or the taking inside of a tantalizing but traumatic event or, just as often, the cumulative trauma of environmental failure. Having failed again and again to find a wished-for caring other, what is wished for instead is just to begin again and again on the road of longing and wishing, to take flight in the ecstatic, to be revved up through it. But, in the next instant, one may fall into fear, loneliness, anger, and rage, which block the capacity for creativity while being the very conditions of possibility for creativity.

I do not know whether the psychoanalytic terms of precocious self-sufficiency, including experiences of ecstasy, exactly fit each or any of the members of the Corona group or whether these terms simply can or should be applied to the populations living in Corona past and present. I do know that, as a group, we did come to share a sensitivity to the collision of the inside and the outside. We do share a sense of each other's childhoods, a shared experience of an impinging environment, abuse, and disregard, but also of effort, love, and even courage in some of these very same environments. Somehow, each of us found some way to forgiveness and creativity at least to some extent, but not, however, without returning feelings of anger, rage, and disregard for others and even each other. But it is together that we channel the creative ecstatic force of Corona.

In our performances, Corona is that place of desire for ecstatic experience. The sounds, the colors, the smells, the feel of the bodies moving in the street, surely can put you there: ecstatic feelings, feelings of pleasure and pain, often tinged with guilt for having made it out, if you have, or even when you have but have returned. It is a place you want to get away from, return to, and stay, but never forever. It is home, and there is no way out really; or to put it another way, there are wishes to start again, so many wishes to start again and again. Corona is vibrating with these wishes. The streets are buzzing with them, along with whatever makes the place scary to some, outsiders maybe, but even insiders, whatever makes the place a magnet for government and nongovernment programs and policy, whatever makes the place a place for an urbanized securitization of life.

Stuff happens there that makes it into sociology books, documentaries, newspapers, TV story lines, and program and policy documents. "Ecstatic Corona" makes of this stuff a matter of political action and political thought that find their way into the performance with the aim of putting an end to the stories about Corona as a place in which the focus is on either a classed ethnoracism informing an unjust sociality that breeds criminality or a cultural resiliency in an affective richness, a glorification of feeling brown or black or ethnic or queer or poor, or sick or tired. Corona is that; it is never just that; it isn't that at all. Or to put this another way, "Ecstatic Corona" is an attempt to uncover the ethnographic and autobiographic compulsion to return to Corona's trauma, returning again and again to the scene of the trauma, often to insist that perhaps nothing happened there or something else happened there. This, in order to return once again. We might follow Catherine Malabou and describe this as "a compulsive mechanical return" that may well be a matter of denial but also "betrays an expectation, the expectation of the arrival of another way of being."[9] It is to turn the compulsion of the death drive into a force of creativity, the force of what Malabou calls a "destructive plasticity."

The very first sounds of "Ecstatic Corona" are those of Elijah singing. "Oh Corona, tectonic homeland. Survival guilt. I tell you now I am virus. I am plasma. I am elemental mineral. Oh Corona, sweet sister, I know you're hurting. I want you laughing. Maybe next time. Maybe tomorrow. Maybe no time. Maybe tomorrow. Maybe no time." When I first heard Elijah singing it was during a practice for the Remix Festival. I cried. I hear the haunting and haunted sound of his voice and then I hear the words, words from conversations he and I had about biopolitics and technology, the plasmatic and the viral, when walking in Corona. And when I listen again, I realize that, with these very first words and sounds, Corona is not just my Corona, not even our Corona. It is an event with time, in time.

At once, Corona is and is not located, a place out of time and a place in time: the time of our sisters hurting, a time of healing in a future, but maybe not, the unending time of survival guilt. The trauma is not just mine, not just ours, not just of a place, but also of our times, for some of us more than others. And I turn again to Mac and Elizabeth dancing, their bodies dramatizing urban racial violence as they mimic the exhaustion of resisting the constant harassment of police and as they enact domestic violence, pounding at each other and returning to each other again and again in an erotic embrace. I hear my mother screaming. I see my parents dancing.

Our experiences of ourselves in Corona, as well as our experiences of Corona, informed "Ecstatic Corona." But in creating our second performance, "The Children of the Mercy Files," we moved beyond Corona as a geographical place to a more abstract view of it. At the same time, "The Children of the Mercy Files" is a more personal, even more a private expression of each of our experiences of racism, sexism, neocolonialism, and ableism in relationship to institutions. The performance first came to our minds in a conversation one night at my apartment, when we were celebrating our performance of "Ecstatic Corona" at the Remix Festival. There were the six of us, and one of us had brought a friend who had just been released from the psychiatric unit of a nearby hospital. He seemed unconcerned about being hospitalized; it was not his first time and there was something about his relationship to his faith, to Jesus, he told us, that both explained how he got to the hospital and how he found it to be an acceptable or simply to-be-lived-through experience. All of us got engaged in a discussion of our experiences within institutions, our living institutionalized lives: being queer, being a foreign student, having HIV, immigrating to the United States, spending time in jail, working in a detention center for kids. Although it would be another year before we would be invited again to the Remix Festival to perform "The Children of the Mercy Files," it was on this night that that performance was first imagined.

If "The Children of the Mercy Files" and "Ecstatic Corona" differ from each other, it is in the way each expresses what is defining the weakening of the distinction of the arts and art documentation from the technical and bureaucratic documentation, what Michel Foucault described as the "tendency" or "line of force" that was leading to the "pre-eminence" of biopower "over all other types of power—sovereignty, discipline, and so on," a shift from societies of discipline to societies of control.[10] Less about law and more about the state's policing through administrative functions that target populations, control depends on calculations and analyses showing the population to possess its own regularities, rates, and statistical probabilities, all constituting "specific aggregate effects," irreducible to an individual case. This, what Foucault called the "normalization" of populations, serves as background for what I have described as a "population racism" that functions now in the transformation of institutional life in turning civil society institutions—the school, the family, the union, the places of worship and health services—into sites not only for amassing, analyzing, and circulating data but also for modulating the affect and effects of continuously calculated assessments, including enforced self-assessments.[11] Intensifying the capacities of measuring risk in order to distribute inequitably life chances among populations, population racism constitutes a racist *actuarialism* that is productive rather than merely representational.

This is what "Ecstatic Corona" takes part in: it renders the biopolitical governing of populations in Corona, looking back to the period of post–civil rights agitation and forward to the lives of those who constitute the many ethnoracial groups, the so-called new immigrant groups, now living in Corona. In doing so, however, "Ecstatic Corona" treats biopolitics as racist, violent, a matter of heartbreaking disregard. With a rush of images and movements and the resounding noise of the ongoing goings on of Corona, "Ecstatic Corona" also refuses the constraints of biopolitics as each of us affectively performs the complexity of individual life in excess of population. Nonetheless, "Ecstatic Corona" also points to the postbiopolitical, when governance and economy no longer require an individual to be representative of a population. Nor is it necessary to see the individual as part of the system as a whole, when, instead, the network is the surround that both penetrates and dividualizes or discretizes the individual. As boundaries of institutions and individual bodies have been made to tremble, and as they come crashing down, some of us will be more debilitated than others, some will be more liberated than others. And this, the aftermath of the biopolitical, is the subject of "The Children of Mercy Files."

The first words spoken in "The Children of the Mercy Files" are located in a mental health facility. We all stand in the dark listening to a recording of the muffled voices of patient and attendant. As the lights come up, the words then spoken are more clear. They are a paraphrase of Stefano Harney and Fred Moten's words: *Perhaps then it needs to be said that the crack dealer, terrorist, and political prisoner share a commitment to war, and society responds in kind with wars on crime, terror, drugs, communism. But this war on war crusades as a war against the asocial, that is, those who live without a concern for sociality. But this cannot be. After all it is professionalization itself that is devoted to the asocial, that reproduces the knowledge of how to neglect sociality in its very concern for what it calls asociality.*[12]

More so than "Ecstatic Corona," "The Children of the Mercy Files" is a threading of what each of us wrote individually and before we knew what the others had written. The script is more particular to each of us, to each one's experience of institutional life. Yet, during the performance, something comes through the words, the dance, the singing, the images, something other than each of us: it is mercy. In the performance, we are seeking mercy as it dances in and through our bodies, most especially in Elizabeth's body as mercy becomes woman, goes mad, and returns to haunt the performance, announcing her death. We seek her not recognizing that she is already a ghost, that she is lost to us, that we look for her in vain among the dirt and ashes that cling to those institutions that imprison, that isolate, that injure, that maim, no matter how much individual affect workers mean to do good, try to do good, and mostly fail. Madness in mercy dancing unto death, like the failure of care enfolded in precocious self-sufficiency, results in a hypervigilance that makes some of us keep distance as best we can or as long as we can from these institutions, while it exhausts others into indifference, indifferent to the pull of institutions while expectant of their containing control—always going bad, always going mad, always going sick, always going dead.

The video and photographs remixed during the performance of "The Children of the Mercy Files" are from a long-abandoned detention home. Windows are broken, parts of the roof are gone, the paint is cracked, strips of it hanging—haunting. Any barrier between the inside and the outside is all but gone as weeds push through cement floors and vines grow through the windows, making their way to inside walls. There are also images of the visit we made to an operating mental institution where we spent the day talking and walking around the grounds. The building is closed off to us by a large cyclone fence, and the guards warn us against getting closer every time we try. It is as if nothing and no one is inside, awaiting every projection from the outside. Weeds are growing among patches of Queen Anne's lace and wildflowers, purple, yellow, and blue. There is the rippling sound of water under a bridge—refreshing. We would like to stop and wash each other there but we move on; we keep walking. The last words of "The Children of the Mercy Files" are finding their way into my head. In the performance's last moments, each of us will speak them. Five times, they will be spoken. I hear the voices of the others and mine too:

Something is repeating in the room but I don't know what it is. Something is repeating. I am praying in the dark, kneeling beside the bed, prayers mixing with tears and blood. What happened before the repeating started? What will happen to make it end?

"The Children of the Mercy Files" is slow, dark, and sad; the anger is smoldering, if not at times explosive; the eroticism is touched by despair. Yet, the performance cries for and aspires to forgiveness even as Mercy ends up spread thin across institutions that fail her, haunted as they are by their decline, the erasure of their histories, and the deadening of their future plans; each institution is transformed, displaced by the life of a hi-tech swarm of numbers. Yet, the institutions continue to hold each of us, hold us down as each of us waits for his or her number to be written on the body, where it cannot be seen. We may have been left to die.

But the number may be an indication not only of being next, next to die, but also of being chosen, an opening to the spirits of the swarm, like a legion of demons, or the spirits of a dark media, as Eugene Thacker has described it, where every possibility of solitude, refusal, and silence is haunted by the imperative to communicate that nonetheless is informed by the impossibility of communication.[13] "The Children of the Mercy Files" is the communication of this impossibility of communication in the biopolitical moment of failed institutions and a lack of human services, in the breakout of nonhuman number. It is an aesthetic that senses in this swarm of numbers a feeling for the future in the present. The poetry of words, sounds, songs, and dance point to this: aesthetic expression to communicate the impossibility of communication.

This impossibility of communication draws the performance to the turn in philosophical discourse to aesthetics, especially to the shift in focus from the aesthetic of the sublime to the aesthetic of the beautiful. With the sublime, there is the experience of the overwhelming disjuncture between imagination and understanding, along with a conscious recognition of this failure of human comprehension. In terms of the aesthetic of the beautiful, however, "what is regarded as beautiful is not experienced as a passive thing or as something that merely produces an effect in us but rather as inviting or requiring something from us, a response that may be owed to it . . . as if the beautiful thing had an independent life of its own . . ."[14]

The turn to aesthetics and to the beautiful, however, can seem troubling, as Steven Shaviro has noted, as capitalism has seemingly appropriated the concept and its practices. But drawing on Whitehead, Shaviro nevertheless suggests that beauty is about the creativity in each thing; as he puts it, each actuality "does in fact change the world, at least to the extent of adding itself to the world as something new."[15] The aesthetic of the beautiful, although not a politic in itself, takes up what Hansen, also following Whitehead, describes as "the potentiality in the contrast among already existing actualities," or "the real potentiality of the settled world at each moment of its becoming"—the world becomes different with each new actuality.[16] It is this worldly potentiality that is to be felt and with which to mobilize and be mobilized, even though there is no assurance of therapeutic effects. As in psychoanalysis, there is only an appreciation of the difference in the contrast among already existing actualities and perhaps a growing appetite for that difference.

It is in these terms that "Ecstatic Corona" and "The Children of the Mercy Files" are study, performance, and mobilization, making it possible for the Corona group and I to make something beautiful of our personal difficulties. In performance, these remain personal, even as, in their beauty, they become resonant with the difficulties of these posttraumatic times of biopolitics and beyond biopolitics, the difficulties of the networking of family, community, nation, and world. The performances are an aesthetic enactment of the collision of the inside and the outside of the subject, a making beautiful of the traumatic relationship that we have with Corona, with all the Coronas.

After each performance, we sit as a group to answer questions, to take up comments. These discussions—often nearly an hour long—have become for us an integral part of each performance. Each time, what is discussed is unique to that performance and its audience. What becomes apparent to us, if not to the audience as well, is how we are changing together and separately. The mood each performance generates in our group, as well as between us and the audience, meets with different aspects of each of our lives and our cultural and political sense of the world around each of us in the moment. Each of us tells stories we have told before, but they are new in that they are newly shared with a particular audience, and we too have new ears, eyes, hands, and feet to hear, see, and feel differently. And sometimes, surprisingly, one of us says something about him or herself that some of us or all of us did not know. The surprise is that an intimate matter is to be spoken in the midst of strangers. But perhaps it is in these moments that strangers are made part of the performance, that there is an enacted collision of the inside and the outside, of private and public. The collision is given its due, its pain, its beauty, and we all become more indebted to each other than ever before. As if the audience is walking with us in Corona, we are freed to tell them something that had been held or withheld in an unvoiced aloneness.

The three-room apartment in which I grew up felt like a prison, and imprisonment had come to feel ordinary. This ordinary feeling, however, created a condition of possibility for writing, writing to break out of the prison that I re-created—moving out and coming back to it again and again. At its best, this self-affecting, if not self-afflicting, writing becomes criticism, invention, poetry. Poetry makes beautiful those traumas that are not easily engaged, not so much to make them more palpable, although there is that, but to perform the struggle of moving away from a wounding to enable poetry as well as philosophical and critical thinking.

Acknowledgments

It gives me great pleasure that a number of my essays and experimental compositions are collected in this volume. Each reached for the edge of thought as it made its way to the present—thought about media, governance, economy, sociality, and unconscious processes. Without others, this reach in thought would not have been possible. First and foremost, I acknowledge my graduate students, many of whom now are professors and colleagues. Thank you for the learning we did together in class discussions, reading groups, and group presentations. You make my life as a scholar, teacher, and writer an experience of joy and wonder. I thank each of you: Manolo Guzmán-Estavillo, David Staples, John Andrews, Grace Cho, Hosu Kim, Jamie Skye Bianco, Rose Kim, Jean Halley, Elizabeth Bullock, Elizabeth Wissinger, Colin Ashley, Polly Sylvia, Aleksandra Wagner, Ananya Mukherjea, Jeff Bussolini, Jonathan Wynn, Claudio Benzecry, Alyson Spurgas, Nick Bazzano, Arto Artinian, Bibi Calderaro, Ali Lara, Kim Cunningham, Kate Jenkins, Heather Wiley, Steve Garlick, Benjamin Eleanor Adam, Greg Narr, Omar Montana, Christina Nadler, Chun-Mei Chuang, Salvador Vidal-Ortiz, Karamary Van Cleaf, Ariel Ducey, Mitra Rastegar, Iréne Hultman Monti, Lyndsey Karr, Sandra Moyano Ariza, Goeun Lee, Talha İşsevenler, Jan Marie Desartes, Deborah Gambs, Sandra Trappen, Bahar Aykan, Asye Akalin, R. Joshua Scannell, Benjamin Haber, Karen Gregory, Craig Willse, Greg Goldberg, Aaron Weeks, Melissa Ditmore, and Rachel Schiff.

I also recognize my colleagues and friends who inspire, support, and deeply enrich my life and work. I thank Jasbir K. Puar, Anne Hoffman, Elizabeth Bernstein, Kerwin Kaye, Ros Petchesky, Samira Haj, Paul Pangaro, Ann Burlein, Una Chung, Steven Seidman, Alan Frank, Anahid Kassabian, Amit Rai, Betty Teng, Michelle Fine, Ann Pelligrini, Jill Herbert, Jonathan Cutler, Katherine Behar, Stefano Harney, Joseph Schneider, Kyoo Lee, Andre Lepecki, Joe Rollins, Lynn Chancer, Hester

Eisenstein, Mary Clare Lennon, and colleagues at the Graduate Center, Queens College, and New York University Performance Studies.

During the same years in which these essays and experimental compositions were written, I also was engaged in returning to Corona, the neighborhood in Queens where I lived until I was eleven years old. My experience of these growing-up years profoundly affected me and has been central to my work with Elijah Kuan Wong, Mac Morris, Elizabeth Garcia, Omar Montana, Yeong Ran Kim, and Jansiel Polanco, who, together with me, produce performances about Corona and the precarious times of the contemporary moment. Working with the Corona group has been an inspiration and a sheer pleasure; I look forward to our future work together. The Corona group also informs my practice as a psychoanalyst, just as my own psychoanalysis and being a psychoanalyst has informed the essays and experimental compositions in this book. The Institute for Contemporary Psychotherapy, where I trained and now serve on the training committee, has offered friendship and a unique support for my work as a scholar, teacher, writer, and analyst. I especially thank James Stoeri, Ann Roberts, and other of my supervisors, advisors, and instructors, Leah Lipton, Leslie Goldstein, Mark Mellinger, and Mary Anne Lowell.

I thank my family, Christopher, Elizabeth, Lucy, and Clara, all of whom delight me and all of whom I love dearly. You mean the world to me. I also am grateful for the love and friendship of my sister Virginia and her family.

I especially thank Rachel Schiff, who edited the Introduction as I wrote it—twice. Without her live-editing and continuous support, the book would not have come together as it has. I thank Joseph Schneider and Amit Rai for their instructive and supportive readings of the manuscript. I also thank the University of Minnesota Press, especially Danielle M. Kasprzak, who supported this book from its inception to its completion.

Notes

INTRODUCTION

1. In my early work, I drew on Richard Beardsworth's reading of Derridean deconstruction as bringing an "originary technicity " to an "originary Being," where, therefore, originary is under erasure. Originary technicity is meant to undo oppostions that an ontology of presence grounds, such as nature and culture, body and machine, the living and the inert, human and nonhuman. See Richard Beardsworth, *Derrida and the Political* (New York: Routledge, 1998), 145–57.

2. Patricia Ticineto Clough, *The End(s) of Ethnography: From Realism to Social Criticism*, 2nd ed. (New York: Peter Lang, 1998); Clough, *Auto-affection: Unconscious Thought in the Age of Teletechnology* (Minneapolis: University of Minnesota Press, 2000).

3. Patricia Ticineto Clough, "The New Empiricism: Affect and So-ciological Method," *European Journal of Social Theory* 12, no. 1 (2009): 43–61.

4. See Michel Foucault, *Birth of Biopolitics: Lectures at the Collège de France 1978–1979,* trans. Graham Burchell (New York: Palgrave Macmillan, 2008).

5. Patricia Ticineto Clough and Craig Willse, "Gendered Security/National Security: Political Branding and Population Racism," in *Beyond Biopolitics: Essays in the Governing of Life and Death,* ed. Patricia Ticineto Clough and Craig Willse (Durham, N.C.: Duke University Press, 2011), 46–64.

6. Brian Massumi, *Parables for the Virtual* (Durham, N.C.: Duke University Press, 2005), 30.

7. Patricia Ticineto Clough et al., "Notes toward a Theory of Affect-Itself," *ephemera: theory and politics in organization* 7, no. 1 (2007): 60–77.

8. Luciana Parisi and Tiziana Terranova, "Heat-Death: Emergence and Control in Genetic Engineering and Artificial Life," *CTHEORY,* October 5, 2000, http://ctheory.net/ctheory_wp/heat-death/.

9. Gilles Deleuze, "Postscript on the Societies of Control," *October* 59 (Winter 1992): 3–7.

10. Keith Ansell Pearson, *Germinal Life: The Difference and Repetition of Deleuze* (New York: Routledge, 1999), 170.

11. My own interest in cybernetics, media, and measure dates back to the early 1970s when I studied cybernetics at the Biological Computer Lab (BCL) under the direction of Heinz von Foerster. In those years, Humberto Maturana was a frequent visitor as he developed his thinking about autopoiesis in living systems in the context of a second-order cybernetics, a cybernetics of cybernetics.

12. David Bohm and Basil J. Hiley, *The Undivided Universe: An Ontological Interpretation of Quantum Theory* (New York: Routledge, 1993), 5.

13. Patricia Ticineto Clough, "War by Other Means: What Difference Do(es) the Graphic(s) Make?" in *Digital Cultures and the Politics of Emotion: Feelings, Affect, and the Politics of Technological Change,* ed. Athina Karatzogianni and Adi Kuntsman (London: Palgrave MacMillan, 2012), 21–32; Mia Kirshner et al., *I Live Here* (New York: Pantheon, 2008).

14. See Brian Massumi, "National Enterprise Emergency: Steps Toward an Ecology of Powers," in Clough and Willse, *Beyond Biopolitics,* 19–45. Along with Massumi's essay, a number of essays appearing in *Beyond Biopolitics* would focus on terrorism and counterterrorism in relationship to racism and a preemptive logic, most notably, essays by Jasbir K. Puar, Eyal Weizman, Amitabh Rai, Eugene Thacker, Sora Han, May Joseph, Una Chung, Fred Moten, and Stefano Harney.

15. Brian Massumi, "The Future Birth of the Affective Fact," in *The Affect Theory Reader,* ed. Melissa Gregg and Gregory Seigworth (Durham, N.C.: Duke University Press, 2010), 52–70.

16. Luciana Parisi, "Nanoarchitectures: The Synthetic Design of Extensions and Thoughts," in Karatzogianni and Kuntsman, *Digital Cultures and the Politics of Emotion,* 33–51.

17. Patricia Ticineto Clough, "Feminist Theory: Bodies, Science, and Technology," in *Handbook of Body Studies,* ed. Bryan Turner (New York: Routledge, 2012).

18. Luciana Parisi, *Contagious Architecture: Computation, Aesthetics, and Space* (Cambridge, Mass.: MIT Press, 2013), 9.

19. Graham Harman, "On Vicarious Causation," *Collapse* 2 (2007): 221.

20. Steven Shaviro, "The Universe of Things" (presentation, *Object Oriented Ontology, A Symposium,* Atlanta, Ga., April 23, 2010), quoting Graham Harman, *Guerrilla Metaphysics: Phenomenology and the Carpentry of Things* (Chicago: Open Court, 2005), 7.

21. Timothy Morton, "Objects in the Mirror Are Closer Than They Appear," *Singularum* 1 (2012): 2–17.

22. Nigel Thrift, "The Insubstantial Pageant: Producing an Untoward Land," *Cultural Geographies* 19, no. 2 (2012): 141–68.

23. Bruno Latour et al., "'The Whole is Always Smaller Than Its Parts'—A Digital Test of Gabriel Tardes' Monads," *The British Journal of Sociology* 63, no. 4 (2012): 595.

24. Ibid., 590–615.

25. Randy Martin, "After Economy? Social Logics of the Derivative," *Social Text* 31, no. 1 (Spring 2013): 83–106.

26. See George Steinmetz, "The Epistemological Unconscious of US Sociology and the Transition to Post-Fordism: The Case of Historical Sociology," in *Remaking Modernity: Politics, History, and Sociology,* ed. Julia Adams, Elisabeth S. Clemens, and Ann Shola Orloff (Durham, N.C.: Duke University Press, 2005).

27. Patricia T. Clough, Karen Gregory, Benjamin Haber, and R. Joshua Scannel, "The Datalogical Turn," in *Non-Representational Methodologies: Re-Envisioning Research,* ed. Phillip Vannini (New York: Routledge, 2015), 155.

28. Mark B. N. Hansen, *Feed Forward: On the Future of Twenty-First-Century Media* (Chicago: University of Chicago Press, 2013).

29. Hansen is specifically differing with readings of Whitehead offered by Shaviro, Massumi, and to a lesser extent, Parisi.

30. Hansen's focus on entities as intensities draws on the work of Judith Jones. See Judith Jones, *Intensity, An Essay in Whiteheadian Ontology* (Nashville, Tenn.: Vanderbilt University Press, 1998).

31. Hansen, *Feed Forward,* 121.

32. Patricia Ticineto Clough, "Rethinking Race, Calculation, Quantification, and Measure," *Cultural Studies ↔ Critical Methodologies* 16, no. 5 (2016): 435–41. Also see Denise Ferreira da Silva for an important discussion of blackness, measure, and indeterminacy "1 (life) ÷ 0 (blackness) = ∞ – ∞ or ∞ / ∞: On Matter Beyond the Equation of Value," *e-flux* 79 (February 2017), http://www.e-flux.com/journal/79/94686/1-life -o-blackness-or-on-matter-beyond-the-equation-of-value/.

33. Clough, "Rethinking Race, Calculation, Quantification, and Measure," 437; Roderick Ferguson, *The Reorder of Things: The University and its Pedagogies of Minority Difference* (Minneapolis: University of Minnesota Press, 2012), 93.

34. Jasbir Puar, "The 'Right' to Maim: Disablement and Inhumanist Biopolitics in Palestine," *borderlands* 14, no. 1 (2015): 1–27, http://www .borderlands.net.au/vol14no1_2015/puar_maim.pdf.

35. Benjamin Bratton, *The Stack: On Software and Sovereignty* (Cambridge, Mass.: MIT Press, 2015).

36. Wendy Hui Kyong Chun, *Updating to Remain the Same: Habitual Media* (Cambridge, Mass.: MIT Press, 2016).

37. Clough, *Autoaffection*; Nigel Thrift, *Knowing Capitalism* (London: Sage, 2005), 213; N. Katherine Hayles, "Traumas of Code," *Critical Inquiry* 33, no.1 (Autumn 2006): 136–57.

38. Thrift, *Knowing Capitalism*, 213.

39. Hayles, "Traumas of Code," 138.

40. Mark B. N. Hansen, *Bodies in Code: Interfaces with Digital Media* (New York: Routledge, 2006).

41. Ibid., 25–103.

42. Ibid., 61.

43. Ibid., 94.

44. Harold Searles, *The Nonhuman Environment: In Normal Development and Schizophrenia* (Madison, Conn.: International Universities Press, 1960). Writing of the relationship between schizophrenia and the nonhuman, Searles, while arguing that the schizophrenic shows a variety of "failures" to establish the distinction between human and nonhuman and, therefore, to establish the expected relationship between the two, nonetheless goes on to propose that the indistinction of human and nonhuman of early infancy and childhood never fully ends for anyone and is especially reinvigorated at various times in "normal" human development when the boundaries of identity are volatile, as for example in adolescence. We might also think of the reinvigoration of the indistinction as a response to volatility in relationship to the massive extension of digital media and computational technologies.

45. Sue Grand, "Unsexed and Ungendered Bodies: The Violated Self," *Studies in Gender and Sexuality* 4 (2003): 338.

46. Ibid., 333.

47. Catherine Malabou, *The New Wounded: From Neurosis to Brain Damage,* trans. Steven Miller (New York: Fordham University Press, 2012), 11.

48. Sylvia Wynter, "Human Being as Noun? Or Being Human as Praxis, Towards the Autopoietic Turn/Overturn: A Manifesto," *Scribd,* August 2007, https://www.scribd.com/doc/237809437/Sylvia-Wynter-The-Autopoetic-Turn.

49. Jean-Luc Nancy, *Being Singular Plural,* trans. Robert Richardson and Anne OByrne (Stanford, Calif.: Stanford University Press, 2000).

50. Chun, *Updating to Remain the Same,* 163.

51. Jean-Luc Nancy, *The Inoperative Community* (Minneapolis: University of Minnesota Press, 1991).

52. Patricia Ticineto Clough, "Ecstatic Corona: From Ethnography to Performance," appearing for the first time in this collection.

53. Nancy, *The Inoperative Community,* xxv.

54. Christopher Bollas, *The Infinite Question* (New York: Routledge, 2009), 2.

55. Patricia Ticineto Clough and Craig Willse, "Beyond Biopolitics: The Governance of Life and Death," in Clough and Willse, *Beyond Biopolitics,* 1–16.

56. Ibid., 4, quoting Nasser Hussain, "Beyond Norm and Exception: Guantanamo," *Critical Inquiry* 33, no. 4 (2007): 741.

57. Clough and Willse, "Beyond Biopolitics," 15.

58. Ibid.

59. Martin, "After Economy?" 103.

NOTES TOWARD A THEORY OF AFFECT-ITSELF

1. Antonio Negri, "Value and Affect," *boundary 2,* no. 26 (1999): 77–88; Michael Hardt and Antonio Negri, *Empire* (Cambridge, Mass.: Harvard University Press, 2000), 34–41.

2. George Caffentzis, "Immeasurable Value? An Essay on Marx's Legacy," *The Commoner,* no. 10 (2005): 10, http://www.commoner.org .uk/10caffentzis.pdf.

3. See George Caffentzis, "Crystals and Analytic Engines: Historical and Conceptual Preliminaries to a New Theory of Machines, *ephemera: theory and politics in organization* 7, no. 1 (2007): 24–45. The laws of thermodynamics generalize energy (as being neither created nor destroyed, that is, conserved in every transfer) to such a high scale of abstraction that capitalists could begin to imagine all sorts of not-yet-imagined sources of energy, allowing them even to dream of ways to transmit energy from one form to another without expenditure or cost. The second law of thermodynamics, however, deflates this dream with the concept of entropy, the heat death of a steam engine that points to the impossibility of using energy without cost. Energy dissipates or becomes unavailable for work in a closed mechanical system. Additional work is needed to reenergize the machine, which, however, further increases entropy. Thus, a response to entropic heat death is called forth in the ongoing development of technology to make production or the use of

energy as efficient as possible while allowing capital to become more impervious to workers' refusal to work. Today, information is thought in terms of a new law that is: "information can neither be created nor destroyed," which speaks to the physicality of information and to what below we will take up as the informational measuring of matter. See Charles Seife, *Decoding the Universe: How the New Science of Information Is Explaining Everything in the Cosmos, from Our Brains to Black Holes* (New York: Viking Press, 2006), 189–221.

4.   George Caffentzis, "The Work Energy Crisis and the Apocalypse," in *Midnight Oil: Work, Energy, War, 1973–1992* (New York: Autonomedia, 1992), 220. Also see Caffentzis's "Why Machines Cannot Create Value; or, Marx's Theory of Machines," in *Cutting Edge: Technology, Information, Capitalism, and Social Revolution,* ed. Jim Davis, Thomas Hirschl, and Michael Stacks (London: Verso, 1997). Here Caffentzis argues that, just as thermodynamics provided a uniform approach to energy in industrial labor, with the invention of the Turing machine, computers provide a uniform approach to the computational procedures of all labor usually identified as skilled labor but "implicit in all parts of the division of social labor" (52). However, Caffentzis does not imagine how digital technologies would permit us to "see" information at all scales of matter, to realize the computational skills immanent to organic and nonorganic matter alike—that is, matter as self-measuring.

5.   F. David Peat, "Active Information, Meaning and Form," accessed October 19, 2016, http://www.fdavidpeat.com/bibliography/essays/fzmean.htm. See also Seife, *Decoding the Universe.*

6.   Karl Marx introduces the labor theory of value in chapter 1 of *Capital,* vol. 1 (New York: Penguin, 1990). He explains that "what exclusively determines the magnitude of the value of any article is therefore the amount of labor socially necessary, or the labor-time socially necessary for its production," including the qualification that "the labor that forms the substance of value is equal human labor, the expenditure of identical human labor" (129).

7.   Because the labor theory of value also speaks to the production of surplus value extracted from the human laborer's waged work, theorists who have taken up Marx's labor theory of value have emphasized the importance of the human laborer. There is a resonance of this in those theorists of affective labor who often point to a general potentiality but only in relationship to humanness. For example, Akseli Virtanen argues that the potential of labor power has always implied that there is something that remains potential. In his article "General Economy:

The Entrance of Multitude into Production," *ephemera: theory and politics in organization* 4, no. 3 (2004): 209–27, he states that affective labor makes this potentiality more visible only as the "general potentiality and linguistic-relational abilities which *distinguish* human-beings" (209). As Virtanen puts it, "for the first time the common mode of existence of human beings, the potential dimension of human existence as the power to do anything appears to us without the mediation of a meaning, product or common cause" (227). This "without the mediation of meaning" suggests to us that there needs be a rethinking of the mattering of potentiality, the potentiality of matter in terms of information, given that information, as we will discuss below, is a matter of form, not meaning.

8. Cf. Caffentzis, "The Work Energy Crisis and the Apocalypse."

9. Michael Hardt and Antonio Negri, "Marx's Mole is Dead!" *Eurozine*, February 13, 2002, https://libcom.org/library/marx-s-mole-is-dead-globalisation-and-communication-michael-hardt-antonio-negri; Maurizio Lazzarato, "Immaterial Labor," in *Radical Thought in Italy: A Potential Politics,* ed. Michael Hardt and Paulo Virno, trans. Paul Colilli and Ed Emery (Minneapolis: University of Minnesota Press, 1996).

10. Marx, *Grundrisse: Outlines of the Critique of Political Economy,* trans. Martin Nicolaus (London: Penguin, 1973), 706.

11. Virtanen, "General Economy," 223.

12. Paulo Virno, *A Grammar of the Multitude,* trans. Isabella Bertoletti et al. (New York: Semiotext(e), 2004), 98.

13. Humberto Maturana and Francisco Varela, *Autopoiesis and Cognition* (Boston: Reidel, 1980).

14. For further critique of the body-as-organism, see *The Affective Turn: Theorizing the Social,* ed. Patricia Ticineto Clough with Jean O'Malley Halley (Durham, N.C.: Duke University Press, 2007).

15. Keith Ansell Pearson, *Germinal Life: The Difference and Repetition of Deleuze* (New York: Routledge, 1999), 154.

16. Brian Massumi, *Parables for the Virtual: Movement, Affect, Sensation* (Durham, N.C.: Duke University Press, 2002), 25.

17. Ibid.

18. Ibid., 9.

19. We are following Timothy Murphy, who draws a comparison between the work of David Bohm, which we take up below, and Deleuze's conceptualization of the virtual. Deleuze distinguished the virtual-actual circuit from the possible-real circuit: in contrast to the possible, which is to be realized, the virtual calls forth actualizations that have no resemblance to the virtual. Actualization is not a specification of a prior generality.

Actualization out of virtuality is creation out of heterogeneity. Actualization is an experiment in virtuality, an affecting or materializing of a virtual series. See Timothy S. Murphy, "Quantum Ontology: A Virtual Mechanics of Becoming," in *Deleuze and Guattari: New Mappings in Politics, Philosophy, and Culture*, ed. Eleanor Kaufman and Kevin John Heller (Minneapolis: University of Minnesota Press, 1988), 211–29.

20. Massumi, *Parables for the Virtual*, 37.

21. Murphy, "Quantum Ontology," 222.

22. Ibid.

23. A number of Bohm's commentators point to his use of the holographic image to further elaborate the way in which unfoldment explicates the implicate at various scales of matter. While the holographic image is one in which all of its parts contain the whole, Bohm prefers the more dynamic term "holomovement" (rather than static imagery of the hologram) to suggest that the whole of the material world is continuously including our sense experiences, nervous system, brain, etc. See Michael Talbot, *The Holographic Universe* (New York: Harper Perennial, 1991).

24. See Murphy's discussion of Bohm, Bohr, and Heisenberg in "Quantum Ontology." Also see David Bohm and Basil J. Hiley, *The Undivided Universe: An Ontological Interpretation of Quantum Theory* (New York: Routledge, 1993).

25. Murphy, "Quantum Ontology," 15.

26. Ibid., 216.

27. Ibid.

28. David Bohm, "A New Theory of the Relationship of Mind and Matter," *Philosophical Psychology* 3, no. 2 (1990): 271–86. See also Bohm and Hiley, *The Undivided Universe*.

29. Bohm, "A New Theory of the Relationship of Mind and Matter," 279.

30. Bohm and Hiley, *The Undivided Universe*, 35.

31. Ibid., 28.

32. Ibid., 36.

33. See Massumi, *Parables for the Virtual*, 36–37. Massumi offers a discussion of quantum effects and the way they feed forward and back through all scales of matter.

34. Murphy, "Quantum Ontology," 225.

35. Luciana Parisi, *Abstract Sex: Philosophy, Bio-technology and the Mutations of Desire* (New York: Continuum, 2004).

36. Lynn Margulis, *Symbiosis in Cell Evolution* (San Francisco: W. H. Freeman, 1981); Margulis and Dorion Sagan, *Microcosmos: Four Billion*

Years of Evolution from Our Microbial Ancestors (New York: Summit Books, 1986).

37. Parisi, *Abstract Sex,* 175. Parisi's comparison of genetic technologies and mitochondrial replication points to the creative mutation possible in technological processes of genetic engineering. Melinda Cooper has also drawn on the work of microbiologists, including Margulis and Sagan, to show how microbial communication offers a model for the "biological turn" in the war on terror. She argues that the ability of bacteria to exchange sequences of DNA across species and genera has only recently been recognized to be useful for biological warfare. This ability of bacteria also has led to a general mode of governance and economy based on the precipitation of random mutation, which we will discuss below. See Melinda Cooper, "Pre-empting Emergence: The Biological Turn in the War on Terror," *Theory, Culture and Society* 23, no. 4 (2006): 11–135. Both Parisi and Cooper complexify those treatments of genetic technologies that link them to what Kaushik Sunder Rajan calls "biocapitalism"; see Rajan, *Biocapital: The Constitution of Postgenomic Life* (Durham, N.C.: Duke University Press, 2006).

38. Parisi, *Abstract Sex,* 157.

39. Luciana Parisi and Steve Goodman, "The Affect of Nanoterror," *Culture Machine* 7, no. 6 (2005), http://www.culturemachine.net/index.php/cm/article/view/29/36.

40. Ibid.

41. Massumi, "The Future Birth of the Affective Fact" (presentation, *Conference Proceedings: Genealogies of Biopolitics,* Concordia University, October 2005), 2, https://www.scribd.com/document/242453979/Affective-Fact-Massumi.

42. Ibid.

43. David Harvey, *The New Imperialism* (New York: Oxford University Press, 2003), 137–82.

44. In many of the treatments of affective labor we explore, there is an implicit or explicit recognition of the importance of Foucault's notion of biopower, as well as his treatment of economy in relation to governmentality. This is because Foucault recognized the tie between the state, power, and life. He traced the entrance of the life of the individual and of the species into politics at the moment when the managing of the household became a model for managing the state, when the sovereign's power shifted from the principality or the territory to the concern and management of the people—that is, the art of governing. In Foucault's account, this occurs from the sixteenth century through the eighteenth,

when the model of the good father overseeing the working of the family, its economy, becomes the managerial model for the state. In his essay "Governmentality," in *The Foucault Effect,* ed. Graham Burchell, Colin Gordon, and Peter Miller (Chicago: University of Chicago Press, 1991), 87–104, Foucault argues that the art of government requires the entrance of economy into political practice "to set up an economy at the level of the entire state which means exercising towards its inhabitants and the wealth and behavior of each and all, a form of surveillance and control as attentive as the head of a family over his household and his goods" (92). The economical state is engaged in the different flows and relationships of population/territory/things in terms of health, wealth, and a general security of the people. Here, the state intervenes in the economy where the economy relies on statistical measures of the population's needs, regularities, and irregularities and where subsets of the population such as the family become objects and vehicles of discipline. More recently, theorists like Massumi have drawn on Foucault's work on neoliberal government to further address governmentality. Massumi makes use of *The Birth of Biopolitics* to outline the relationship of governance and economy in order to capture the workings of what we have been referring to as preemptive power. See Foucault, *The Birth of Biopolitics: Lectures at the Collège de France, 1978-1979,* trans. Graham Burchell (New York: Palgrave MacMillan, 2008).

45. Brian Massumi, "National Enterprise Emergency: Refiguring Political Decision," (presentation, *Beyond Biopower: State Racism and the Politics of Life and Death Conference,* New York, March 2006).

46. Wendy Brown, "Neoliberalism and the End of Liberal Democracy," *Theory and Event* 7, no. 1 (2003): 1–28; Thomas Lemke, "'The Birth of Biopolitics': Michel Foucault's Lecture at the Collège de France on Neoliberal Governmentality," *Economy and Society* 30, no. 2 (2001): 190–207.

47. Massumi, "The Future Birth of the Affective Fact," 8.

48. Ibid., 7.

49. Ibid., 8.

WAR BY OTHER MEANS

1. Mia Kirshner, J. B. MacKinnon, Paul Shoebridge, and Michael Simmons, *I Live Here* (New York: Pantheon Books, 2008).

2. On the inside of the box there is a disclaimer: "The text, testimonies, opinions and artwork included in *I Live Here* are the work of the

individual authors and artists who collaborated on this project, and none of the people interviewed or the material derived was corroborated by AIUSA research. While AIUSA strongly supports freedom of expression, the organization considers some of the depictions in *I Live Here* potentially inappropriate for young people."

3.   The descriptions I offer below draw on the images and bits of stories from each of the four books in the boxed collection. My choices of images and stories already are part of my response to the books and as such are meant to reproduce the feelings I first had in reading and looking at the books. While these are my choices, I do think they are fairly representative of the collection as a whole. I want to thank Jasmin Zine, who reminded me of Susan Sontag's remarks relevant to my choices of images and stories: "So far as we feel sympathy, we feel we are not accomplices to what caused the suffering. Our sympathy proclaims our innocence as well as our impotence. To that extent, it can be (for all our good intentions) an impertinent—if not an inappropriate—response. To set aside the sympathy we extend to others beset by war and murderous politics for a consideration of how our privileges are located on the same map as their suffering, and may—in ways that we prefer not to imagine—be linked to their suffering, as the wealth of some may imply the destitution of others, is a task for which the painful, stirring images supply only the initial spark" (*Regarding the Pain of Others* [New York: Farrar, Straus and Giroux, 2003], 102).

4.   Christine Harold, "On Target: Aura, Affect, and the Rhetoric of 'Design Democracy,'" *Public Culture* 21 (2009): 599–618.

5.   Luciana Parisi and Steve Goodman, "Mnemonic Control," in *Beyond Biopolitics: Essays on the Governance of Life and Death,* ed. Patricia T. Clough and Craig Willse (Durham, N.C.: Duke University Press, 2012), 252–71. For Parisi and Goodman, affective potential can be "conceived as a time-span that lasts a second or fraction of a second and 'which lives actively in its antecedent world'" (265).

6.   Ibid., 267.

7.   Brian Massumi, "National Enterprise Emergency: Steps Toward an Ecology of Powers," in Clough and Willse, *Beyond Biopolitics,* 25–65.

8.   Tiziana Terranova, "Another Life: The Limits of Sovereignty and the Nature of Political Economy in Foucault's Genealogy of Biopolitics," *Theory, Culture and Society* 26, no. 6 (2009): 234–62.

9.   There has been much discussion among critical theorists of these formations noting the use of particular bodies like those often displayed in *I Live Here* to draw certain sympathies or arouse affect. See, for

174 NOTES TO WAR BY OTHER MEANS

example: Rey Chow, *The Protestant Ethnic and The Spirit of Capitalism* (New York: Columbia University Press, 2002); Jenny Sharpe and Gayatri Chakravorty Spivak, "A Conversation with Gayatri Chakravorty Spivak: Politics and the Imagination," *Signs: Journal of Women in Culture and Society* 28, no. 2 (2003): 609–24; Inderpal Grewal, *Transnational America: Feminisms, Diasporas, Neoliberalisms* (Durham, N.C.: Duke University Press, 2005); Sara Ahmed, "Affective Economies," *Social Text* 22, no. 2 (2004): 117–39; Aihwa Ong, *Neoliberalism as Exception: Mutations in Citizenship and Sovereignty* (Durham, N.C.: Duke University Press, 2006); and Jasbir Puar, *Terrorist Assemblages: Homonationalism in Queer Times* (Durham, N.C.: Duke University Press, 2007).

10. Timothy Murray, *Digital Baroque: New Media Art and Cinematic Folds* (Minneapolis: University of Minnesota Press, 2008), 225.

11. Thomas Lamarre, *The Anime Machine: A Media Theory of Animation* (Minneapolis: University of Minnesota Press, 2009).

12. See Michel Foucault, *Security, Territory, Population: Lectures at the Collège de France, 1977–78* (New York: Picador, 2007), and *Birth of Biopolitics: Lectures at the Collège de France 1978–1979,* trans. Graham Burchell (New York: Palgrave Macmillan, 2008).

13. Massumi, "Requiem for Our Prospective Dead (toward a Participatory Critique of Capitalist Power)," in *Deleuze and Guattari: New Mappings in Politics, Philosophy, and Culture,* ed. Eleanor Kaufman and Kevin Jon Heller (Minneapolis: University of Minnesota Press, 1998), 57.

14. Foucault, *Security, Territory, Population,* 70.

15. I first developed the notion of "population racism" in my "The New Empiricism: Affect and Sociological Method," *European Journal of Social Theory* 12, no. 1 (2009): 43–61.

16. It is important to note that the arguments I am making are from the perspective of the deployment of ontopower. Another or other perspectives might prevail from those regions presented in projects like *I Live Here,* where such regions are treated in wildly limited terms.

17. See Patricia Ticineto Clough, Greg Goldberg, Rachel Schiff, Aaron Weeks, and Craig Willse, "Notes toward a Theory of Affect-Itself," *ephemera: theory and politics in organization* 7, no. 1 (2007): 60–77.

18. See *Crisis in The Global Economy: Financial Markets, Social Struggles, and New Political Scenarios,* ed. Andrea Fumagalli and Sandro Messadra (New York: Semiotext(e), 2010).

19. There is much yet to be developed in a discussion of measure in relationship both to contemporary governance and capitalism that most likely also will pressure rethinking the methods of the social sciences.

Here, my introduction to the need to discuss aesthetic measure draws on Steven Shaviro's work on beauty versus the sublime. See Steven Shaviro "Beauty Lies in the Eye," *symploke* 6, no. 1 (1998): 96–108, and *Without Criteria, Kant, Whitehead, Deleuze, and Aesthetics* (Cambridge, MA: MIT Press, 2009). Also, for a discussion of the causality of allure, see Graham Harman, "On Vicarious Causation," *COLLAPSE* 2 (2007): 187–221.

20. Lauren Berlant, "Introduction: Compassion and Withholding," in *Compassion: The Culture and Politics of an Emotion,* ed. Lauren Berlant (New York: Routledge, 2004).

21. I am drawing from Kathleen Woodward's discussion of neoliberal compassion in her chapter "Calculating Compassion," in Berlant, *Compassion,* 59–86.

PRAYING AND PLAYING TO THE BEAT
OF A CHILD'S METRONOME

1. These words are taken from the "Magnificat," a prayer first sung by the Virgin Mary announcing to her cousin Elizabeth that she, Mary, had been chosen to be the mother of the Son of God. Also called the "Canticle of Mary," the "Magnificat" appears in the Gospel of Luke (1:46–55).

2. I am thinking of, among others: Giorgio Agamben, *The Time That Remains: A Commentary on the Letter to the Romans,* trans. Patricia Dailey (Stanford, Calif.: Stanford University Press, 2003); Slavoj Žižek, *The Puppet and the Dwarf: The Perverse Core of Christianity* (Cambridge, Mass.: MIT Press, 2003); Alain Badiou, *Saint Paul: The Foundation of Universalism,* trans. Ray Brassier (Stanford, Calif.: Stanford University Press, 2003); Jacques Derrida, "A Silkworm of One's Own," in *Veils,* ed. Hélène Cixous and Jacques Derrida, trans. Geoffrey Bennington (Stanford, Calif.: Stanford University Press, 2001), 49–92; and finally and earlier, Gilles Deleuze, "Nietzsche and Saint Paul, Lawrence and John of Patmos," in *Essays Critical and Clinical,* trans. Michael A. Greco (Minneapolis: University of Minnesota Press, 1997).

3. I am gesturing here to Alain Badiou's philosophical discourse.

4. I am drawing on Niklaus Largier, *In Praise of the Whip: A Cultural History of Arousal,* trans. Graham Harman (New York: Zone Books, 2007), and Michel Foucault, *Abnormal: Lectures At the Collège de France, 1974–1975,* trans. Graham Burchell (New York: Picador, 1999). In referring to acts of flagellation, mysticism, and convulsion as counterpastoral,

Foucault is pointing to the challenge these acts posed to the church's pastoral role as the source of its power.

5.   I am drawing these thoughts and words from Jean-Luc Nancy, *Noli me tangere: On the Raising of the Body*, trans. Sarah Clift, Pascale-Anne Brault, and Michael Naas (New York: Fordham University Press, 2008), 10.

6.   Gil Anidjar, "Secularism," *Critical Inquiry* 33 (Autumn 2006): 61.

7.   Nancy, *Noli me tangere*, 43.

8.   I am drawing on the rich and moving account of rock-and-roll by John Mowitt in his *Percussion: Drumming, Beating, Striking* (Durham, N.C.: Duke University Press, 2002). See also, Anahid Kassabian, *Hearing Film—Tracking Identifications in Contemporary Hollywood Film Music* (New York: Routledge, 2001).

9.   I am following Mowitt in drawing on a number of texts by Freud, along with: Didier Anzieu, *The Skin Ego*, trans. Chris Turner (New Haven, Conn.: Yale University Press, 1989); Jean Laplanche and Jean-Bertrand Pontalis, "Fantasy and the Origins of Sexuality," in *Formations of Fantasy*, ed. Victor Burgin and Cora Kaplan (London: Metheun, 1986); and Jean Laplanche, *Life and Death in Psychoanalysis*, trans. Jeffrey Mehlman (Baltimore, Md.: Johns Hopkins University Press, 1970).

10.   I am drawing again on Mowitt. While it has been argued that rock-and-roll is neither essentially black nor white, African nor North American, Mowitt shifts the debate to suggest a percussive genealogy. For him, rock-and-roll is "an idiom formed at the frontier that rather like a scar, arose as whites and non-whites collided with each other on, or bumped each other off, a social playing field that was, and remains, far from level" (*Percussion*, 27). Mowitt also points to Joan Dayan's discussion of vodou in *Haiti, History, and the Gods* (Oakland: University of California Press, 1995), where she argues that vodou practices do not always go back to Africa, but "rather . . . were responses to the institution of slavery, to its peculiar brand of sensuous domination," thus reconstituting "the shadowy and powerful magical gods of Africa as everyday responses to the white master's arbitrary power" (36). It is Dayan's comment I have paraphrased above: "The dispossession accomplished by slavery became the model for possession in vodou: for making a man not into a thing but into a spirit" (ibid.). Remembering that Christianity was the ground upon which vodou was elaborated in relationship to slavery, I want to underscore the knotted resonances here among beating, sexuality, psyche, spirit, vodou, and Christianity and to point to Mowitt's instruction: "Possession might be understood to bear not on the loss of control, but on the sense (indeed, the overwhelming sense) that one is,

even at one's limits, but at a moment in a rush of restricted possibilities that constitute the social at any given time. Ecstasy is thus not about surrender. It is about the disorienting recognition of one's dependence on a relationship, on a field of relations, that an identity manages poorly, if at all" (*Percussion,* 85).

11. I don't mean to imply a direct relationship between vodou and the invention of the metronome. I am, rather, inspired to play with Mowitt's use of metronome to describe the backbeat as the "metronome" of a band of musicians.

12. I am drawing my argument about the Kantian sublime and what follows from Eugene Thacker's discussion of swarming and demonic power in "Pulse Demons, Swarm and Algorithm," *Culture Machine* 9 (2007), http://www.culturemachine.net/index.php/cm/article/view/80/56.

GENDERED SECURITY / NATIONAL SECURITY

1. *New York Times Magazine*, September 8, 2002.

2. In relation to advertising, marketing, and therefore, spending, it is difficult not to think of then-President Bush, who, immediately after September 11, 2001, reminded Americans that they should keep on shopping as if to save American democracy by preventing an interruption of the economy.

3. The critiques of human security became part of the debates about the deployment of gender in human rights policy; there too, cultural critics debated the universality of gender norms and using the woman as "victim" in promoting policy and advocacy.

4. We will be drawing on Patricia Ticineto Clough's development of political branding in "War by Other Means: What Difference Do(es) the Graphic(s) Make?" presented at the Society for Social Studies of Science, October 28–31, 2009.

5. Connecting contemporary calls to "save Muslim women" to nineteenth-century Christian missionary work, Abu-Lughod insists, "as feminists in or from the West, or simply as people who have concerns for women's lives, we need to be wary of this response to events and aftermath of September 11, 2001." See Lila Abu-Lughod, "Do Muslin Women Really Need Saving? Anthropological Reflections on Cultural Relativism and Its Others," *American Anthropologist* 3 (2002): 783–90. Abu-Lughod extended this line of argument in a critique of the United Nations and discourse of "Muslim women's rights" in Abu-Lughod, "Dialectics of Women's Empowerment: The International Circuitry

of the *Arab Human Development Report 2005,*" *International Journal of Middle East Studies* 1 (2009): 83–103. Further critiques of the mobilization of "feminism" against "Islamic fundamentalism" are offered by: Charles Hirschkind and Saba Mahmood, "Feminism, the Taliban, and Politics of Counter-Insurgency," *Anthropological Quarterly* 75, no. 2 (2002): 339–54; Jenny Sharpe and Gayatri Chakravorty Spivak, "A Conversation with Gayatri Chakravorty Spivak: Politics and the Imagination," *Signs: Journal of Women in Culture and Society* 28, no. 2 (2003): 609–24; Inderpal Grewal, *Transnational America: Feminisms, Diasporas, Neoliberalisms* (Durham, N.C.: Duke University Press, 2005); Aihwa Ong, *Neoliberalism as Exception: Mutations in Citizenship and Sovereignty* (Durham, N.C.: Duke University Press, 2006); and Jasbir Puar, *Terrorist Assemblages: Homonationalism in Queer Times* (Durham, N.C.: Duke University Press, 2007). Rey Chow offers a critique of feminist human rights discourse in *The Protestant Ethnic and the Spirit of Capitalism* (New York: Columbia University Press, 2002). And for a general discussion of relationships between feminism, militarism, and racism, see the essays collected in Chandra Talpade Mohanty, Minnie Bruce Pratt, and Robin L. Riley, *Feminism and War* (London: Zed Books, 2008).

6.   As in Clough's essay "War by Other Means," we here are following Christine Harold's term "aesthetic capitalism," which she coins in relationship to Steven Shaviro's discussion of the "age of aesthetics." As such, Harold argues that, in an aesthetic capitalism, "capital can no longer rely simply on an explosion of surface-level sign value; it must instead 'go deep,' developing commodities that are imbued with value not through their production but through the various models of their use." See Christine Harold, "On Target: Aura, Affect, and the Rhetoric of "Design Democracy," *Public Culture* 21, no. 3 (2009): 611. We also have taken note of the idea of gender as brand in Lisa Adkins's discussion of gender in terms of the information economy, what she calls the "new economy" in "The New Economy, Property, and Personhood," *Theory, Culture and Society* 22, no. 1 (2005): 111–30, and what we discuss as an affect economy. For Adkins, in the new economy, the relationship of ownership, property, and person is changing. This change involves a "patenting" of things previously coded as natural and/or social, "a process, which has been described as type or kind becoming brand" (115). In the new economy, the value of processes is not determined by ownership so much as by "audience effect" (117). For a rich discussion of "branding" in relation to contemporary political discourse that favors attention and affect rather than logic, see Jakob Arnoldi's discussion of

"informational ideas" in "Informational Ideas," *Thesis Eleven* 89, no. 1 (2007): 58–73.

7. Luciana Parisi and Steve Goodman, "Mnemonic Control," in *Beyond Biopolitics: Essays on the Governance of Life and Death,* ed. Patricia Ticineto Clough and Craig Willse (Durham, N.C.: Duke University Press, 2011).

8. Tiziana Terranova, "Another Life: The Limits of Sovereignty and the Nature of Political Economy in Foucault's Genealogy of Biopolitics," *Theory, Culture and Society* 26 (2009): 234–62.

9. In an affect economy, human attention is shifted away from the logics of the cinematic gaze, even from the logics of television that draw the subject into the production of value, by watching capital-invested time images. In an affect economy, digital logics are more about a tactile connectivity, the modulation through contact of the intensities of affective energies. See Clough's discussion of political economy, attention, and teletechnologies in *Autoaffection: Unconscious Thought in the Age of Teletechnology* (Minneapolis: University of Minnesota Press, 2000). For a more detailed discussion of affect economy, also see *The Affective Turn: Theorizing the Social,* ed. Patricia Ticineto Clough with Jean Halley (Durham, N.C.: Duke University Press, 2007), and Patricia Ticineto Clough, Greg Goldberg, Rachel Schiff, Aaron Weeks, and Craig Willse, "Notes toward a Theory of Affect-Itself," *ephemera: theory and politics in organization* 7, no. 1 (2007): 60–77.

10. Michel Foucault, *The History of Sexuality,* vol. 1, *An Introduction,* trans. Robert Hurley (New York: Vintage, 1979): 138.

11. Ibid., 145–46.

12. Michel Foucault, *Society Must Be Defended: Lectures at the Collège de France, 1975–76* (New York: Picador, 2003), 243.

13. Such a linear progression has also been critiqued by scholars who have emphasized the centrality of imperialism and colonialism to the rise of technologies of biopower. See Ann Laura Stoler, *Race and the Education of Desire: Foucault's History of Sexuality and the Colonial Order of Things* (Durham, N.C.: Duke University Press, 2012).

14. Foucault, *The History of Sexuality,* 146.

15. The term "population racism" is introduced in Patricia Clough, "The New Empiricism: Affect and Sociological Method," *European Journal of Social Theory* 12, no. 1 (2009): 43–61, and Clough, "The Affective Turn: Political Economy, Biomedia and Bodies," *Theory, Culture and Society* 25, no. 1 (2008): 1–22.

16. Foucault, *Society Must Be Defended,* 254.

17. The concept of biovalue is introduced in Catherine Waldby, *The Visible Human Project: Informatic Bodies and Posthuman Medicine* (New York: Routledge, 2000). A further elaboration of the concept is offered by Kaushik Sunder Rajan, *Biocapital: The Constitution of Postgenomic Life* (Durham, N.C.: Duke University Press, 2006).

18. Aihwa Ong, *Neoliberalism as Exception,* 5.

19. Foucault, *Birth of Biopolitics: Lectures at the Collège de France 1978–1979,* trans. Graham Burchell (New York: Palgrave Macmillan, 2008), 121.

20. Randy Martin, *An Empire of Indifference: American War and the Financial Logic of Risk Management* (Durham, N.C.: Duke University Press, 2007), 63.

21. Brian Massumi, "Future Birth of the Affective Fact" (presentation, *Conference Proceedings: Genealogies of Biopolitics,* Concordia University, October 2005), which would eventually be published in *The Affect Theory Reader,* ed. Melissa Gregg and Gregory Seigworth (Durham, N.C.: Duke University Press, 2010): 52–70.

22. Michel Foucault, *Security, Territory, Population: Lectures at the Collège de France, 1977–1978,* trans. Graham Burchell (New York: Picador, 2007), 70.

23. Ibid., 75.

24. Tiziana Terranova, "Futurepublic: On Information Warfare, Bio-racism and Hegemony as Noopolitics," *Theory, Culture and Society* 24, no. 3 (2007): 135. Terranova is drawing on Maurizio Lazzarato, *La politica dell'evento* (Cosenza: Rubbittino, 2004).

25. Terranova, "Futurepublic," 139.

26. Ibid., 140.

27. Julian Dibbell, "The Life of a Chinese Gold Farmer," *New York Times Magazine,* June 17, 2007, 36–41.

28. Julian Dibbell, *Play Money: or, How I Quit My Day Job and Made Millions Trading Virtual Loot* (New York: Basic Books, 2006).

29. Ibid., 23.

30. Chow, *The Protestant Ethnic and The Spirit of Capitalism.*

31. Ibid., 21.

32. Ibid., 160.

33. Juliet Lapidos, "Storage Company Ads Too Political For Some Tastes," *New York Sun,* March 30, 2007, http://www.nysun.com/article/51510.

34. "Manhattan Mini Storage Ad: Does This Cross over Too Far into Bad Taste?" *Reddit,* July 23, 2007, http://reddit.com/info/20pfq/comments.

35. "Does This Ad Go a Little Too Far?" *Subwayfox*, June 23, 2007, http://subwayfox.net/index.php?q=node/297.

36. In February 2009, the mayor of Los Alamitos, California, came under criticism for sending out an email with an image depicting the White House lawn planted with rows of watermelons, accompanied by the text, "No easter egg hunt this year." He was eventually forced to resign as a result. See "White House Watermelon Email from Mayor Dean Grose Inspires Outrage," *African America,* February 25, 2009, http://www.africanamerica.org/topic/white-house-watermelon-email -from-california-mayor-dean-grose-inspires-outrage?page=1.

MY MOTHER'S SCREAM

1. These words and thoughts are taken from Kaja Silverman, *The Acoustic Mirror: The Female Voice in Psychoanalysis and Cinema* (Bloomington: Indiana University Press, 1988), 80.

2. These words and thoughts are taken from Jean-Luc Nancy, *Listening* (New York: Fordham University Press, 2007), 12–13.

3. These words and thoughts are taken from Fred Moten and Stefano Harney, "Blackness and Governance," in *Beyond Biopolitics: Essays on the Governance of Life and Death,* ed. Patricia Ticineto Clough and Craig Willse (Durham, N.C.: Duke University Press, 2011), 351–61.

4. These words and thoughts are taken from Douglas Kahn, *Noise Water Meat: A History of Sound in the Arts* (Cambridge, Mass.: MIT Press, 2001), 227, 233.

5. These words and thoughts are taken from Steve Goodman, *Sonic Warfare: Sound, Affect, and the Ecology of Fear* (Cambridge, Mass.: MIT Press, 2009), 10.

6. Steve Goodman summarizing the thought of Jacques Attali in ibid., 7.

7. These words and thoughts are taken from Brian Massumi, *Parables for the Virtual: Movement, Affect, Sensation* (Durham, N.C.: Duke University Press, 2002), 14. Steve Goodman also draws on Massumi's discussion of the echo in *Sonic Warfare* (45).

8. These words and thoughts are taken from Goodman, *Sonic Warfare,* 82.

9. Ibid., 122.

10. The words and thoughts are taken from Luciana Parisi, "The Labyrinth of the Continuum: Topological Control and Mereotopologies of Abstraction" (unpublished presentation, 2009) and her "Symbiotic

Architecture: Prehending Digitality," *Theory, Culture and Society* 26, nos. 2–3 (March/May 2009): 347–79.

FEMINIST THEORY

1. Donna Haraway, *Modest Witness@Second Millennium: Female Man Meets OncoMouse* (New York: Routledge, 1997).
2. Judith Butler, *Bodies That Matter: On the Discursive Limits of "Sex"* (New York: Routledge, 1993); Butler, *Gender Trouble: Feminism and the Subversion of Identity* (New York: Routledge, 1991).
3. Pheng Cheah, "Mattering," *Diacritics* 26, no. 1 (1996): 113.
4. Ibid., 120. The critiques of Butler's work concern only her very early work on queering the body.
5. Elizabeth Grosz, *Volatile Bodies: Toward a Corporeal Feminism* (Bloomington: Indiana University Press, 1994); Grosz, *Space, Time, and Perversion: Essays on the Politics of Bodies* (New York: Routledge, 1995).
6. Grosz, *Volatile Bodies*, 21.
7. Ibid.
8. Ibid., 164.
9. Gilles Deleuze, *Essays Critical and Clinical*, trans. Daniel W. Smith and Michael Greco (Minneapolis: University of Minnesota Press, 1997), 63.
10. Grosz, *Space, Time, and Perversion*, 125–37.
11. Elizabeth Grosz, *Time Travels: Feminism, Nature, Power* (Durham, N.C.: Duke University Press, 2005); Grosz, *The Nick of Time: Politics, Evolution, and the Untimely* (Durham, N.C.: Duke University Press, 2004).
12. Grosz, *Time Travels*, 21.
13. Ibid.
14. Henri Bergson, *Creative Evolution* (New York: Random House, 1944), 161, quoted in Grosz, *The Nick of Time*, 139.
15. Eugene Thacker, *The Global Genome: Biotechnology, Politics, and Culture* (Cambridge, Mass.: MIT Press, 2005), 201.
16. Luciana Parisi and Tiziana Terranova, "Heat-Death: Emergence and Control in Genetic Engineering and Artificial Life," *CTHEORY*, October 5, 2000, http://www.ctheory.net/articles.aspx?id=127.
17. Donna Haraway, "The Promises of Monsters: A Regenerative Politics for Inappropriate/d Others," in *Cultural Studies*, ed. Lawrence Grossberg et al. (New York: Routledge, 1992), 298.

18. Gilles Deleuze, "Postscript on Societies of Control," *October* 59 (1991): 3–7.

19. Humberto Maturana and Francisco Varela, *Autopoiesis and Cognition* (Boston: Reidel, 1980).

20. Parisi and Terranova, "Heat-Death."

21. N. Katherine Hayles, *How We Became Posthuman: Virtual Bodies in Cybernetics, Literature, and Informatics* (Chicago: University of Chicago Press, 1999).

22. Keith Ansell Pearson, *Germinal Life: The Difference and Repetition of Deleuze* (New York: Routledge, 1999), 170.

23. Ibid., 154.

24. Parisi and Terranova, "Heat-Death."

25. Ibid.

26. Michel Foucault, *Security, Territory, Population: Lectures at the Collège de France 1977–1978,* trans. Graham Burchell (New York: Palgrave Macmillan, 2007); Foucault, *The Birth of Biopolitics: Lectures at the Collège de France 1978–1979,* trans. Graham Burchell (New York: Palgrave Macmillan, 2010).

27. Tiziana Terranova, "Futurepublic: On Information Warfare, Bioracism, and Hegemony as Noopolitics," *Theory, Culture and Society* 24, no. 3 (2007): 136.

28. Ibid., 137.

29. Ibid., 136.

30. *The Affective Turn: Theorizing the Social,* ed. Patricia Ticineto Clough with Jean O'Malley Halley (Durham, N.C.: Duke University Press, 2007).

31. Brian Massumi, "National Enterprise Emergency: Steps Toward an Ecology of Powers," in *Beyond Biopolitics: Essays on the Governance of Life and Death,* ed. Patricia Ticineto Clough and Craig Willse (Durham, N.C.: Duke University Press, 2012), 25–65.

32. Luciana Parisi, *Abstract Sex: Philosophy, Bio-technology and the Mutations of Desire* (New York: Continuum, 2004).

33. Karen Barad, "Getting Real: Technoscientific Practices and the Materialization of Reality," *differences: A Journal of Feminist Cultural Studies* 2, no. 10 (1998): 87–129.

34. Luciana Parisi, "The Adventures of a Sex," in *Deleuze and Queer Theory,* ed. Chrysanthi Nigianni and Merl Storr (Edinburgh: Edinburgh University Press, 2009), 81.

35. Ibid.

36. Parisi is drawing on Whitehead, *Adventures in Ideas* (New York: The Free Press, 1933) and *Process and Reality*.

37. Whitehead, *Process and Reality*, 195, quoted in Steven Shaviro, "The Universe of Things" (presentation, *Object Oriented Ontology, A Symposium*, Atlanta, Ga., April 23, 2010), 10.

38. Parisi, "The Adventures of a Sex," 72–91.

A DREAM OF FALLING

1. These thoughts and words are from Jean-Luc Nancy, *The Fall of Sleep*, trans. Charlotte Mandell (New York: Fordham University Press, 2009), 7, 13–14.

2. I take this expression from Eugene Thacker, *The Horror of Philosophy*, vol. 1, *In the Dust of This Planet* (Washington, D.C.: Zero Books, 2010).

3. I take these thoughts and words from Christopher Bollas, *The Shadow of the Object: Psychoanalysis of the Unthought Known* (New York: Columbia University Press, 1987), 14.

4. I take these thoughts and expressions from Eugene Thacker's work, especially *After Life* (Chicago: University of Chicago Press, 2010).

5. I am drawing on Michel Foucault, *Birth of Biopolitics: Lectures at the Collège de France 1978–1979*, trans. Graham Burchell (New York: Palgrave Macmillan, 2008); Foucault, *Security, Territory, Population: Lectures at the Collège de France, 1977–1978* (New York: Picador, 2007); Tiziana Terranova, "Another Life: The Limits of Sovereignty and the Nature of Political Economy in Foucault's Genealogy of Biopolitics," *Theory, Culture and Society* 26 (2009): 234–62.

6. I take these thoughts and expressions from Graham Harman, *Prince of Networks* (Melbourne: Re.press, 2009). Here, in his treatment of allure, Harman is drawing on the work of Alfred North Whitehead on allure and the aesthetic.

7. Here I am drawing on the thoughts and expressions of Steven Shaviro, *Without Criteria* (Cambridge, Mass.: MIT Press, 2009), 5–6.

8. Bollas, *The Shadow of the Object*, 34–35, 64–81.

9. I am drawing here on the thought of Gilles Deleuze, *Proust and Signs: The Complete Text*, trans. Richard Howard (Minneapolis: University of Minnesota Press, 2004).

THE DATALOGICAL TURN

1. Matt Sledge, "CIA's Gus Hunt on Big Data: We 'Try to Collect Everything and Hang on to It Forever,'" *Huffington Post*, March 20,

2013, http://www.huffingtonpost.com/2013/03/20/cia-gus-hunt-big
-data_n_2917842.html.

2.   Big Data is a loosely defined term that is generally applied to massive amounts of data (on the order of peta- and exabytes) that accrue over time. The size of the data is such that it cannot be parsed using common databased tools, requiring specialized methods such as parallel computing to glean meaningful information.

3.   Luciana Parisi, *Contagious Architecture: Computation, Aesthetics, and Space* (Cambridge, Mass.: MIT Press, 2013), 9.

4.   Ibid., 13.

5.   Sledge, "CIA's Gus Hunt on Big Data."

6.   George Steinmetz, "The Epistemological Unconscious of U.S. Sociology and the Transition to Post-Fordism: The Case of Historical Sociology," in *Remaking Modernity: Politics, History, and Sociology,* ed. Julia Adams, Elisabeth Clemens, and Ann Shola Orloff (Durham, N.C.: Duke University Press, 2005), 109–57.

7.   Nigel Thrift, *Non-Representational Theory* (London: Routledge, 2008).

8.   Patricia Ticineto Clough, *The End(s) of Ethnography: From Realism to Social Criticism,* 2nd ed. (New York: Peter Lang, 1998); Patricia Ticineto Clough, "The Case of Sociology: Governmentality and Methodology," *Critical Inquiry* 36, no. 4 (2010): 627–41.

9.   Mike Savage and Roger Burrows, "The Coming Crisis of Empirical Sociology," *Sociology* 41, no. 5 (2007): 885–99.

10. Jacques Derrida, *Specters of Marx: The State of the Debt, the Work of Mourning and the New International,* trans. Peggy Kamuf (New York: Routledge, 2006).

11. Michel Foucault, *Security, Territory, Population: Lectures at the Collège de France 1977–1978,* trans. Graham Burchell (New York: Palgrave Macmillan, 2007).

12. Steinmetz, "The Epistemological Unconscious of U.S. Sociology," 129.

13. N. Katherine Hayles, *How We Became Posthuman: Virtual Bodies in Cybernetics, Literature, and Informatics* (Chicago: University of Chicago Press, 1999).

14. Humberto Maturana and Francisco Varela, *Autopoiesis and Cognition: The Realization of the Living* (Dordrecht: Springer, 1980), 78.

15. Niklas Luhmann, *Social Systems,* trans. John Bednarz (Stanford, Calif.: Stanford University Press, 1996).

16. IBM, "What is Big Data?—Bringing Big Data to the Enterprise," accessed October 29, 2016, http://www-01.ibm.com/software/data

/bigdata/ (the presentation of this information on this webpage has since been replaced with videos on big data and IBM services/platforms for working with it).

17. Thomas H. Davenport and D. J. Patil, "Data Scientist: The Sexiest Job of the Twenty-first Century," *Harvard Business Review,* October 2012, http://hbr.org/2012/10/data-scientist-the-sexiest-job-of-the-21st-century/ar/1.

18. Tiziana Terranova, "Free Labor: Producing Culture for the Digital Economy," *Social Text* 18, no. 2 (2000): 33–58.

19. We are drawing on Whitehead's notion of prehension: "Each actual entity is 'divisible' in an indefinite number of ways and each way of division yields its definite quota of prehensions. A prehension reproduces itself in the general characteristics of an actual entity: it is referent to an external world, and in this sense will be said to have a 'vector character'; it involves emotion, and purpose, valuation, and causation. In fact, any characteristic of an actual entity is reproduced in a prehension." See Alfred North Whitehead, *Process and Reality: An Essay in Cosmology* (New York: Free Press, 1978), 19. Or, as Steven Shaviro would read Whitehead, prehension is any nonsensuous sensing or perception of one entity by another involving "a particular selection—an 'objectification' and an 'abstraction,' of the 'data' that are being prehended. Something will always be missing, or left out." See Steven Shaviro, *Without Criteria: Kant, Whitehead, Deleuze, and Aesthetics* (Cambridge, Mass.: MIT Press, 2009), 49–50.

20. Tiziana Terranova, *Network Culture: Politics for the Information Age* (London: Pluto Press, 2004).

21. Jane Burry and Mark Burry, *The New Mathematics of Architecture* (New York: Thames & Hudson, 2012).

22. Luciana Parisi, "Symbiotic Architecture: Prehending Digitality," *Theory, Culture and Society* 26, nos. 2–3 (2009): 357.

23. Jacob Aron, "Frankenstein Virus Creates Malware by Pilfering Code," *New Scientist,* August 15, 2012, https://www.newscientist.com/article/mg21528785-600-frankenstein-virus-creates-malware-by-pilfering-code/.

24. Jiawei Han, Micheline Kamber, and Jian Pei, *Data Mining: Concepts and Techniques* (Waltham, Mass.: Elsevier, 2012).

25. Bruno Latour et al., "'The Whole is Always Smaller Than Its Parts'—A Digital Test of Gabriel Tardes' Monads," *British Journal of Sociology* 63, no. 4 (2012): 590.

26. Parisi, *Contagious Architecture,* 13–14; see also, Shintaro Miyazaki, "Algorhythmics: Understanding Micro-Temporality in Computational Cultures," *Computational Culture: A Journal of Software Studies,* Sep-

tember 28, 2012, http://computationalculture.net/article/algorhythmics-understanding-micro-temporality-in-computational-cultures.

27. Celia Lury, Luciana Parisi, and Tiziana Terranova, "Introduction: The Becoming Topological of Culture," *Theory, Culture and Society* 29, nos. 4–5 (2012): 3–35.

28. Chris Anderson, "The End of Theory: The Data Deluge Makes the Scientific Method Obsolete," *Wired,* June 26, 2008, http://www.wired.com/science/discoveries/magazine/16-07/pb_theoryen.

29. Whitehead, *Process and Reality.*

30. A derivative is a financial instrument whose value is based on one or more underlying assets. In practice, it is a contract between two parties that specifies conditions (especially the dates, resulting values of the underlying variables, and notional amounts) under which payments are to be made between the parties. The most common types of derivatives are: forwards, futures, options, and swaps. The most common underlying assets include: commodities, stocks, bonds, interest rates, and currencies; see https://en.wikipedia.org/wiki/Derivative_(finance).

31. Randy Martin, "After Economy? Social Logics of the Derivative," *Social Text* 31, no. 1 (Spring 2013): 83–106.

32. Elie Ayache, "Author of the Black Swan," *Wilmott Magazine,* July 2007, 40–49.

33. Ibid., 42.

34. Martin, "After Economy?" 97.

35. Gregory J. Seigworth and Matthew Tiessen, "Mobile Affects, Open Secrets, and Global Illiquidity: Pockets, Pools, and Plasma," *Theory, Culture and Society* 29, no. 6 (2012): 64. Seigworth and Tiessen describe liquidity to "refer more broadly to the globally integrated financial system's need to meet its future obligations (for nominal monetary growth or 'profit' and for ongoing economic expansion, in part by keeping the funds flowing through the perpetual outlay/creation of more 'credit' and, correspondingly, more debt)" (69).

36. Ibid., 69.

37. Ibid., 70.

38. Martin, "After Economy?" 91.

39. Ibid., quoting Dick Bryan and Michael Rafferty, *Capitalism with Derivatives: A Political Economy of Financial Derivatives, Capital and Class* (New York: Palgrave Macmillan, 2006), 37.

40. Martin, "After Economy?" 85–87.

41. Nigel Thrift, *Non-Representational Theory: Space, Politics, Affect* (New York: Routledge, 2007).

42. Ibid., 7, 12.

43. Nigel Thrift, "The Insubstantial Pageant: Producing an Untoward Land," *Cultural Geographies* 19, no. 2 (2012): 141–68.

44. Foucault, *Security, Territory, Population.*

45. Latour et al., "'The Whole Is Always Smaller Than Its Parts,'" 591.

46. Ibid., 2.

47. Seigworth and Tiessen, "Mobile Affects, Open Secrets, and Global Illiquidity," 68.

48. Ibid.

49. Ibid., 62–63.

50. In our tracing the move away from system, however, we have not developed a position on network. But surely the datalogical turn touches on thinking about networking. So *flat networky topography* is good enough language for us for now. What is more important here is the thinking about liquidity in relationship to what no longer is to be thought of as system.

51. Mark Hansen, "Beyond Affect? Technical Sensibility and the Pharmacology of Media" (presentation, *Critical Themes in Media Studies,* New York, 2013), 13.

52. Ibid., 14.

53. Michel Feher, "Self-Appreciation; or, The Aspirations of Human Capital," *Public Culture* 21, no. 1 (2009): 21–42.

54. Ibid.

55. We are thinking here of Foucault's treatment of practice in his *Hermeneutics of the Subject: Lectures at the Collège de France 1981–1982,* trans. George Burchell (New York: Palgrave Macmillan, 2005).

THE OBJECT'S AFFECTS

1. John Donne, *A Sermon, Preached to the King's Majestie at Whitehall* (1625), quoted in Juliet Mitchell, *Siblings, Sex and Violence* (Cambridge, UK: Polity, 2003), 59. These words, taken from John Donne's 1625 poem, *Sermon,* actually are "And God was displeased with me before I was I."

2. See also Amy Knight Powell, *Deposition: Scenes from the Late Medieval Church and the Modern Museum* (New York: Zone Books, 2012), 21–42, 121–58. Knight Powell argues that, through the fifteenth century, the deposition from the cross was so frequently represented that it rivaled the representation of the crucifixion, and thus, these representations together prefigure not only the iconoclasm of the Reformation but also the disposition of the image itself.

3.   I am referring here to what, in philosophy and critical theory, has been called the "ontological turn" that is especially concerned with the agencies or affective capacities of objects. Here, objects refer to any entity or thing without their being opposed to subjects or without privileging the epistemological position of human consciousness. See also *The Speculative Turn: Continental Materialism and Realism,* ed. Levi Bryant, Nick Srnicek, and Graham Harman (Melbourne: Re.press, 2011).

4.   I am especially referring here to: Graham Harman, *Guerrilla Metaphysics: Phenomenology and the Carpentry of Things* (Chicago: Open Court, 2005); Harman, "On Vicarious Causation," *Collapse* 2(2007): 187–21; Steven Shaviro, "The Universe of Things," (presentation, *Objected Oriented Ontology: A Symposium*, Atlanta, Ga., April 23, 2010); Shaviro, "The Actual Volcano: Whitehead, Harman, and the Problem of Relations," in Bryant, Srnicek, and Harman, *The Speculative Turn,* 279–90; Timothy Morton, "Objects in Mirror Are Closer Than They Appear," *Singularum* 1 (2012): 2–17; Morton, "An Object-Oriented Defense of Poetry," *New Literary History* 43 (2012): 205–24.

I am especially referring here to: Harman, *Guerrilla Metaphysics*; Harman, "On Vicarious Causation"; Shaviro, "The Universe of Things"; Shaviro, "The Actual Volcano"; Morton, "Objects in Mirror"; Morton, "An Object-Oriented Defense of Poetry."

5.   Anne Winston-Allen, *Stories of the Rose: The Making of the Rosary in the Middle Ages* (University Park: Pennsylvania State University Press, 1997).

6.   Caroline Walker Bynum, *Fragmentation and Redemption: Essays on Gender and the Human Body in Medieval Religion* (New York: Zone Books, 1991), 119–50.

7.   Eugene Thacker, *The Horror of Philosophy,* vol. 1, *In the Dust of This Planet* (Washington, D.C.: Zero Books, 2011).

8.   Sue Grand, *The Reproduction of Evil: A Clinical and Cultural Perspective* (Hillsdale, N.J.: Analytic Press, 2000), esp. 4.

RETHINKING RACE, CALCULATION, QUANTIFICATION, AND MEASURE

1.   Roderick Ferguson, *The Reorder of Things: The University and Its Pedagogies of Minority Difference* (Minneapolis: University of Minnesota Press, 2012).

2.   See Michel Foucault, *The Order of Things: An Archaeology of the Human Sciences* (New York: Vintage Books, 1994).

3.   By data-fication, Hansen and I are pointing to the data mining of social media, tracking devices, biometric and environmental passive microsensors—the full analytic capacities of twenty-first-century digital technologies. See: Patricia Ticineto Clough et al., "The Datalogical Turn," in *Nonrepresentational Methodologies: Re-envisioning Research,* ed. Phillip Vannini (London: Routledge, 2015), 146–64; Mark B. N. Hansen, *Feed-Forward: On the Future of Twenty-First-Century Media* (Chicago: University of Chicago Press, 2015).

4.   Ferguson, *The Reorder of Things,* 34.

5.   Ibid., 34.

6.   Jordan Crandall, "The Geospatialization of Calculative Operations: Tracking, Sensing and Megacities," *Theory, Culture and Society* 27 (2010): 68–90.

7.   Michel Foucault, *Security, Territory, Population: Lectures at the Collège de France, 1977–1978,* trans. Graham Burchell (New York: Palgrave Macmillan, 2007); Foucault, *The Birth of Biopolitics: Lectures at the Collège de France, 1978–1979,* trans. Graham Burchell (New York: Palgrave Macmillan 2008).

8.   Randy Martin, "After Economy? Social Logics of the Derivative," *Social Text* 31, no. 1 (2013): 83–106.

9.   Foucault, *The Birth of Biopolitics,* 259.

10.   Ibid., 259–60.

11.   Ferguson, *The Reorder of Things,* 75.

12.   Ibid., 73.

13.   Patricia Ticineto Clough and Craig Willse, "Human Security / National Security: Gender Branding and Population Racism," in *Beyond Biopolitics: Essays on the Governance of Life and Death,* ed. Patricia Ticineto Clough and Craig Willse (Durham, N.C.: Duke University Press, 2011), 46–64.

14.   For my earlier discussion of population racism, see "The New Empiricism: Affect, and Sociological Method," *European Journal of Social Theory* 1 (2009): 43–61. To engage what is an ongoing discussion of the centrality of race to the biopolitical calculating of populations, also see Alex Weheliye, *Habeas Viscus: Racializing Assemblages, Biopolitics, and Black Feminist Theories of the Human* (Durham, N.C.: Duke University Press, 2014). Weheliye is critical of Foucault's periodization of racism, raising a concern about introducing state racism after colonialism. Also see Jasbir Puar, "The 'Right' to Maim: Disablement and Inhumanist Biopolitics in Palestine," *borderlands* 14 (2015): 1–27. In taking up Weheliye's concerns in her treatment of Israel's maiming of populations of Palestine, Puar points further to the importance of distinguishing

settler colonialism from colonialism. She goes on to note that Foucault's treatment of biopolitics as a matter of preserving the health of a national population is now surpassed in the settler colonialism of Palestine, where illness is no longer a hindrance to governance or economy, as "maiming" seems preferred. This argument might be related to one that, as I suggested above, can be gleaned from Foucault's *The Birth of Biopolitics,* where he also argues that containing illness is no longer an aim of neoliberal biopolitics.

15. Stephanie Smallwood, *Saltwater Slavery: A Middle Passage from Africa to American Diaspora* (Cambridge, Mass.: Harvard University Press, 2008), quoted in Ferguson, *The Reorder of Things,* 91.

16. Ferguson, *The Reorder of Things,* 91.

17. Ibid., 93.

18. Mike Savage and Roger Burrows, "The Coming Crisis of Empirical Sociology," *Sociology* 4, no. 5 (2007): 885–99.

19. Ibid., 889.

20. Ibid.

21. See the collection *The Nonhuman Turn,* ed. Richard Grusin (Minneapolis: University of Minnesota Press, 2015).

22. Bruno Latour et al., "'The Whole Is Always Smaller Than Its Parts'—A Digital Test of Gabriel Tardes' Monads," *British Journal of Sociology* 63, no. 4 (2012): 590–615.

23. Ibid., 2.

24. Hansen, *Feed-Forward,* 40.

25. Ibid., 8–9, 52.

26. Ibid., 45, 192.

27. Alexander Galloway, "Love of the Middle," in *Excommunication: Three Inquiries in Media and Mediation,* ed. Alexander Galloway, Eugene Thacker, and McKenzie Wark (Chicago: University of Chicago Press, 2014), 25–76.

28. Ibid., 62.

29. Ibid.

30. Martin, "After Economy?" 91.

31. Ibid.

32. Elie Ayache, "Author of the Black Swan," *Wilmott Magazine,* July 2007, 42.

33. Ibid., 41.

34. Ibid., 44.

35. Hansen, "Our Predictive Condition, or, Prediction in the Wild," in Grusin, *The Nonhuman Turn,* 118.

36. Crandall, "The Geospatialization of Calculative Operations," 75.

37. Hansen, "Our Predictive Condition," 119.

38. Alfred North Whitehead, *Process and Reality* (New York: Free Press, 1979), quoted in Hansen, "Our Predictive Condition," 121.

39. Hansen, *Feed-Forward,* 85.

40. Ibid., 120. In his reading of Whitehead, Hansen is differing from those theorists who have linked potential to the virtuality of Whitehead's conception of conscrescence, such as Steven Shaviro, Luciana Parisi, and Brian Massumi. Although Hansen is critical of Parisi's take on the virtuality of conscrescence, I nonetheless recognize the importance of her treatment of the incomputable in algorithms as a nonhuman indeterminacy or agency. (For further discussion of Parisi, see Ezekiel Dixon-Román, "Algo-Ritmo: More-Than-Human Performative Acts and the Racializing Assemblages of Algorithmic Architectures," *Culture Studies ↔ Critical Methodologies* 16, no. 5 [2016]: 482–90.) However I find Hansen's take on potentiality in data, or in the contrast among already existing actualities, to be a much more convincing take on Whitehead, when reading Whitehead, that is, in the context of the data mining of social media, tracking devices, biometric and environmental passive microsensors, and the data-fication of twenty-first-century media.

41. Ibid., 210.

42. Hansen, "Our Predictive Condition," 121.

43. The relationship between Martin's and Hansen's views of surplus cannot be fully developed here. But I would suggest that the potentiality Hansen discusses in relationship to already existing actualities might be the condition of the derivative's appropriating and modulating that potentiality.

44. Martin, "After Economy?" 100.

45. Ibid.

46. McKenzie Wark, "Furious Media: A Queer History of Heresy," in Galloway, Thacker, and Wark, *Excommunication,* 158, 160.

47. Wendy Hui Kyong Chun, "Race And/As Technology, or How to Do Things to Race," in *Race After the Internet,* ed. Lisa Nakamura and Peter Chow-White (New York: Routledge, 2012), 38–60.

48. Chun, "Race And/As Technology," 39.

49. Bernard Stiegler, *Technics and Time, 1: The Fault of Epimetheus,* trans. Richard Beardsworth and George Collins (Stanford, Calif.: Stanford University Press, 1998).

50. Hansen, *Feed-Forward,* 52.

51. Ferguson, *The Reorder of Things,* 232.

52. Martin, "After Economy?" 87.

53. Matthew Fuller and Andrew Goffey, *Evil Media* (Cambridge, Mass.: The MIT Press, 2012).

54. Stefano Harney and Fred Moten, *The Undercommons: Fugitive Planning and Black Study* (New York: Minor Compositions, 2013), 41.

55. Ibid., 40.

AND THEY WERE DANCING

1.   I take these words and thoughts from Erin Manning, "The Elasticity of the Almost," in *Planes of Composition,* ed. Andre Lepecki and Jenn Joy (London: Seagull Books, 2009), 117–18.

2.   I take these words and thoughts from Jenn Joy, "Anatomies of Spasm," in Lepecki and Joy, *Planes of Composition,* 71–122. She is quoting Gilles Deleuze, *Francis Bacon: The Logic of Sensation* (Minneapolis: University of Minnesota Press, 2002), 16.

3.   Ibid.

4.   I am drawing on the history of Southern Italian women in Jennifer Guglielmo, *Living the Revolution* (Chapel Hill: University of North Carolina Press, 2010).

5.   I take these words from Gilles Deleuze on Nietzsche (*Pure Immanence: Essay on A Life,* trans. Anne Boyman [New York: Zone Books, 2001], 94).

6.   I take these thoughts from Randy Martin, *Knowledge LTD* (Philadelphia, Pa.: Temple University Press, 2015), 160. He is drawing on Susan Leigh Foster, *Choreographing Empathy, Kinesthesia in Performance* (London: Routledge, 2011).

7.   I take these thoughts and words from Jordan Crandall, "The Geospatialization of Calculative Operations: Tracking, Sensing and Megacities," *Theory, Culture and Society* 27, no. 6 (2010): 68–90.

8.   I take these thoughts and words from Jose Gil, "Paradoxical Body," in Lepecki and Joy, *Planes of Composition,* 96–97.

9.   I am drawing on the thoughts and words of Gilles Chatelet, *Figuring Space: Philosophy, Mathematics and Physics* (Dordrecht: Kluwer Academic Publishers, 2000).

10.   I take these thoughts from Donald Winnicott, "Fear of Breakdown," *International Review of Psycho-Analysis* 1 (1974): 103–7.

11.   I take the history of dance referenced in this last paragraph from Martin, *Knowledge LTD,* 143–212.

ECSTATIC CORONA

1. Patricia Ticineto Clough, *The End(s) of Ethnography: From Realism to Social Criticism,* 2nd ed. (New York: Peter Lang, 1992).

2. Boris Groys, *Art Power* (Cambridge, Mass.: MIT Press, 2013).

3. Boris Groys, "Comrades of Time," *e-flux* 11 (December 2009): http://www.e-flux.com/journal/11/61345/comrades-of-time/.

4. Mark B. N. Hansen, *Feed-Forward: On the Future of Twenty-First-Century Media* (Chicago: University of Chicago Press, 2014). By "worldly sensibility," Hansen is referring to "the wide swath of environmental data" made available through the data mined from social media, tracking devices, and biometric and environmental passive microsensors (120).

5. Steve Goodman, *Sonic Warfare: Sound, Affect, and the Ecology of Fear* (Cambridge, Mass.: MIT Press, 2009), 95.

6. Luce Irigaray, *Speculum of the Other Woman* (Ithaca, N.Y.: Cornell University Press, 1985), 194–95.

7. Michael Eigen, "Mystical Precocity and Psychic Short Circuits," in *The Mind Object: Precocity and Pathology of Self-Sufficiency,* ed. Edward Corrigan and Pearl-Ellen Gordon (Northvale, N.J.: Jason Aronson, 1995), 126.

8. Peter Shabad and Stanley Selinger, "Bracing for Disappointment and the Counterphobic Leap into the Future," in Corrigan and Gordon, *The Mind Object,* 209–27.

9. Catherine Malabou, *Ontology of the Accident: An Essay on Destructive Plasticity,* trans. Carolyn Shread (Malden, Mass.: Polity, 2012), 87.

10. Michel Foucault, *Security, Territory, Population: Lectures at the Collège de France, 1977–1978* (New York: Picador, 2007), 108–9.

11. Ibid., 63; Patricia Ticineto Clough, "The New Empiricism: Affect and Sociological Method," *European Journal of Social Theory* 12, no. 1 (2009): 43–61.

12. Stefano Harney and Fred Moten, *The Undercommons: Fugitive Planning and Black Study* (Wivenhoe, N.Y.: Minor Compositions, 2013), 46.

13. Eugene Thacker, "Dark Media," in *Excommunication: Three Inquiries in Media and Mediation,* ed. Alexander Galloway, Eugene Thacker, and McKenzie Wark (Chicago: University of Chicago Press, 2013), 77–149.

14. Richard Moran, "Kant, Proust, and the Appeal of Beauty," *Critical Inquiry* 38, no. 2 (2012): 213.

15. Steven Shaviro, "The Universe of Things" (presentation, *Object Oriented Ontology, A Symposium*, Atlanta, Ga., April 23, 2010).

16. Hansen, *Feed-Forward,* 120.

Previous Publications

"Notes toward a Theory of Affect-Itself" was published in *ephemera: theory and politics in organization* 7, no. 1 (2007): 60–77.

"War by Other Means: What Difference Do(es) the Graphic(s) Make?" was published in *Digital Cultures and the Politics of Emotion: Feelings, Affect, and Technological Change,* ed. Athina Karatzogianni and Adi Kuntsman (Houndmills, Basingstoke, Hampshire: Palgrave Macmillan UK, 2002), 21–32.

"Praying and Playing to the Beat of a Child's Metronome" was published in *Subjectivity* 3, no. 4 (December 2010): 349–65.

"Gendered Security / National Security: Political Branding and Population Racism" was published as "Human Security / National Security: Gender Branding and Population Racism," in *Beyond Biopolitics: Essays on the Governance of Life and Death,* ed. Patricia Ticineto Clough and Craig Willse (Durham, N.C.: Duke University Press, 2011), 46–64. Copyright 2011 Duke University Press. Reprinted by permission. www.dukeupress.edu.

"My Mother's Scream" was published in *Sound, Music, Affect: Theorizing Sonic Experience,* ed. Marie Thompson and Ian Biddle (London: Bloomsbury, 2013), 65–71.

"Feminist Theory: Bodies, Science, and Technology" was published in *The Routledge Handbook of the Body,* ed. Bryan S. Turner (New York: Routledge, 2012), 94–105.

"A Dream of Falling: Philosophy and Family Violence" was published in *Objects and Materials: A Routledge Companion,* ed. Penny Harvey, Eleanor Conlin Casella, Gillian Evans, Hannah Knox, Christine McLean, Elizabeth B. Silva, Nicholas Thoburn, and Kath Woodward (New York: Routledge, 2014), 156–61.

Index

Patricia Ticineto Clough is professor of sociology and women's studies at the Graduate Center and Queens College, City University of New York, and a psychoanalyst practicing in New York City. She is author of *Autoaffection: Unconscious Thought in the Age of Technology* (Minnesota, 2000), *Feminist Thought: Desire, Power, and Academic Discourse,* and *The End(s) of Ethnography: From Realism to Social Criticism.* She is editor of *The Affective Turn: Theorizing the Social,* with Craig Willse; editor of *Beyond Biopolitics: Essays on the Governance of Life and Death*; and editor of *Intimacies: A New World of Relational Life,* with Alan Frank and Steven Seidman.